# HIGH GOTHIC ART

# ART OF THE WORLD

A SERIES OF REGIONAL HISTORIES
OF THE VISUAL ARTS

# HIGH GOTHIC ART

MARCEL AUBERT

WITH THE COLLABORATION OF
J. A. SCHMOLL AND CONTRIBUTIONS BY
HANS H. HOFSTÄTTER

METHUEN – LONDON

FIRST PUBLISHED IN 1964

© HOLLE VERLAG GMBH, BADEN-BADEN, GERMANY

PRINTED IN HOLLAND

Translated by Peter Gorge

## TITLE-PAGE

Fishermen netting pikes. From the frescos in the *Chambre de la Gard-Robe* in the papal palace, Avignon. *Cf. p. 90.* The *Chambre de la Garde-Robe*, which adjoins the pope's bedchamber, was the favourite room of Clement VII. Its walls are covered with frescos illustrating the courtly diversions of the age, such as fishing, bathing, and, above all, every form of the chase; falconry, ferreting, and bird-catching. The settings throughout are woods and gardens; the rich foliage of the fruit-laden trees extends almost to the full height of the wall, so that only a narrow strip of the sky can be seen below the ornate beamed ceilling. Our illustration shows four men at a fish-pond; two are trying to catch the pike in the water with nets, while the others are diverting them with bait.

Two masters have been suggested in connection with these frescos: the first is Robin de Romans—who was paid for the paintings in the papal palace, though his actual share in the work was small—the second, more likely artist is Matteo di Giovanetto of Viterbo, who was active at the papal court from 1343–1366 and who painted the frescos in the St. John's chapel and the Martyrs' chapel. The fresco of St. Elizabeth in the St. John's chapel, in particular, shows a very similar treatment of the plants, while the figures of the fishermen are of a Sienese grace. Even the school of Simone Martini was at one time suggested, the more so because the fish tank with its suggestion of the third dimension—despite the 'wrong' perspective—recalls the attempts of the Sienese master at spatial effects. The awareness of nature manifest throughout these frescos goes hand in hand with the scientific interest of the age in natural phenomena, in botany and zoology. Undoubtedly, what had already found expression in the hunting scenes of the Arras tapestries—which were known to Clement VII—or in Simone Martini's Virgil illustrations to Petrarch (Ambrosiana, Milan) was still active. It would seem as if all these experiences centred around Avignon. John the Good had the rooms of his palace at Vaudreuil painted with similar motifs, and Charles V, the Wise, followed his example at the Hotel Saint-Pot in Paris and later at the Louvre, as did his brother, Jean de Berry, in Bourges. In Italy, this feeling for nature finds expression a little later in Ambrogio Lorenzetti's fresco 'Peaceful city' in the Palazzo Publico in Siena. French miniatures and tapestries illustrating such scenes now occur in increasing numbers.

With its emphasis on nature, the fresco in the papal palace at Avignon stands at the threshold of High and Late Gothic and anticipates the beginnings of the Early Renaissance in Italy.

# FOREWORD

The author, Professor Marcel Aubert, Membre de l'Institut and for many years President of the Société archéologique de France, was unable to complete the manuscript for this book. He died in Paris on December 28, 1962. In consequence ways had to be found of completing a work primarily concerned with the art of the High Gothic in its country of origin and its spread throughout Europe — the original French title had been *Le Triomphe de l'Art Gothique* — bearing in mind the intentions of the author. That this was possible is due to the editor, Professor Dr. J.A. Schmoll gen. Eisenwerth (Saarbrücken), who, as the close collaborator of Professor Aubert, made many important contributions — among them the chapter on German Brick Gothic to the text — and to Dr. Hans H. Hofstätter who, at the request of the editor and the German publishers, contributed the chapter on German Gothic, the captions, bibliography, chronology and glossary. With the editor, Dr. Hofstätter was also responsible for the choice of illustrations. The publishers hope that such co-operation, based an mutual understanding, has resulted in a rounded picture of the epoch covered by this volume, which will be supplemented in the near future by LATE ROMANESQUE AND EARLY GOTHIC, by W. Sauerländer, and LATE GOTHIC, by J.A. Schmoll.

THE PUBLISHER

# LIST OF PLATES

# LIST OF MAPS

# LIST OF FIGURES

The drawings in this volume are by Heinz Prüstel, Mainz.

The map on p. 203 was re-drawn after a map in Editions de Visscher, Brussels. The map on p. 204 was re-drawn from F. van der Meer, *Atlas van de Westerse Beschaving*, Amsterdam (Elsevier), map 21.

# ACKNOWLEDGMENTS

We take this opportunity of expressing sincere thanks to the museums and institutions listed below for their kindness in allowing reproduction of the plates on the following pages:

| | | | |
|---|---|---|---|
| Bibliothèque Nationale, Paris | 107 | Ehem. Staatliche Museen, Berlin | 153, 179 |
| Louvre, Paris | 111, 112, 113 | Universitätsbibliothek, Heidelberg | 159 |
| Louvre, formerly Soltykoff Coll. | 109 | Kunstsammlungen der Veste Coburg | 151 |
| Wallraf–Richartz-Museum, Cologne | 157 | Frauenhaus, Strasbourg | 141 |
| Ehem. Kaiser-Friedrich-Museum, Berlin | 147 | Dom opera, Siena | 173 |

The plates on the following pages were kindly supplied by:

| | | | |
|---|---|---|---|
| Castelli, Lübeck | 133 | Publications Filmées d'Art et d'Histoire, Paris | 33, 87, 107 |
| Editions CGC, Paris | 101, 103 | Dr. Rathschlag, Cologne | 115 |
| Photo Giraudon, Paris | 109, 111, 112, 113 | Foto Scala, Florence | 161, 165, 167, 171, 173 |
| W. Hartl, Klagenfurt | 155 | Hugo Schmölz, Cologne | 143, 149 |
| Foto Hinz, Basle | 105 | Max Seidel, Mittenwald | 29, 31, 41, 47, 65, 67, 69, 71, 73, 75, 77, 79, 81, 83, 99, 129, 141, 145, 179 |
| Institut für Film und Bild, Munich | 159 | | |
| A. F. Kersting, London | 119, 123 | Jack Skeel, Ashford (Kent) | 121 |
| J. A. Lavaud, Paris | 3, 61, 95, 163 | Foto Steinkopf, Berlin | 147, 153, 179 |
| Foto Marburg | 127 | Foto Stober, Fribourg | 131 |

The plates on pp. 139 and 157 are based on blocks kindly placed at our disposal by Prof. Dr. Edgar Lehmann, Berlin and Verlag M. Du Mont Schauberg, Cologne respectively.

The map on p. 203 was re-drawn after a map in Editions de Vissher, Brussels. The map on p. 204 was re-drawn from F. van der Meer, Atlas van de Westerse Beschaving, Amsterdam (Elsevier), map 21.

# CONTENTS

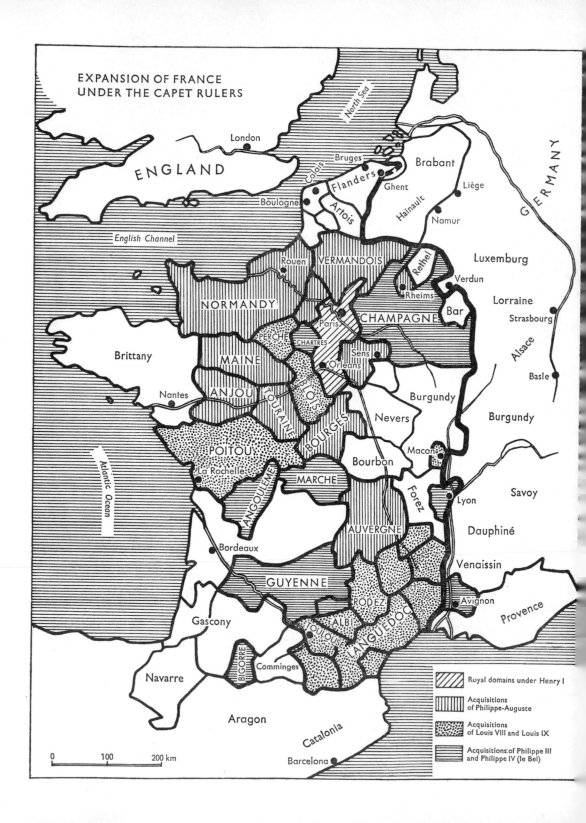

EXPANSION OF FRANCE
UNDER THE CAPET RULERS

London

ENGLAND

North Sea

Calais
Bruges
Flanders
Boulogne
Ghent
Artois
Brabant
Liège
Hainault
Namur

GERMANY

English Channel

Rouen
VERMANDOIS
Rethel
Verdun
Rheims
Luxemburg

NORMANDY
Paris
CHAMPAGNE
Bar
Lorraine
Strasbourg

Brittany

PERCHE
CHARTRES
Sens
Orleans

MAINE
Alsace

ANJOU
TOURAINE
BLOIS
Basle

Nantes

Burgundy
Nevers
Burgundy

BOURGES

POITOU
La Rochelle

MARCHE
Bourbon
Macon

Savoy

ANGOULEME
Forez
Lyon

Atlantic Ocean

AUVERGNE
Dauphiné

Bordeaux
Venaissin

GUYENNE
RODEZ
Avignon
Provence

Gascony
ALBI
LANGUEDOC

TOULOUSE

BIGORRE
Comminges

Navarre

Aragon

Catalonia
Barcelona

| | |
|---|---|
| ▨ | Royal domains under Henry I |
| ▥ | Acquisitions of Philippe-Auguste |
| ▦ | Acquisitions of Louis VIII and Louis IX |
| ▤ | Acquisitions of Philippe III and Philippe IV (le Bel) |

0    100    200 km

# I. CHRISTIAN EUROPE 1220–1350

The epoch covered by this volume is one of the most splendid in Europe's history; it is the century of the absolute monarchy of St. Louis and of the rule of Frederick II in Italy, of the triumph of the Gothic and of medieval court art; it is the age of Amiens cathedral, of the *Summa theologica* of St. Thomas Aquinas and of Dante's *Divina Comedia*.

This epoch embraces, at least in broad outline, the years between 1220 and 1350. But these dates must not be considered rigid frontiers; occasionally, where certain developments demand it, we have to go beyond them.

Thirteenth-century Europe is dominated by the need for order and a longing for unity, the unity of thought, religion, culture, and art. Under the pro-  *European unity* tection of the Byzantine empire and the eastern marches of Christendom — Hungary, Serbia, and Roumania, who are stemming the tide of the new barbarians, the Mongols, Saracens and Turks — this unity gradually emerges. For centuries, the Byzantine empire had resisted the advance of the Arabs and the Turks. After a long death struggle, final defeat comes on 29th May, 1453. The Hungarians — under the rule of a branch of the house of Anjou-Naples — are now cast in the role of the defenders of western Christen- dom against the Mongols in the east. Like the Huns centuries earlier, nomad  *Mongolian threat* Mongol tribes, united by Jenghiz Khan (1155 or 1167–1227) into a great empire extending from the China Sea to Russia and the Balkans, advance towards the west. In 1241, Batu, the grandson of Jenghiz Khan, defeats a German-Polish army led by Henry II of Silesia at Liegnitz, and at the same time Bela IV of Hungary is completely routed by a second Mongolian army in the Theiss valley. The gates to Europe are now open to the Mongols, but, miraculously, the death of Ugeder Khan supervenes. The funeral cele- brations and the election of the new Khan cause Batu's sudden retreat. In Asia Minor the Mongol flood is checked by Sultan Baibar in 1260; only the rise of Tamerlane (1336–1405) brings renewed danger. During that time connections between Christians and Mongols become as rich and varied as between Christians, Arabs and Jews, whose civilizations extend throughout the Mediterranean region.

The rapid spread of Islam in the seventh and eighth centuries contributes  *Spread of Islam* greatly to the development of close relationships between east and west. Wars are followed by trade, and trade leads to closer spiritual links. The Arabs, filled with the wisdom and culture of the Indians, Greeks and Persians, which they had acquired through their great gift of assimilation, revive the sciences, above all astronomy, medicine, magic and mathematics. In the thirteenth century, a pupil of the Mussulmans, Leonardo Fibonacci, who taught at Pisa, introduced Arabic numerals in the west. (The cultural links between Christians, Jews and Arabs will be discussed later in this volume.)

*Trade links* — In Christian Europe, one of the main reasons for the unity that flowered in the thirteenth century and lasted into the fourteenth is to be found in the trade links that were evolved increasingly despite bad roads, heavy tariffs, and brigandry. In Flanders and Brabant, English wool is transformed into soft fabrics of glowing colours. Through the Champagne, Burgundy and Lombardy, goods from the north reach the south of Italy and the Near East, while spices, perfume, silk and jewellery travel in the opposite direction to the north. As far as possible, transport by sea, being safer and cheaper, is given preference. The North Sea and the Baltic assume importance as trade-routes to northern Europe. In the Mediterranean the fleets of Genoa, Pisa and Venice predominate.

*Conditions in France* — France belonged to a few great feudal nobles, who did not hesitate to challenge the king to battle. St. Louis, however, makes use of his right as sovereign and, thanks to his skilful administration and his great prestige, is able to enlarge and consolidate his kingdom. Even where his rule is not absolute, he imposes his law, his order, and his superior culture. Gradually, some degree of prosperity is established in the thirteenth and the early fourteenth century. Only the famine of 1315–17 and the Black Death of 1340–1350 — which claims nearly a third of the population — bring about fundamental social changes. All kinds of difficulties now begin; towns are in rebellion, outbursts of cruelty occur everywhere. Between 1337 and 1453 France is occupied by the English and the *Grandes Compagnies*. Degradation is complete.

*England* — The King of England, France's most dangerous adversary at the time, had his domains firmly organized, both at home and abroad.

*Germany* — In Germany unity was less marked. Seven Electorates had been formed, three ecclesiastical — Trier, Mainz and Cologne — and four — the Rhine, *Italy* — Saxony, Brandenburg and Bohemia — secular. In Italy, where the cities of Genoa, Milan, Pisa and Florence exercised considerable political influence through the wealth of their merchants and bankers, and where the arts passed through an incomparable renaissance at the princely courts, the *Spain* — situation was similar. Spain, divided into several kingdoms, was still partly *Emperor and Pope* — under Moorish occupation. In Germany, the emperors, anxious to establish their supreme authority over the empire, met with the resistance of the princes, the towns and, above all, the papacy, which proclaimed the supremacy of the Holy See over the kings of Europe. These struggles for power were a source of constant unrest in Germany and Italy in the thirteenth and fourteenth centuries.

*Spread of Christianity* — Christian Europe, whose frontiers were at first still vague, now draws wider and wider regions into its orbit. The kingdoms of Aragon, Castile and Portugal are wrested from the Moors; Cordoba in 1236, Seville twelve years later,

Granada not until 1492. In the south of France the heresy of the Albigensians is put down. Genoa, Pisa and Venice chase the fleet of the Saracens from the Mediterranean. In the east, the March Brandenburg is formed on hitherto Slav soil. Prussia and the Baltic provinces are conquered by the Teutonic Order. The kingdom of Bohemia receives a new impetus in the fourteenth century through kings from the house of Luxemburg. Poland and Hungary enlarge their territories, partly at the expense of the Byzantine empire. Sweden, Norway and Denmark are converted to Christianity; their kings call in the Cistercians, who found abbeys which develop into important religious, cultural and economic centres.

But Byzantine influence lives on in Russia and several western Slav countries, among them Serbia, Bulgaria and Moldavia-Wallachia. Numerous links exist between east and west, chiefly through trade. In Asia, the principal intermediary is the Byzantine empire, in Syria the Frankish kingdoms of Jerusalem and Egypt play a similar part. There are also close contacts with the Moslem world throughout the Mediterranean, in Spain no less than in Sicily. Polychrome decoration and domed interiors are to no small degree derived from the architecture of the east. *Byzantine influence*

Yet the papacy remains the leading force in Christendom. Because it *Papacy* champions the supremacy of ecclesiastical over secular authority, Germany and Italy are involved in wars between the Guelphs, who are the allies of the pope and the Sacerdotium, and the supporters of imperial power, the Ghibellines. The whole age is overshadowed by the struggle between Rome and Frederick Barbarossa, king of Sicily and Holy Roman Emperor and one of the most outstanding minds of the Middle Ages. Not much later, Pope Boniface VIII finds himself in conflict with Philippe le Bel of Burgundy; Philippe's adviser, Nogaret, who supports his master's plans for a national church, makes an attempt on the pope's life at Anagni on 11th October, 1303. Five weeks later, Boniface dies. From 1309 to 1377, the popes are in exile at Avignon. Under the pressure of the Capet, Bertrand de Got, archbishop of Bordeaux, is elected pope as Clement V on 3rd June, 1305; because of the uncertain political situation in Italy, he is brought to Avignon, *Exile of Avignon* as are his successors, the severe Cistercian, Benedict XII, and Clement VI, another former archbishop of Bordeaux. Through them, the papacy is brought into the closest dependence on France. A papal palace is built at Avignon, and Italian artists — Simone Martini, Lippo Memmi and their pupils — are brought to France to decorate it with frescos.

On 17th January 1377, Pope Gregory X Ireturns to Rome, since the hostility *Return to Rome* of the Italians, due to the absence of the popes, is proving a serious threat to the papal state. The popes now rule from the Vatican, and no longer, as in the past, from the Lateran. Under Urban VI (1378–1389) and his anti-pope, Clement VII (1378–1394), the Christian west splits into two hostile camps. Heresy and rebellion break out everywhere. The European unity that *Schism* marked the age of the High Gothic has come to an end. This unity, towards which Christian Europe strove in the twelfth and thirteenth centuries, originated in part in the Île-de-France and France itself; it was a unity of thought, culture and art — the Gothic.

*France and England* Despite the efforts of two Capet kings, Louis VI and Louis VII, the territory of the French crown was small; it extended from Valois to Orleans, Melun, Sens and Bourges. The duchy of Guyenne, acquired by Louis VII through his marriage with Eleanor, the rich heiress of the Duke of Aquitaine, broke its link with the crown to become part of the domain of Henry Plantagenet, Count of Anjou and Maine, Duke of Guyenne and Count of Poitou, who was crowned King of England in 1154. A series of long drawn-out wars now begins. Philippe-Auguste conquers Vexin, then Normandy (1204), Anjou, Touraine, Maine and Poitou (1205). The King of England forms a powerful anti-French coalition which is thoroughly defeated by Philippe at Bouvines (1214), thanks to the courage of the militia and the citizens of the towns of the north, Perche and Ponthieu, commanded by his brother Guérin. The battle of Bouvines marks the beginning of France's cultural and economic unity, which was to be realized in the thirteenth century.

*St. Louis* With the personality of Louis IX (1226–1270), St. Louis, France assumes the leading role in the Christian west. The king's justice, kindness and charity, the repute of his piety and his virtues, endow the French monarchy with an incomparable splendour. He is the *roi des rois de la terre*, whose judgement is accepted by all. The centre of his kingdom is Paris, the permanent residence of the Capet kings since Philippe-Auguste. The court of the Valois was a centre of culture and chivalry; under Philippe VI (1328–1350) and John the Good (1350–1364) it passed through the greatest glories and the greatest disasters, through times that needed the wisdom of a ruler like Charles V (1364–1380), who could count on the support of the great strategist of his age, the Connétable Duguesclin, to hold together a kingdom seriously weakened by inflation and ravaged by the troops of the English and the *Grandes Compagnies*.

Eudes de Châteauroux, a former Cistercian, later cardinal and papal legate, exclaimed in the middle of the thirteenth century 'La France est le four, où cuit le pain intellectuel de l'humanité' (France is the oven where the *Paris as a cultural* bread for the human mind is baked). The schools of Paris surpass even Laon *centre* and Chartres. From the end of the twelfth century onwards, the greatest minds of the age, such as Abélard and Thomas Aquinas (1225–1274), are active there and, by their presence, attract pupils from all over the Christian world, from Anjou, Poitou, Gascony, Normandy, Brittany, Flanders, England, Spain, Rome, and from the Holy Roman Empire. The intellectual centre on the hill of St. Geneviève had become justly famous through the profound knowledge of the men who were teaching dialectics, grammar and rhetoric, through the beauty of their Latin poetry and prose, which amounted to a veritable renaissance of Classic literature, and through the synthesis of Christian theology and Greek philosophy that brought forth a

FIG. 1 – *Seal of the University of Paris. 13th cent. The inscription reads: S(igillum) Universitatis Magistror(um) et Scolariu(um) Parisius*

picture of the world described by Etienne Gilson, one of to-day's leading authorities on Thomist philosophy and the history of philosophy at the Sorbonne, as follows: 'The greatest difference between the men of that age and our own lies in their almost complete ignorance of what the natural sciences could be... To a thinker of that age, the whole point about anything was that it was not what it appeared, but the symbol of a higher reality, or that it had an altogether different meaning... What the twelfth century lacked is the concept of nature as an independent reality, as a self-sufficient entity, however feeble.'

*Nature and idea*

This new picture of the world, based on Aristotle's writings on natural history, originates in Paris in the thirteenth century.

*Foundation of the Sorbonne*

Around 1200 the teachers and students of the schools of Paris combine into a single community, following the examples of Bologna, Oxford and Cambridge. This is the origin of Paris university. Its recognition by Philippe-Auguste and Pope Innocent III follows, and its charter as a *universitas magistrorum et scholarium Parisiis studentium* is officially acknowledged by the papal legate, Robert du Courçon, in 1213. Gradually, the university loosens its links with the church, and the bishop's chancellor only keeps the right to bestow the *licentia discendi*. Via Toledo, Cordoba, Seville, Sicily and southern Italy, the meeting places of east and west, translations of Aristotle with their Arabic commentaries — as well as Greek works about philosophy, natural science, mathematics, astronomy, trigonometry and medicine, which had been collected by the Arabs — reach Paris.

FIG. 1

The university of Paris received every encouragement from the French kings and the popes. Students came from all over the world, and many outstanding masters taught there, among them John of Salisbury, William of Occam, Roger Bacon and Duns Scotus. Many colleges were founded to protect the interests of the students; the English had six for theology alone. French thought and language spread everywhere. 'The learning of the schools of

Paris is to the Holy Church like a tree of life in the earthly Paradise and like a brilliant light in the house of the Lord', wrote Alexander IV in 1255, 'In Paris, the human race, struck with the blindness of its innate ignorance, regains vision and beauty through the perception of the true light that reflects Divine wisdom'. In 1292 Nicholas IV grants the masters of the university of Paris an unheard-of privilege: they are allowed to teach anywhere in the world, without having to take any further examinations. Charles V calls the Sorbonne 'beloved daughter of the King'.

*Spiritual development*

In Europe's spiritual development, the Gothic plays an outstanding part; ideas now begin to move. The thirteenth century turns to the intellect, the fourteenth to the emotions. The thirteenth century classifies and builds, the fourteenth disputes about the truths of religion and tries to achieve a compromise between the mysticism of a Pseudo-Bonaventura and Aristotle's realism, between St. Francis of Assisi and Jacobus de Voragine. The

*13th century*
*Synthesis*

thirteenth century is a century of synthesis, of the *summae* of history, philosophy, literature and art. The scholastic *summae* of Albertus Magnus and Thomas Aquinas are constructed with the severe and vigorous logic of a cathedral. The *speculum universale* of Vincent de Beauvais conceives the world in formulae and definitions; the *speculum naturale* describes the infinite diversity of creation, which is mirrored in the picture cycles of the great cathedrals; the *speculum doctrinale* glorifies manual skills (in the pictures of the seasons) and the labours of the mind, *trivium* and *quadrivium*, crowned by philosophy and theology. The *speculum morale* shows how the virtues overcome vice, the *speculum historiale* presents the story of man's salvation in the Old and the New Testament and the history of mankind from the Creation to the Last Judgement. In the group under the rose window in the south transept at Chartres, the Evangelists stand on the shoulders of the Prophets, whose vision is less than theirs.

*14th century*
*Dissolution of*
*synthesis*

The fourteenth century, dissolving all synthesis, emphasizes the distinction between philosophy and theology; the dawn of modern thought has begun. The university of Paris forms the centre of all these disputes. Former students, among them Albert von Sachsen, first rector of Vienna university (d. 1390), and the first rector of Heidelberg, Marsilius von Inghen (d. 1396), spread its doctrine throughout the west. Here, under the influence of scholastic thought, the striving for a sole universal truth evolves.

*Literature*

France's intellectual lead in the Middle Ages also extends to all forms of literature, which, evolved here, are soon taken up everywhere in Europe. Mystery plays and the *Chansons de Gestes* of the twelfth century yield to lyric poetry and the courtly novel. We can almost speak of a renaissance of Classic literature, distinguished by grace, elegance and charm and by the more refined style of life of a society where women are assuming increasing importance. In the thirteenth century this culture attains its peak with the concept of an ideal mystic love, the neo-Platonic love of perfect beauty; it is the triumph of grace and the spirit of chivalry over male brute force, the

FIG. 2 – *Back of an ivory mirror with a Minne scene. French, early 14th cent., diam. c. 4³/₈ ins. Museo Nazionale, Florence. Cf. below and p. 116*

courtly 'Minne' — of Provençal origin — whose cult spreads all over France. It is taken up by Eleanor of Aquitaine and her daughters, Marie of Champagne, Countess of Flanders, and Alix of Blois, as well as other leading women of the time, among them Erengard of Narbonne and Maria Countess of Ponthieu, who set up *Cours d'amour*, courts of love. The influence of courtly lyric and the courtly novel is soon felt in England, Flanders, Germany, Spain and Italy; it is manifest in the works of Dante (1265–1321) and Petrarch (1304–1374) who saw his Laura for the first time on 6th April, 1327, in the church of Sainte-Claire at Avignon. In France, 'courtly love' in its most sublime form, as the accentuation of human into Divine love, grows into the cult of the Madonna, which, slightly later, attains its noblest flowering in German literature and art. At the same time, another new impulse becomes active in art and literature; it has its source in the cities of the Champagne, Flanders and Picardy, especially Arras, and is sustained by the new middle class, the wealthy merchants, senators and bankers who begin to assume more and more importance in the development of France, particularly in the growth of the cathedrals, parish churches, chapels and convents. Courtly poetry, the preserve of the aristocracy, is replaced by masks and comedies, in which the satirical and down-to-earth spirit of the bourgeoisie triumphs. The *Roman de la Rose* was begun *c.* 1236 by Guillaume de Lorris as a courtly novel. It achieved considerable success as a compendium of the courtly arts. Forty years later, Jean de Meung completed the work as the triumph of clerical scholasticism and the victory of bourgeois, un-courtly Minne.

This bourgeois, down-to-earth mood also speaks out of the tales of Chaucer (b. 1340), who gives us an insight into the every-day life not only of the king and his court, but also of the artisan, the cleric, the monk, and the artist. But plays and tales in the thirteenth century are not confined to the middle class; some originate even at the French court in Naples. In Germany,

*Minne cult*

FIG. 2

*Dante and Petrarch*

*Madonna cult*

*Roman de la Rose*

*Chaucer*

19

literature passes through similar changes; after the song of the Nibelungs, we find the admonitory verse of the Meistersinger, who are chiefly drawn from the artisan class.

But the great contribution of French art is in the realm of architecture. Gothic architecture, whose characteristic feature, rib-vaulting, originated in the Île-de-France, was to achieve great triumphs, first in a newly united France, then throughout Europe. Attempts had already been made throughout the twelfth century, in central Italy and Lombardy as well as in Normandy and England, though these can be considered no more than a preparation.

Within medieval art, the architecture of the church reigned supreme. This is not the place to investigate the origins of Gothic architecture; we would merely recall that it was evolved in the Île-de-France, a fertile landscape covered with rich pastures, cornfields and vineyards, a country that produced a beautiful, easily worked stone — the kingly limestone, not too hard yet weather-resistant, of a wonderful firmness that allows the boldest constructions. Through its position at the confluence of the Marne and Oise with the Seine, the Île-de-France became an important trade centre. It was to be the very heart of France, yet, at the end of the tenth century, it was still desolate as the result of many invasions, depopulated and ravaged by hordes of robbers. Only the Capet kings finally put an end to banditry, established the safety of towns and abbeys, restored trade-routes and secured the freedom of peasants, monks and merchants. In the twelfth century, the king's peace spreads over the Île-de-France, bringing wealth and prosperity, the conditions essential to all art.

The piety of the Capet kings, rooted in their natural disposition no less than political considerations, and of the clergy, whose strength was rapidly growing and from whose ranks the leaders of powerful religious movements were to emerge, found expression in the building of vast cathedrals. With the political and economic support of the monarchy, these were raised throughout France to the greater glory of God and the Virgin (Notre Dame). At the beginning of the thirteenth century, most of the great cathedrals of the royal domain were either completed or under construction. As the rule and authority of the king spread in France, so new building huts were opened outside the Île-de-France, the region of which it has been said that it not merely gave France 'law and political unity, but also the twin foundations of her culture and leading position in Europe: a literary language of infinite clarity and a highly creative form of art' (Luchaire).

The first Capet kings built a large number of convent churches and cathedrals; Guillaume de Saint-Pathus, the biographer of St. Louis, delights in listing the considerable sums the king expended on the building of churches — 100,000 livres for the abbey of Royaumont, 40,000 livres for the Sainte-Chapelle in Paris, and further monies for the churches of the predicant order in Paris, as well as in Pontoise, Vernon, Compiègne, Senlis, Rouen, Caen, etc.

The enthusiasm of the community for the house of God, which is also the house of the faithful who assemble there on feast days to dream of the glories of Paradise amidst the portal sculpture and the painted glass, is also a source of financial support; offertories are placed into churches under construction or into the counting houses of leading merchants, collections are made in town and country, even in the adjoining dioceses. Sums are advanced from the income of diocese and chapter; the clergy, the king, the aristocracy, as well as wealthy merchants and citizens who combine in brotherhoods, raise further contributions. Where necessary, general appeals are made. 'It is largely the poor widow's mite on which the cathedral of Paris was raised' reports the papal legate, Eudes de Châteauroux, and we could quote many, many other contemporary examples of the readiness of the people to bring sacrifices, regardless of their own circumstances.

Yet, despite this glowing zeal, the sums gathered were by no means adequate, and the buildings approached completion only very gradually bay by bay. Often, the building huts had to close for lack of funds; in consequence, building operations were often spread over many years. Though Chartres took only thirty years, work at Amiens continued for sixty, at Paris and Rheims for ninety, at Bourges it lasted a century, and Beauvais was never finished.

*Building periods*

In the second half of the twelfth century, as at St. Denis, Rouen and Chartres, the faithful, organized in brotherhoods, offered their services to the building hut. But, unable to cut stone or wood, to raise walls or to help in the construction of vaults and roofs, they could only perform the simplest tasks. The shortage of stonemasons, carpenters, blacksmiths, tilers, sculptors and glass-painters was serious in the extreme.

The head of the building hut was the master-mason. He sees the building as it will be after its completion. He knows foreign cathedrals, or cathedrals going up elsewhere in his own country, and longs that his own should be of greater dimensions, even brighter, and even more beautiful. Himself a stone-mason and chosen from the most capable of his craft, he knows all the secrets of his calling, passed on to him by his predecessors. He is also conversant with the other trades of the building hut he controls. After a six-year apprenticeship with a master, he travelled the country from building hut to building hut, recording at the same time his increasing skill, as Villard de Honnecourt had done. Villard de Honnecourt's sketch-book, which fortunately survives, contains notes and instructions of every kind, as well as drawings of machines and tools for raising blocks of stone, plans, details, sketches for cornices and sculpture — in fact everything that attracted his attention in the course of his travels from Cambrai and Saint-Quentin to Chartres, Meaux, Laon, Rheims, Lausanne and as far as Hungary. His architecture is a pragmatic science, supported by the geometric and algebraic formulas his master had taught him.

*Organization of the building hut*

FIGS. 3, 4, 5

After the bishop or the canons had approved the plan and perhaps also the

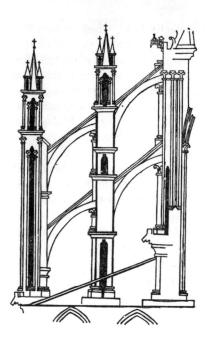

Fig. 3 – *The buttressing of the choir at Rheims Cathedral. From the sketch-book of Villard de Honnecourt*

model of the future cathedral, the master-mason, using a rope, marks the plan on the ground, then still partly covered by a variety of buildings, among them most probably an old church which has to be preserved at least in part so that worship can continue until the new building is ready to receive altar and relics. The master-mason draws up the plan, sketches the façade, and prepares drawings for the statues and the stonework in general; be supervises the stonemasons and the carpenters, where necessary he lends a hand with the more intricate tasks. He also completes the statues, invents lifting gear and introduces the workmen into the order of the hut. He himself has an office, a *chambre de traits*, in the building hut. His assistants include a superintendent, or *contremaître*, the *parlier* — in German still called *Polier* — who is in charge of the journeymen, and a comptroller responsible for the accounts. The master-mason receives a fixed annual salary and a house, sometimes also a plot of land or a vineyard, gloves and a master's coat, extra payment by the day for special tasks and provision for himself, his servant and his horse. He is not allowed to leave the lodge for other work without the special permission of his patron. If he has to give up his work because of illness or old age, he is granted a pension.

*Social standing of the master-mason*

The medieval master-masons were mostly outstanding personalities who enjoyed the patronage of bishops, abbots and nobles; occasionally, they even gained the personal friendship of the king, like Eudes de Montreuil, the

FIG. 4 – *The choir windows of Rheims Cathedral. Drawn after Villard de Honnecourt. Cf. pp. 21, 37*

companion of St. Louis during his captivity, or Raymond du Temple, the favourite of Charles V. From the end of the thirteenth century onwards their names are frequently recorded; Jean de Chelles is named on the south transept of Notre-Dame in Paris, similarly Pierre de Chelles, who was undoubtedly his son or grandson. The choir screens of Paris Cathedral are inscribed with the names of Jean Ravy and his nephew Jean de Bouteiller, who were active there from 1300 to 1351. Often, the names of architects are incised in the labyrinth, which is usually let into the pavement of the first nave bay: Robert du Luzarche and Pierre and Renaud de Corment at Amiens, Jean d'Orbais, Jean le Loup, Gaucher de Reims, Bernard de Soissons and Robert de Coucy at Rheims. They also appear on tombstones — Jean Deschamps at Clermont Cathedral, Hugues Libergier at Saint-Nicaise in Rheims, Jean Vast at Beauvais, and, above all, Pierre de Montreuil, *prince des maîtres tailleurs de pierre*, the 'prince of all stonemasons', the great architect who, with Jean de Chelles, infused a new life into Gothic architecture in the middle of the thirteenth century. With his wife Anna, he was buried in 1267 in the Lady Chapel at Saint-Germain-des-Prés, next to the

FIG. 6

FIG. 5 – *Standing male nude with staff. From the sketch-book of Villard de Honnecourt*

FIG. 6 – *Labyrinth. Drawn after Villard de Honnecourt*

new refectory which, like the chapel, was his work. Pierre de Montreuil was the brother of Eudes de Montreuil, and the uncle of Raoul, a son of Eude, who completed the nave of Saint-Denis.

Finally, some names have reached us through contemporary writings, among them Villard de Honnecourt, Chaumes, and Valrinfroy. Often, master-masons came from the same family.

The great architects were so busy in their *chambre de traits* that they sometimes gave little attention to the hut or the actual work. Nicolas de Biard, a well-known preacher of the time, takes them severely to task in a sermon of 1261: 'les maîtres de l'œuvre, ayant à la main la règle et les gants, disent aux autres "par ci le me taille" — mais ils ne taillent pas eux-mêmes, et cependant, ils reçoivent des honoraires plus élévés. Ainsi les évêques...' 'The master-mason, rule and gloves in hand, says to the others: "cut me this" — but they don't cut anything themselves, yet they are better paid. Likewise the bishops...' — for these always made him angry.

In the course of time, particularly after the middle of the thirteenth century, cathedrals become more and more elaborate, walls are pierced increasingly, the vaulting becomes lighter and lighter, the play of thrust and counter-thrust is more and more delicately balanced. Constantly, the architect has to increase his skill and knowledge in every branch of his art.

VAULTING The vaulting caps are stretched between pointed arches; thrust and counter-thrust are concentrated at the four corners of the vaulting bays, which have to be adequately buttressed by mighty stone arms — in turn supported by buttress piers — that rise above the aisle roofs to the base of the nave vaulting.

*Flying buttresses* FIG. 3 These buttresses were used from the end of the twelfth century, in Paris after 1180, at Chartres after the fire of 1194. At first they were mostly placed too low, to be increased according to need. They assure the balance of the high vaulting, at the same time making it possible to dispense with the tribunes which had seemed an essential structural device to the masters of the second half of the twelfth century, concerned to strengthen the building with a solid belt all round. With the disappearance of the tribune, the nave window could be made larger, an aim ceaselessly striven after by medieval architects.

The same impulse is responsible for the slender ascending lines, no longer interrupted by horizontal bands, and the reduction of the nave wall from four storeys to three. At the same time the capitals lose their characteristic Romanesque heaviness; they are now decorated with buds, followed in the fourteenth century by flowers and foliage, and eventually harden into bas-relief. This upward striving is characteristic of the architecture of the thirteenth and fourteenth centuries; it represents an aspect of beauty that corresponds to the profound magic of contemporary mysticism. Transverse ribs, supported by flying buttresses, allow the vaulting to become higher and higher, letting more and more light into the nave. The nave, at Senlis only 59 ft. high, at Noyon 72, and at Laon 79, has risen to 98 ft. at Sens, 106 in Paris, 113 at Chartres, over 122 ft. at Bourges, 132 ft. at Rheims, 147 ft. at Amiens and Metz and, finally, to 157 ft. at Beauvais.

In the middle of the thirteenth century the building was further deprived of PLATE P. 41 its solidity by piercing the triforium also towards the outside, replacing the masonry with glass, as at St. Denis, Troyes and Metz and in the choirs of Amiens and Beauvais. From the second half of the thirteenth century onwards, the thick outer walls that their builders had not dared to pierce with any but the narrowest openings, — as at Senlis and Notre-Dame de Paris — are filled-in with increasingly larger stained-glass windows, as on the transepts at Notre-Dame in Paris (1250–1260) and in the Sainte-Chapelle (1243–1258), a veritable shrine in glass. Here we really have the answer to PLATE PP. 29, 47 this search for light which would seem to have been one of the fundamental traits of the further development of Gothic architecture.

I have already shown in earlier study of Notre-Dame (cf. bibliography) that *Metaphysics of light* medieval architects did not merely aim to close their buildings with solid vaults to make them weather- and fireproof, but that they also strove to bring in more and more light by making the windows as large as possible. This abundance of light, the goal of all medieval architects and achieved fully from the middle of the thirteenth century onwards, did not merely serve to meet the desire for better natural lighting: it was to present to the worshippers religious truths in glass paintings, to 'enlighten' them, because light itself is of Divine origin. Like the mosaics of Christian basilicas, the wall-paintings in Romanesque churches and the reliefs and sculptures of the Gothic cathedral, stained-glass windows show '*aux simples gens qui ne savent pas l'escripture ce qu'ils doivent croire*' — to the common people, who do not know the Scriptures, what they ought to believe, in the words of Gerson, who did nothing but pass on the advice of the Church Fathers, of Synods and Councils of the Church, and of the Abbot Suger and St. Bernard. Glass paintings bring a warm and radiant atmosphere, enhanced by the coloured portions of the building, into our cathedrals. Thus the nave, where the faithful gather to seek healing, strength, instruction and refuge from the dangers and temptations of this world, shines and sparkles.

The significance of the stained-glass windows is accentuated by the contemplations of the mystics. In his writings the Abbot Suger quotes Dionysius the Areopagite, who was inspired by Plotinus, Porphyry and Augustinus, the Neo-Platonists of the third, fourth and early fifth centuries. Others whose teachings exercised great influence at the time were Gilbert de la Porée and the scholastics Rupert von Deutz, Walafried Strabo, Albertus Magnus, Thomas Aquinas and Bonaventura. Light, so they taught, was of Divine origin. It is an attribute of God and proof of his working; through it, His word is transmitted to the faithful. The mystery of transparency is already a miracle, for light is a substance, yet it is distinguished from other substances because it is able — exactly like God Himself — to penetrate other substances without breaking them: for that reason, it is also the symbol of the Immaculate Conception.

*Architectural symbolism*   Though not trying to follow the commentators of the Middle Ages in their at times rather esoteric interpretation of the symbolism of the architecture of the cathedral, we must yet recognize its existence. The cathedral is the image of the City of God, the Heavenly Jerusalem, the image of Paradise, as the liturgy of the consecration ceremony confirms. The nave walls display the events of the Old and the New Testament. The piers and columns are the Prophets and Apostles who support the vaulting of which Christ Himself is the keystone; the transparent windows that protect us from rain and storms and bring us clarity are the teachers (Honorius), and the portal, decorated with painted and gilt statues, is the gate to Paradise. The House of God, according to Gilbert de la Porée, Hugues de Saint-Victor, Robert Grossetête and the Abbot Suger, should be lit up by the sun, blinding through its clarity like Paradise itself. God is light, and light gives beauty to the world. The brightness of the cathedral therefore has to be increased by making the windows as large as possible, from the arcades up to the ceiling.

This, undoubtedly, was also the aim of Hugues de Noyer, who, as Bishop of Auxerre from 1183 to 1206, had the windows of the cathedral enlarged so much that 'the church, hitherto dark and sombre, in the manner of old buildings, now shone with the brightest radiance'.

The same longing filled all the great thirteenth- and fourteenth-century architects and bishops, whose most outstanding works we shall discuss in the following pages.

# II. GOTHIC ARCHITECTURE IN FRANCE

Notre-Dame, in Paris, is the last of the group of Early Gothic Cathedrals in which the galleries still had to support the structure at the expense of brightness within. Though flying buttresses came into use while the nave was under construction, the original scheme, begun with the choir, was continued. The cathedral was begun by Bishop Maurice de Sully in 1163, slightly later than Laon, where its forms are already to some extent anticipated. Of a clear and straightforward composition, Notre-Dame has a large nave, intersected by short, barely projecting transepts, and double aisles. The choir ambulatory is also double, although there are as yet no radiating chapels. In the traditional manner, the nave wall is divided into four storeys. The ground-floor arcades rest on sturdy piers, above are the tribunes, followed by rosette windows and, finally, the clerestory, whose small lancet windows have as yet no tracery; towards 1230, these are enlarged, dispensing with the rosettes. In the nineteenth century Viollet-le-Duc restored the original arrangement in the first nave bay after the crossing. The line of the piers dividing the inner and outer aisles shows alternating supports, both on the north and on the south side. The heavier, clustered piers correspond to the bases of the transverse arches and of the transverse ribs of the sexpartite cross-vaulting of the nave. They suggest the presence of flying buttresses which can be considered the earliest of the Gothic and whose date of origin lies

*Île-de-France*
*Notre-Dame*
APPX. PL. 2, 10

FIGS. 7, 8, 9

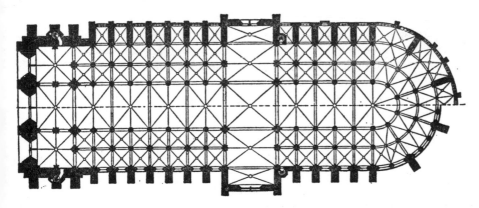

FIG. 7 – *Paris Cathedral. The lower half is shown before the addition of radiating chapels, i.e. before 1250*

27

FIG. 8 – *Paris, Notre-Dame. Nave wall: the two bays on the right are shown in their original state, with four storeys, those on the left after the merging of the lancets with the wheel windows. Cf. p. 27*

somewhere in the last quarter of the twelfth century, for the choir, begun in 1163 and consecrated on 19th May, 1182, was already far advanced in 1177. The nave was built between 1180 and 1200. About four years after the death of Maurice de Sully in 1196, his successor, Eudes de Sully, began the façade, which was finished in 1245. The chapels between the flying buttresses of the nave came later, the chevet chapels later still. The façade of the north transept dates from *c.* 1250, that of the south transept was begun on 12th February, 1258. The broad and majestic west front, whose mighty wall is hollowed by three portals, is held together by the tall gallery of kings, which

PLATE P. 29

Paris, Notre-Dame. The rose and gable storey of the south transept, by Jean de Chelles; begun in 1258, at the same time as the radiating chapels which surround the entire building. A principal work of the mature *style rayonnant*, completed *c.* 1276. The rose window, *c.* 40 ft. in diameter, is of later origin than that of the north transept. *Cf. p. 25, 28, 99*

rises to the very zone of the rose. The great rose window, with its firm, yet slender tracery, measures nearly 31 feet in diameter. Filigree-like arcading links the composition.

*St. Etienne, Bourges* The cathedral of St. Etienne, in Bourges, was begun in 1195 by Saint
PLATES PP. 31, 79, Guillaume — who died in 1209 — and completed *c.* 1270–1280. The large
81 *housteau*, the vast rose window on the west front, dates from the end of the fourteenth century and is the work of Guy de Dammartin, architect to the Duc de Berry. With the infinite grace of its proportions, its triangular cross-section and the clever staggering of all vertical and diagonal lines, Bourges, even more than any other Gothic cathedral, gives an impression of powerful upward movement. The plan and some of the detail recall Notre-Dame. But here the similarity ends. The vaulting of the aisles (30 ft. and 69 ft.) ascends in stages, as if to enclose and balance the nave (102 ft.), already adequately supported by flying buttresses. A similar arrangement has been used on the choir at Le Mans (built 1217–1245) and at Coutances, where the choir dates from the third quarter of the thirteenth century. The example of Bourges was outstanding; its influence spread as far as Toledo.

*Meaux* Meaux Cathedral, begun at the end of the twelfth century, still has tribunes. The nave, with double aisles — which, however, do not extend beyond the transepts — the columnesque arcade piers and the galleries above the outermost aisle all are reminiscent of Notre-Dame. Yet the eastern section tells an entirely different story. With a deep apse and three radiating chapels, it surprises by the simplicity of its composition and the beauty of its proportions. Villard de Honnecourt has drawn it in his sketch-book. Choir and nave were considerably altered in the fourteenth century, when a series of radiating chapels was added round the choir, and the tribunes — of which traces can still be seen on the piers — were removed. At Bourges, the situation was altogether different; tribunes as a feature had been dispensed with from the beginning, although it was decided to retain their purely structural aspect.

In certain regions, particularly on the frontiers of Burgundy, the Champagne and the Île-France, large cathedrals rose, among them Sens — of the same

The choir ambulatory of the double-aisled cathedral of St. Etienne, Bourges, completed in 1218. Like Paris, Bourges has a semi-circular apse, no longer usual in churches of that period, with a double ambulatory and small, oriel-like radiating chapels. The inner ambulatory and the dividing wall between the inner and outer aisle, like the nave wall above the ground-floor arcades (completed in 1260), have a low, almost stunted, triforium, each bay being divided into six arcades of equal height (on the nave wall these are staggered), spanned by a round-headed relieving arch. With the tall nave arcades, these triforium galleries produce the effect of an airy and richly differentiated interior. *Cf. p. 30*

age as Saint-Denis — and the choirs of Vézelay and of Saint-Germain-des-Prés in Paris, whose rib-vaulting is heavily buttressed to take the downward thrust without having to resort to tribunes. The nave wall is divided into three zones: ground-floor arcades, triforium and a row of very small clerestory windows, which, at Sens, were enlarged at the beginning of the thirteenth century, when the flying buttresses around the choir were built. The proportions differ from those of the galleried churches in the Île-de-France. The nave becomes lower and wider. At Sens it is 45 ft. wide and 80 ft. high, in Paris 41 ft. and 108 ft. respectively. Towards the end of the fifteenth century Martin Chambiges built the great flamboyant transept at Sens.

*Langres* Despite its rib-vaulting Langres Cathedral, at the other end of the Champagne, in what used to be northern Burgundy, still recalls Burgundian Romanesque churches such as the cathedral of Autun with its barrel-vaulted nave and rib-vaulted aisles. The choir and ambulatory, as well as the eastern transept façades, were built in 1141–1153 and are therefore of about the same age as Sens. Here, too, we find the same hesitation in the placing and buttressing of the cross ribs. Nave and transepts — three-storied, as at Autun — were built in 1170–1196. Without flying buttresses the architect, despite his skill and experience, has not been able to carry out his ideal plan any more than at Sens.

*Chartres*
PLATE P. 33
FIGS. 10, 11, 12,
13, 14
The first great cathedral to be freed from the limitations of the tribunes is Notre-Dame de Chartres, where flying buttresses allow every boldness of construction. The architect, sure of his knowledge and no longer reluctant to balance the tall vaulting with powerful buttressing, dispensed with galleries and opened up the walls into large windows filled with radiant glass paintings that showed the faithful all the Saints of the Golden Legend against the azure background of the sky. Sculptors now gradually introduce details from observed nature and bring the stone to life; without forgetting its architectural context, they endow monumental sculpture with a new noble bearing. Chartres is one of the great sanctuaries of the Virgin, where crowds of pilgrims come to worship her miraculous statue and the precious robe she had worn in life.

On 5th September, 1134, the façade of the Romanesque cathedral, built by Bishop Fulbert, was destroyed by fire. Soon afterwards, the towers — slightly in front of the old façade — were begun, first the north tower, then, towards 1145, the other. Around 1150 the façade was brought forward to form a line with the towers. Thanks to the general enthusiasm, the building progressed rapidly, for men came from everywhere to share in the labour of the artisans. In the night from June 9th to June 10th, 1194, another fire destroyed the old cathedral with its wooden roof, without, however, damaging the new façade, which had been protected by the vaulting of the first two bays and the gallery above. The decision to rebuild was taken shortly afterwards. The nave, begun first, was already far advanced by 1210; ten years later, it was completed, and the chronicler congratulated the master-mason,

Chartres, Cathedral of Notre-Dame. The west front. The north tower (left), called the *clocher neuf*, was begun in 1134. Originally it stood in front of the façade of Bishop Fulbert's earlier cathedral. The south tower (right), called the *clocher vieux*, was begun in 1145, when the nave was extended towards the west. The façade was brought forward between the towers in 1150; at the same time the — in part slightly earlier — portal sculpture was completed. The storey of the rose window and the upper part of the nave were built between 1210 and 1220. The north tower, damaged by lightning, was given its elaborate spire, designed by Jean de Beauce, between 1507 and 1513. At a total height of 509 ft., it surpasses the south tower whose spire, however, measures nearly 280 ft. — by 30 ft. *Cf. pp. 32f.*

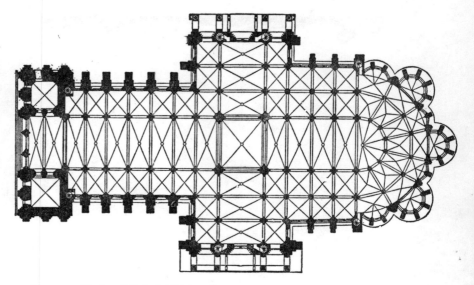

FIG. 10 – *Chartres Cathedral. Cf. pp. 32f.*

Guillaume le Breton, on his 'recently completed' vaulting that was to protect the church against fire in the future. The lower parts of the transepts were built between 1200 and 1220, followed by the choir — of which the canons were able to take possession in 1221 — and, in the succeeding years, the choir ambulatory and the radiating chapels. The upper portions of the transept and the two transept porches belong to the years between 1220 and 1245. On 24th February, 1260, the church was solemnly consecrated. The work of the coming years did little to change the appearance of the cathedral. The graceful steeple of the north tower, by Jean Texier, called Jean le Beauce, was built between 1507 and 1513. On 4th June, 1836, the church was damaged by fire once more; roof tree and towers were destroyed although the vaulting proved firm and the cathedral itself was saved. Today, the vaulting is protected by an iron framework covered with copper sheeting.

APPX. PL. 11 The nave has a length of 558 ft. 6 in. — or 638 ft. 2 in., if we include the Chapel of Saint-Piat, added in the middle of the fourteenth century — and is 45 ft. 5 in. wide. The rib-vaulting, quadripartite and oblong — at Paris and Bourges still sexpartite — rises to a height of nearly 253 feet, each compartment being less than a foot in diameter. It is supported by three groups of flying buttresses — of which one was built slightly later, at the same time as the two choir buttresses — and rests on powerful piers, strengthened by four engaged columns. Here, alternating supports have become purely decorative: a round pier with polygonal clustered shafts is followed

34

FIG. 11 – *Chartres Cathedral. Cross-section. Height of the nave 120 ft. Cf. pp. 32f.*

by a polygonal pier with round shafts. The play of the light interrupts the monotony that a succession of identical piers might have caused. The aisles ascend to a height of 46 ft. The articulation of the walls is reduced to three stories — the ground-floor arcades, the triforium with its arcading of dwarf columns, and the clerestory windows, divided into two lancets surmounted by an eight-lobed rosette. With the transept windows and the great rose windows, of a diameter of 44 ft., these windows, which are of the same height as the ground-floor arcades, give the interior its radiant glow that is unique in French medieval architecture.

The rib-vaulting of the five chevet chapels in the cathedral of Saint Gervais

35

FIG. 12 – *Chartres Cathedral. Nave wall. Cf.pp. 32f.*

FIG. 13 – *Chartres Cathedral. Tracery of the western rose window. 1210–1220. Cf.pp. 32f*

FIG. 14 – *Chartres Cathedral. Tracery of the southern rose window. c. 1220. Cf.pp. 32f.*

FIG. 15
*Soissons*
and Saint Protais at Soissons extends into the corresponding bays of the choir ambulatory, although the plan follows Chartres. The famous round south tower, reminiscent of the towers of galleried churches, was built at the end of the twelfth century, the rest of the building dates from the early thirteenth. On 13th May, 1212, the choir was consecrated. The nave was completed in the middle of the thirteenth century, the façade of the north transept, as well as the upper portions of the towers, in the fourteenth. The consecration ceremony of the whole building was not performed until 25th April, 1479.

*Rheims*
On 6th May, 1210, the cathedral of Notre-Dame in Rheims, where the kings of France were anointed, was destroyed by fire. Its main sections had been built in the middle of the twelfth century. The original galleried church

36

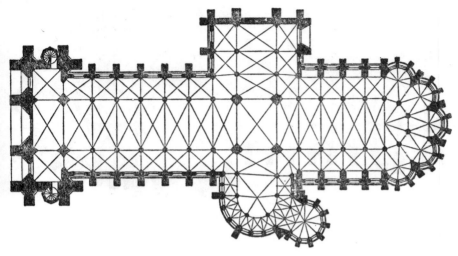

FIG. 15 – *Soissons, Cathedral of St. Gervais and St. Protais*

was thought to have been nearly as large as the present cathedral, an FIGS. 16, 17, 18, 19 assumption confirmed when the old foundations were examined.

A year later, on 12th May, 1211, Archbishop Aubry de Humbert laid the foundation-stone of the new cathedral. Work was begun with the choir, followed by the south front and, in 1241, the north front. The choir was consecrated on 7th September, 1211, on the eve of the anniversary of the birth of the Virgin. The ceremony was performed by Archbishop Henri de Braisne, who died in 1240 and is buried in front of the main altar. He is portrayed in the central window of the chevet.

Villard de Honnecourt, who visited the building hut in the early stages, has left us a record of the chevet chapels and the choir façade in his sketch-books. FIG. 4 The original version was somewhat modified, perhaps because there was not enough money available; indeed, we know that collections, authorized by the Pope in 1221 and 1251, were made in the diocese. The nave, more or less undamaged by the fire of 1210, was restored so that — as in Notre-Dame, in Paris — services should continue without interruption. Space was also needed to display the precious relics and to perform the coronations of two future kings, Louis VIII (August 1223) and Louis IX (29th November, 1226). The new nave, begun 1241 after the completion of the choir and the transepts, was not ready until the end of the thirteenth century.

The names of the architects of Rheims have been recorded in the labyrinth, FIG. 6 formerly on the floor of the third and fourth nave bays but destroyed when the floor was renewed in 1776. Fortunately, a sixteenth-century drawing, by Jacques Cellier, survives. The first name is that of Jean d'Orbais, who

37

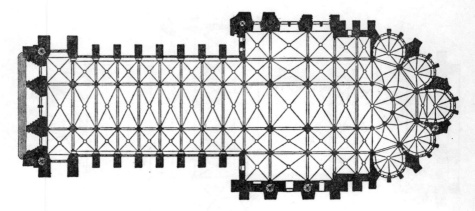

FIG. 16 – *Rheims Cathedral. Cf. pp. 36, 39*

FIG. 17 – *Rheims Cathedral. Cross-section. Height of the nave 123 ft. Cf. pp. 36f.*

FIG. 18 – *Rheims Cathedral. Tracery of the tympanum window of the west portal. After 1255. Cf. pp. 36f.*

FIG. 19 – *Rheims Cathedral. Tracery of the western rose window. Completed c. 1285. Cf. pp. 36, 39*

was probably trained in the building huts of the beautiful abbey churches of his homeland towards the end of the twelfth and the beginning of the thirteenth century. He was the author of the plan, which was hardly changed throughout the building years. Jean d'Orbais began with the eastern sections, first in the south, then in the north. He is responsible for the choir with its double aisles, the ambulatory, and the five radiating chapels — the central chapel is slightly longer than the others — the transepts and the last eastern bays of the nave, as well as the wall of the last three eastern bays of the north transept, which was formerly adjoined by low-ceilinged rooms, possibly sacristies. Jean d'Orbais was active at Rheims for twenty years, from 1241, and his work was completed by Jean le Loup — 'qui fut maître des travaux d'icelle église l'espace de 16 ans et commença les portaux' (who was master-mason at this church for sixteen years and began the portals).

Jean le Loup was head of the Rheims building hut from 1231 to 1247. After the completion of the choir, he laid the foundations for nave, west front and towers. His successor, Gaucher de Reims, an inspired sculptor, 'ouvra aux voussures et portaux' worked on the archivolts and portals on the west front from 1247 to 1255. He was succeeded by Bernard de Soissons, who was master-mason for the next thirty-five years, from 1255 to 1290. According to contemporary records, he 'fit cinq voutes et ouvra à l'O'...' made five vaulting bays and worked on the rose window. A contemporary drawing shows him with a design of the rose window in his hand, while Jean d'Orbais is marking the plan on the ground with a rope and Jean le Loup is holding an angle measure. Gaucher de Reims is portrayed with a stonemason's

APPX. PL. 3

FIG. 19

hammer. Bernard de Soissons is thus responsible for bays five to nine of the naves and the aisles; he also carried the west front, begun by Jean le Loup, beyond the rose window, and was in charge of the sculpture programme after Gaucher de Reims.

Robert de Coucy, Bernard's successor from 1290 to 1311 (he died on 12th November, 1311), closed the four westernmost bays of the nave and completed the façade. It was undoubtedly he who was shown at the centre of the labyrinth. In the fourteenth century the upper stories of the towers and the steep gable between them were begun; the fifteenth century finally saw the completion of the work.

FIG. 16 The cruciform plan is clear and simple. The nave, as far as the crossing, is flanked by two aisles: the choir, with double aisles, terminates in a semi-circular apse with an ambulatory and five radiating chapels. Inside, the cathedral is 586 ft. long, on the outside 623 ft. The rib-vaulting, which rises in the nave to a height of 125 ft. and in the aisles to 54 ft., terminates at the keystone in a pointed arch. Similarly, the vaulting bays are framed by pointed arches — throughout an arrangement calculated to reduce the force of thrust and load with the lightest possible buttressing arches. Above the ground-floor arcades, supported by round piers, each with four engaged shafts, and the triforium gallery with its elegant small columns, the nave windows flood the interior with a glowing light whose rich colour scale is even further enhanced by the stained glass, today to some extent missing or replaced. The façade of Rheims cathedral is one of the most famous of the Gothic — probably *the* most famous, through the elegance of its composition no less than through its wealth of stained glass and the sculpture, which, though in continuation of the tradition of Chartres, Paris and Amiens, fore-shadows in its beauty and originality the style of the fourteenth century. The influence of Rheims, whose sculpture, soon famous throughout Europe, was imitated in Germany, England, Spain, and even Italy, can also be traced to a large number of figures of saints and angels in gold, ivory and wood, undoubtedly minor reflections of the art of the great cathedrals.

*Amiens* Like the cathedrals of Chartres and Rheims a few years earlier and Beauvais slightly later, Amiens, in 1218, also became a victim of the flames. Recon-
FIG. 20 struction was begun under Bishop Evrard de Fouilly, whose bronze tomb — like that of his successor Geoffroy d'Eu — stands in the nave, the earliest portion of the new building. At the death of Geoffroy, in 1236, the façade had risen as far as the gable; the nave was completed, and it was now necessary to demolish the old church of Saint-Firmin to make room for the north

Rheims. Cathedral of Notre-Dame. View from the choir towards inner west wall with its sculpture cycle of 32 figures, unparalleled in the art of the west. For the first time a rose window has replaced the tympanum relief above the central portal. Above is the glazed triforium, surmounted by the western rose window (completed in 1285) which, in contrast to Laon, Paris and Chartres is fitted into the pointed arch by means of

spandrils, thus avoiding the compromise solution of a round-headed arch. The nave walls are divided into three storeys, following the example of Chartres. An important innovation appears for the first time: the traceried window, achieved by merging two windows into one. The nave was completed in 1311. In the perfect harmony of all its parts Rheims surpasses Chartres. *Cf. pp. 36f.*

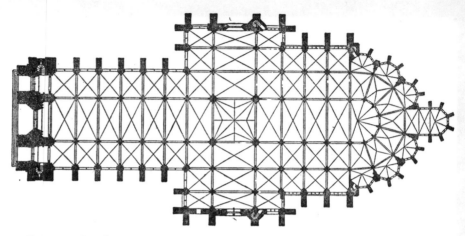

FIG. 20 – *Plan of Amiens Cathedral*

transept. The choir was begun in 1210; in 1247 Bishop Arnould was buried there. The whole population contributed, particularly the *waidiers* (indigo-dyers) who had become rich through the discovery of woad, the source of a beautiful blue dye; they built one of the chapels, on whose reliefs they appear.

In 1269 the choir was completed, and Bishop Bernard d'Abbeville now had the centre window placed into the choir façade. The relics of St. Firmin were brought back in 1279. In the last years of the thirteenth and at the beginning of the fourteenth century, the side chapels were added to the nave and the towers completed, the south tower still in the second half of the old century, the north tower slightly later. The two first chapels on the north front were built in 1375 under Cardinal Làgrange, Bishop of Amiens, who, with King Charles V, and the king's sons, Louis d'Orléans and the Dauphin, Charles, as well as Bureau de la Rivière, is portrayed among the highly expressive sculptures on the façade of the chapel and the adjoining tower.

FIG. 6    Again, as at Rheims, the names of the architects of the cathedral are recorded in the labyrinth which was let into the centre of the nave in 1288. Robert de Luzarches supplied the plan and the model for the building; he is also responsible for the monumental sculpture programme of the west front. The work begun by him was continued by Thomas Cormont and completed by Thomas' son Renaud.

The plan and composition, the proportions, the articulation of the façade and the masterly vaulting display a degree of taste, logic and formal rhythm that make Amiens one of the most perfect cathedrals of the Middle Ages. It is the culmination of Gothic architecture, its highest, most Classic, expression. The plan resembles Rheims, although there are seven, instead of five, radiating chapels, with a much longer centre chapel. The inner length is 437 ft., the outer 522 ft., slightly less than at Rheims. The transepts have a total length of 230 ft., the width of the nave from pier to pier is 48 ft., the width of each aisle 28 ft. 5 ins. The rib-vaulting in the nave rises to a height of 139 feet, in the aisles to 60 ft. The piers, each strengthened by four engaged columns, have cusped and foliated capitals. The nave wall, above the aisles, is interrupted by a triforium, whose attractive traceried triple arcading is surmounted by quatrefoils. In the choir and in the transepts, of a later phase, the triforium opens towards the pierced outer wall. The windows of the nave — which take up almost half the total height — and the windows of the transepts and the chapels give the interior a rich and jewelled light.

Seven years after the fire of Amiens, the old cathedral of Beauvais also burned down. In 1225 Milon de Manteuil began the vast new choir, whose main structure was completed in 1272. It has an ambulatory and seven radiating chapels of equal size, forming a cross. The vaulting of the nave rises to a height of 156 ft., that of the aisles to 69 ft. Above the nave arcades, which rest on slender piers, the pierced wall of the triforium seems to make the tall clerestory windows even larger; on the outside, twin buttresses support the tall vaulting, transmitting the thrust and counter-thrust to strong supporting piers. *Beauvais* FIGS. 21, 22

With every new cathedral the aim was to build higher and higher, and to dispense with the impression of weight altogether. At Beauvais things had been carried too far. In 1284 the nave collapsed. The buttress arches were then doubled, and the former oblong quadripartite vaulting compartments were replaced with sexpartite vaulting. In 1324, under Guillaume de Roye as master-mason and Aubert d'Aubigny as stonemason, the new work was completed. But money had run out, and it was only in the sixteenth century that the church was given its flamboyant transepts by Martin and Pierre Chambiges, Jean de Damas, Michel Laliet and Jean Vast. The tower of the crossing, 502 feet high, proved too great a load for its supporting piers and collapsed on 30th April, 1573. It was almost impossible to find the resources to remedy such vast damage; the nave, in the end, was never built.

With these cathedrals, Gothic architecture in France reached its peak; it cannot be surpassed, nor does it lend itself to further metamorphosis.

In the choirs at Amiens and Beauvais, in Saint-Denis, and — towards the end of the thirteenth and the beginning of the fourteenth century — at Saint-Urbain in Troyes and the cathedrals of Metz and Evreux, an even more radiant light enters through the triforium, pierced and glazed towards the outside. The *claire-voie*, the pierced wall, occurs for the first time at Saint-Leu-d'Esserant; it is the beginning of a new phase. Soon the wall itself will have become one great window, a screen of glass reaching from the ground-floor arcade to the roof, thus reducing the articulation of the façade to even fewer components. The same spirit produces buildings that appear increasingly light and weightless, almost floating upwards. Delicate ribs *Principle of pierced walls* stand out sharply against the vaulting. The simple cusped capitals of the thirteenth century become rounder and assume elaborate foliage.

*Evolution of the façade* The façade grows more elaborate; the rose window, larger in each successive church, comes to resemble a wheel with thin spokes of stone. Towering gables of lace-like transparency, crocketed and enriched with foliage, rise above portals where stained glass now frequently replaces the tympanum. Buttress arches, increasingly delicate, also assume a filigree-like outline.

Almost everywhere, on portals, gables, buttress piers and on the windows along the cornices, the stiff leaves of the thirteenth century yield to more and more elaborate, meticulously carved foliage; crocket flowers open to full bloom. A supreme awareness of the play of light and shade — originally accentuated by painting, of which few traces remain — finds expression on every moulding and every ornament. In the fourteenth century towers are surrounded with narrow arcaded walks or parapets at the base of the helms, which — as far as they materialize at all — now have pierced spires, a feature particularly notable in Germany (Freiburg, the original design for Cologne Cathedral, etc.).

This new type of the Gothic — more perfect and bold, leaner and overbred, richer and more elegant, yet less vigorous and aristocratic than the well-balanced art of the first half of the century — emerges from the Île-de-France from the middle of the century onwards under the guidance of two great Paris masters, Jean de Chelles and Pierre de Montreuil, who gave Gothic art a new face.

*Notre-Dame, Paris. Last building phase* In the second half of the thirteenth century, Notre-Dame, in Paris, had a series of chapels along the aisles, between the buttress piers. The outer walls of these chapels formed one line with the transept façades. It was now decided to increase each transept by one bay to carry it beyond the aisle chapels. The master-mason of Notre-Dame, Jean de Chelles, was commissioned with the work which, according to an inscription carved into the base of the south transept, was begun with the foundation-stone ceremony on Tuesday, 12th February, 1258. Jean de Chelles completed the façade of the north transept; the south transept was the work of his successor, Pierre de Montreuil, who had undoubtedly been his pupil. He is also the architect of the nave and transepts of St. Denis, of the Lady Chapel and the Refectory PLATE P. 47 of Saint-Germain-des-Prés and, most probably, of the Sainte-Chapelle in Paris (1245–1248). Pierre de Montreuil died on 17th March, 1267, having completed the façade of the south transept of Notre-Dame, as well as the first choir chapels and the *porte rouge* on the north front, which was decorated with the most enchanting sculpture.

The two masters were also responsible for the great rose windows above the tall, pierced transept façades, which are more graceful and intricate than the transept walls of the slightly earlier cathedrals of Saint-Denis and Chartres. In all probability they also supervised the execution of the stone sculpture, where a new spirit is manifest, a spirit that was to lend fame to the monu-

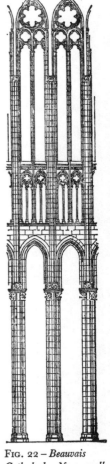

FIG. 21 – *Beauvais. Cathedral of Saint-Pierre, cross-section. Height of the nave vault 156 ft. Cf. p. 43*

FIG. 22 – *Beauvais Cathedral. Nave wall. Cf. p. 43*

mental sculpture of Rheims in the second half of the thirteenth century. The figures are livelier, their bearing is less forced, their gestures show greater inventiveness; their expression is dominated by the smile of eyes and lips, the famous '*sourire de Reims*'. This new, slightly more realistic art lacks some of the hieratic grandeur, of the severity we admire in the earlier figures on the west front. Many scenes, treated like small pictures in stone, seem to have little connection with the dominating architectural concept. Yet the art of

45

the Île-de-France still has sufficient restraint to avoid the exaggerated and the bizarre.

The smaller churches around Paris in the succession of the great cathedrals, above all Notre-Dame, are legion — Arcueil, Bagneux, Montreuil, Beaumont, Gonnesse, Champeaux, Saint-Leu (Esserent), and others.

The art of the masters of the crown lands, the art of the great cathedrals of northern France, spreads rapidly throughout the country; it meets us in the finest cathedrals and great churches of the thirteenth and fourteenth centuries, not only in the Champagne and in Burgundy, whose Gothic art remains closely linked with that of the Île-de-France, but also in certain towns of central France and in the south, where the bishops had close links with the crown and where the masters of the Île-de-France were active. Thus Jean Deschamps, thought to be a native of Amiens, who had seen the new choir and the transepts of Saint-Denis and was conversant with the major works of Jean de Chelles and Pierre de Montreuil, began Clermont Cathedral in 1248, Limoges Cathedral in 1273, Rodez Cathedral four years later and Narbonne Cathedral in 1286. His influence and that of his son Pierre, who was his successor in the various building huts until 1330 or 1340, asserted itself to a high degree in the churches of southern France: at Bordeaux (where Paul Courtrance and M. J. Gardelle have discovered traces of a Bertrand des Champs), at Bayonne, at Saint-Nazaire de Carcassonne and in many buildings beyond the Pyrenées. Jean Deschamps died, rich in years, shortly before 1295. He rests under the floor of one of his churches, Clermont Cathedral.

The traveller through France can soon recognize the buildings more or less influenced by the cathedral art of the north; the most characteristic examples are the cathedral and the church of Saint-Urban in Troyes, the collegiate church of Saint-Quentin, the choir of Saint-Ouen at Rouen, Auxerre Cathedral — whose choir was begun in the first quarter of the thirteenth century and whose nave was completed in the fourteenth — the transepts of Tours Cathedral, the façade of Strasbourg and, in part, the cathedrals of Metz, Châlons-sur-Marne, Toul, Evreux, Sées, Tréguier, Quimper, and Saint-Pol-de-Léon. At the same time, other churches, although contemporary with the buildings directly inspired by the masters of the north, retain their regional character.

*The east and south-east*

Some churches in the east and south-east preserve the plan and even the articulation of the façade customary in the Romanesque and in pre-Romanesque Carolingian times; examples include the cathedrals of Verdun and Besançon — both of which have apses at opposite ends — Toul, Dijon and Lyon, (whose nave was begun in the second quarter of the thirteenth century and completed towards the end, and whose façade is of fourteenth century and later origin), as well as the cathedrals of Vienne, Grenoble and Saint-Jean-de-Maurienne.

Even more characteristic are the cathedrals and major churches of Nor-

The Sainte-Chapelle, Paris. The eastern end of the upper church, by Pierre de Montreuil. Built as the chapel of the royal palace in the manner of the chapels of episcopal palaces; above the lower church, of the basilica type, is a vast chamber which relies for its overpowering effect on the noble structural detail and on the radiance of the stained-glass windows which are among the earliest in Paris. In 1134 scenes, these windows tell stories from the Old and the New Testament and from the lives of the saints. For the first time in French architecture, canopied figures stand at the piers inside the church; they link the arcading, enriched by gilding and enamel, with the windows. The whole composition has rightly been compared to a precious reliquary. *Cf. pp. 44, 103*

mandy, which represent the earlier type in even purer form: Lisieux, Rouen, Coutances, Bayeux, Sées and, in the north and west of Brittany, Dol, Saint-Brieuc, Tréguier and Saint-Pol-de-Léon, where the Norman tradition is still preserved in many respects.

In Normandy, the cathedral art of the Île-de-France already predominated towards the end of the twelfth century, as at Lisieux; from about 1200 onwards it develops its distinct character that was to triumph in the second half of the century. The plans of all these buildings show a long nave, transepts, and a choir with an ambulatory and radiating chapels. The façade is divided into three stories: ground-floor arcades, a tall triforium unrelated to the windows above, with a passage behind the triforium and another at the base of the clerestory windows. Sometimes, at Bayeux and in the choir of Coutances, even the triforium has been dispensed with and the façade is reduced to ground-floor arcades and clerestory windows with a narrow passage running along them. The crossing is frequently surmounted by a lantern dome which — as at Coutances — may be of considerable dimensions; many of these domes recall the central towers of some English cathedrals. The vaulting is sometimes strengthened by ridge ribs, which, at the corners, are met by intermediary ribs. The profile of ribs and cornices is deeply cut and hollowed, exactly as on the piers. The architects of Normandy still delighted in the play of light and shade. Great emphasis is placed on the curve of the arch; small arches are made with the same movement of the compass as the arches surrounding them. The arcades of the semi-circular choir rest on double arcading, the ribs of the vaults on curved corbels. The thirteenth century bell capitals are surmounted by a round abacus. Individual statues or scenes in relief are almost unknown, yet the luxuriating foliage and the decoration of the cornice show an extraordinary inventiveness. Characteristic features are the rosettes, trefoils, quatrefoils and other, often tiny, geometric forms hollowed into the unadorned wall, producing a sharp contrast of a black cavity against the white stone.

Among the most famous of the many churches built in the Champagne during the thirteenth and fourteenth centuries are Saint-Yved, in Braisne, Saint-Jacques, in Rheims, Orbais, Saint-Urban, the cathedrals of Troyes, Bar-sur-Aube, Saint-Quiriace, Saint-Ayoul and Sainte-Croix in Provins, Lagny and Rampillon, and, in Burgundy, the cathedrals of Auxerre, Dijon and Nevers, the choir at Vézelay, Saint-Père near Vézelay, Chablis, Notre-Dame in Dijon, Semur-en-Auxois, and Saint-Martin, in Clamecy.

In the Champagne the vaulting of the choir ambulatory is sometimes based on square bays and the adjoining triangular wedges, in which case the cross ribs spring from the flanking columns of the radiating chapels. Where the aisles have small apsidal terminations, these are arranged diagonally. Frequently, the choir end is straight. Sexpartite vaults are retained until well into the twelfth century. Occasionally, the arcading is based on coupled pillars with a round abacus, as in Normandy. The triforium continues the

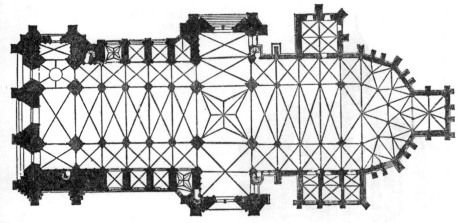

FIG. 23 – *Plan of Auxerre Cathedral*

tracery of the clerestory windows already at a very early stage. A gallery runs along the base of the aisle windows. Ornament, in soft limestone, is elaborate and deeply undercut.

The straight apse occurs particularly often in Burgundy; square choir chapels open towards the transept, as in the churches of the Cistercian order, whose monks, often outstanding architects, spread Burgundian art throughout the Christian world. Large churches have a choir ambulatory, sometimes with a single chapel along the central axis. Sexpartite vaulting continues until well into the thirteenth century. Ribs spring from short shafts, based on

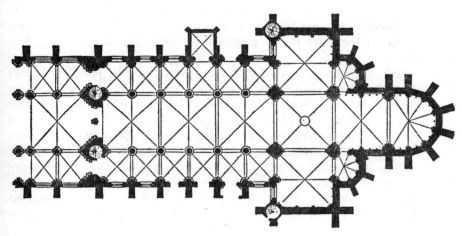

FIG. 24 – *Plan of Dijon Cathedral. Cf. p. 48*

49

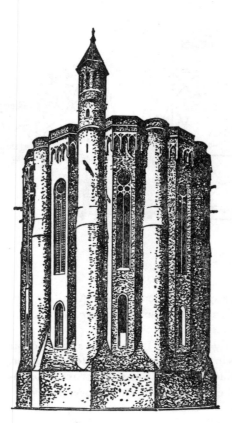

FIG. 25 – *Albi Cathedral. Choir end. Cf.* *below*

corbels carved with masks or elaborate foliage. The triforium is higher than in the Île-de-France; in the spandrils of the slender arcades are vigorously carved heads. A passage runs along the base of the nave clerestory windows. The height of the outer wall is governed by the triforium and the gallery above.

*The south*     The south of France — apart from the cathedrals built by Jean Deschamps and other northern masters and therefore derived in varying degrees from the art of the north — possesses a number of buildings which, through their specific character, form an independent group within the architecture of the Gothic. The nave of Toulouse, completed in 1211, about the time of the siege of the city by Simon de Montfort, is one of the earliest monuments in this group. Its width and height are exactly the same; the choir is more reminiscent of the architecture of the north.

FIGS. 25, 26, 27     The cathedral of Albi, begun on 15th August, 1282, was not consecrated until 23rd April, 1480. A brick structure, it resembles a real fortress, dominated by a donjon; its bell-tower is 256 ft. high.

Mention must also be made of the cathedrals of Béziers, Saint-Bertrand de

FIG. 26 – *Albi Cathedral. Cross-section.*
*Cf. p. 50*

Comminges, Perpignan, Montpellier, Lodève, Lavaur, Marmande, Lombèz, and Mirepoix (1297) — with one of the biggest naves and a width of 71 ft. — as well as Carpentras and the churches of Saint-Martial and Les Célestines at Avignon. All these churches are characteristic for their unaisled naves and their rib-vaulting, supported by tall inner buttress piers which enclose chapels. The unaisled nave, reminiscent of the hall churches of the Romanesque, has another unusual feature; it is built in brick, a material

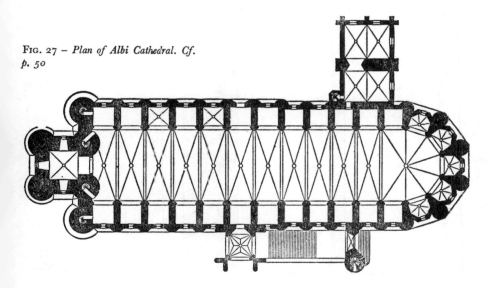

FIG. 27 – *Plan of Albi Cathedral. Cf.*
*p. 50*

preferred in this region on account of its cheapness. Unaisled interiors also allow for more direct contact between the priest and the congregation; in addition, they meet military needs, for the walls can easily be doubled in thickness and, finally, they have the great advantage of comparative cheapness. The interiors of these unaisled churches, wide, bare and lit only by narrow windows, are of a spaciousness that the churches of the north, with their dramatic upward movement, lack. The façade, its block-like form unbroken by chapels and buttresses and pierced only by small windows, gives the impression of strength and power; these churches look like fortresses and many are, indeed, fortified. The nave is generally very wide; in many cases there is no vaulting, in others it was added long after the completion of the church. Sometimes the roof is open, supported by a series of arches that span the nave. Large stepped octagonal towers, modelled on the handsome tower of Saint-Sernin in Toulouse, rise above the nave. Some of the smaller — as well as a few of the larger — churches have open belfries in the gable.

FIGS. 28, 29    The churches of the Jacobin friars at Toulouse and Agen belong to a group of their own. A central colonnade, which supports the vaulting, divides the nave into two sections, one for the monks — in the earlier Dominican church in Toulouse this was smaller — and another for the laity.

FIG. 28 – *Toulouse Jacobin Church. Cross-section. Cf. above*

Fig. 29 – *Toulouse, Jacobin Church. Cf. p. 52*

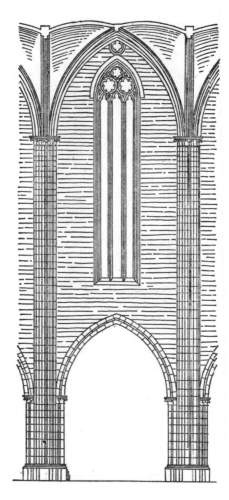

Instead of striving heavenward, like the cathedrals of the north, these southern churches spread out on the ground. They are the pattern of the preaching church, adopted by the architect of Il Gèsu in Rome which, in turn, became the model for many later churches. 'Broadened by the Renaissance, the Gothic of the south ruled for over another two centuries' (Emil Mâle).

In their construction, these churches in the south follow the same principle of rib-vaulting as those of the Île-de-France, however much they may differ from them in other respects, unlike the Angevin churches, the last important group to be discussed in this chapter.

The earliest churches of this type, which spread from Anjou throughout the west of France, as far as Aquitaine, often have unaisled naves, like the twelfth-century cathedrals of Angers, Laval (1136–1158), Saint-Malo, Vannes, Bordeaux, and Fontevrault. The vast interiors of these churches, *Anjou and Aquitaine*

FIG. 30 – *Poitiers Cathedral. Cross-section*

which in plan and façade follow the domed churches of Aquitaine, have tall domical vaulting of a type that appears to reduce the function of the ribs considerably. At the beginning of the thirteenth century the Angevin architects, anticipating structural developments of the distant future, designed a domical vault whose cross ribs only represent a skeleton without any load-bearing function, a system of vaulting which was rapidly adopted not only in the Loire valley, in the south of Brittany and in western France, but also, during the thirteenth and fourteenth centuries, in Spain, England, Germany, the Netherlands and Scandinavia.

In the second half of the thirteenth century the naves, transepts, choirs and aisles at Angers Cathedral, in the Hospital Saint-Jean and in the church of Saint-Serge in the same city, at Puy-Notre-Dame, at Aisnière, at Candes, at Sainte-Radegonde, at Airvault, at Romorantin and at Mennetou-sur-Cher are given a type of vaulting reminiscent of domes or oblong barrel-vaults, although the vaulting compartments are joined like cross-vaults supported by an elaborate system of cross- and ridge ribs, which, deeply embedded in the masonry, extend as far as the delicately profiled shafts that support the vaulting.

*Poitiers*
FIGS. 30, 31  At Poitiers, the two eastern bays, built between 1162 and 1180, have domical rib-vaulting of the same type as that in the nave at Angers; the ribs of the lierne vaults of the six other bays, of the thirteenth century, are so thin that they almost disappear in the mass of the domical vaulting.

These ribs have no load-bearing function; they merely serve to guide the architect in the construction of the vault which rests on the transverse arch

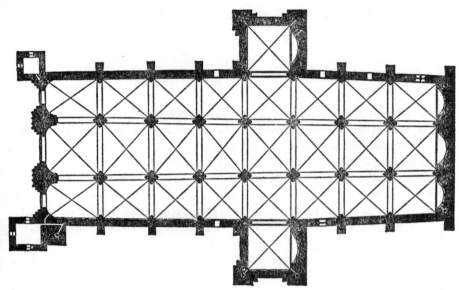

Fig. 31 – *Plan of Poitiers Cathedral. Cf. p. 54*

and the wall arch. Here lies the origin of the lierne vault, which appears everywhere throughout Christian Europe in the fourteenth century and continues in use throughout the Middle Ages. The vaulting now often consists only of lath and plaster. Where aisles occur, as at Poitiers, they are of the same height as the nave they support, exactly as in Romanesque churches, thus preventing the light from falling directly into the nave. All Gothic churches, even those that adhere closely to a regional tradition or appear to depart furthest from the Classical type, follow to a greater or lesser degree the examples of the great cathedrals raised in the Île-de-France and the French heartlands at the time of St. Louis with the help of the Capet rulers as part of a great spiritual and cultural revival that affected the whole country. Rib-vaulting allows the cathedrals to rise higher, in ever greater radiance and seeming weightlessness. Their composition seems to mirror the edifice of medieval thought, of mystic, religious and theological thinking as well as of social striving.

Their iconography embraces the Old and the New Testament, the story of Jesus Christ, of the Virgin Mary and the Saints, the Last Judgement — everything, in fact, that men have to know and believe.

These buildings caused the admiration of the rest of France and of Christian Europe; everywhere they became a source of inspiration. Gothic architecture, which released such a powerful impulse in the thirteenth and fourteenth century, was to live on in many places until the seventeenth and eighteenth; its hold extended even to regions where art had hitherto followed the tradition of Antiquity.

AWARENESS OF
NATURE
FIG. 32

The new spirit that found expression in architecture also set new tasks to the sculpture of the cathedral. Artists, no longer content to repeat forms hallowed by tradition, began to observe the world around them, the flowers in the fields and the trees in the forest, whose praise St. Francis was to sing. They encountered nature with a profound sense of wonder; it was to become for them the path to a new language of ornament. Around 1200 new motifs appear on the façade of Notre-Dame in Paris: rose bushes, strawberry plants, vines, watercress, ferns, acorns, maple-leaves. In the course of the thirteenth century buds open into full foliage; in the fourteenth, we find veritable garlands, branches laden with fruit and flowers; in the fifteenth, the foliage has shrivelled and the branches have become sharp and thorny, like trees at the end of a scorching summer.

*Anatomy*
FIG. 33

The human form in its natural posture and accurate proportions is now also studied. Increasingly substantial, it gradually detaches itself from its background, where it had hitherto stood out as bas-relief; in the thirteenth century, it obtains a third dimension.

The thirteenth-century sculptor does not look for individual detail. He knows that he works for a greater entity and therefore shows types rather than individuals. St. Martin, on the south transept at Chartres, represents the type of an Apostle, a man of action, full of energy and enthusiasm; St. Jerome, opposite, is a typical scholar, unassuming and reserved. St. Theodore, on the adjoining portal, is a young knight, proud and bold, while the Joseph at Rheims is boastful and a flatterer, 'lively, gay and full of tricks, a story-teller and a maker of verses' (H. Focillon).

The sculpture programme is confined almost entirely to the façade. The capitals no longer need to instruct; their decoration would only divert attention from the general upward movement. Throughout the thirteenth century they dwindle in volume and importance; their basic meaning and purpose are expressed in simple and harmonious forms.

The portal sides under the relief-covered tympanum now become the background for large statues and are thus integrated in the general composition of the façade. At first figures are still slender and elongated, although they soon receive more natural proportions, without losing their nobility and restraint. Iconographic motifs become simpler and more defined, so that the worshippers should see their meaning clearly, without any need for com-

FIG. 32 – *Gothic choir-stall. Detail from the sketch-book of Villard de Honnecourt*

mentary. The frightening monsters and exotic beasts disappear. Their place is taken by the gentle animals of home and farm who — like all God's creatures — have a right to their place in the decoration of the church. The symbolism that had governed the whole of the twelfth century is not altogether abandoned in the thirteenth, but it becomes simpler, easier to understand, and more logical: in the cruciform plan of the church, orientated towards the east, as in the past, the dark north front is reserved for the Old, the light-flooded south front for the New Testament, while the west front, touched by the rays of the setting sun, displays the story of the Last Judgement and the end of all things. The Old Testament prepares the New: Isaac, Moses, Joseph and Samuel are Christ's forerunners, David, Jeremiah and Isaiah foretell His Passion, John the Baptist proclaims His Divinity, the aged Simeon hails Him. The Virgin Mary is given a place of honour as the mother of Our Lord and the representative of the Church.

Iconography is by no means a matter for the artist's imagination. It is *Iconography* defined as precisely as the dogma of the Church, for it is a method of teaching, a mode of instruction *par excellence,* laid down by Councils and Popes; 'l'art conduit les âmes par le moyen des choses matérielles aux immatérielles' (art guides the souls with the help of material things to the immaterial), declared the Abbot Suger of St. Denis.

Each subject is portrayed according to a definite canon. The Son of God in the *Maiestas Domini,* surrounded by the Evangelists' symbols and winged apocalyptic creatures, a principal theme of the Romanesque, has been replaced on the façade by the Last Judgement, which is invariably shown in the same arrangement: the Resurrection of the Dead, the weighing of the souls, separation into the good and the wicked, the Judge of the World between Mary, St. John and the angels with the instruments of the Passion; the Ascension, scenes from the childhood of Jesus, the Madonna and Child enthroned or the Adoration of the Kings and, finally, from the end of the twelfth century, as at Senlis, the Death of the Virgin, her Assumption and her Coronation.

The new concept of nature as a reality in itself, with its own significance, is inspired by the Aristotelian picture of the world, which, by way of the Arabs in Cordoba and Toledo, spread gradually to the great universities, decisively transforming medieval thought. In consequence natural forms came to be given preference to signs and symbols.

The thirteenth and fourteenth centuries are also the age of the encyclopedias, the *summae,* in which medieval man ordered and classified all the knowledge of his time. The *Speculum maius* of Vincent de Beauvais comprises — as Emile Mâle has proved so brilliantly — the basic truths of the natural sciences in four main sections: the *speculum naturale, historiale, doctrinale, morale.* The *Summa*

FIG. 33 – *A prophet. After Villard de Honnecourt. Cf. p. 56*

*theologica* of Thomas Aquinas, the most beautiful edifice of thought ever created, places the philosophy of the ancients and of more recent thinkers, as well as the new truths, within the framework of a rational order. Vincent de Beauvais' *Speculum* and Thomas Aquinas' *Summa* take form in the cathedral, which appears as an illustration of their writings, for it shows the same severe dogmatism and religious intensity; here, too, are calm and firm logic and a sense of order. All vagueness, mysteries, transcendental visions and miracles are things of the past. Everything is confirmed in the daylight of a rational, logical catechism; Gothic monumental sculpture proclaims its inherent truth and reality, in art and natural science no less than in the realms of morals and religion. Everything is classified and ordered according to a rational system; composition and execution of every scene are carefully worked out in advance.

This certainty of knowledge that dominates the *summa* and the *specula* endows the sculpture it inspires with a suggestion of gaiety, which contrasts sharply with the mood of the art of the previous epoch. Scenes of great drama, such as the Passion — represented in full only very rarely at the end of the century — at Strasbourg or Rouen, the sufferings of the martyrs, or the torments of the damned, are all steeped in the ideal calm and peace of an atmosphere where all excess of suffering, even suffering itself, are banished, where faith and reason rule equally, and where everything seems destined for eternity. The terror-striking figure of the apocalyptic God has been replaced on the tympanum by the Christ in Glory from the St. Matthew's Gospel; though a severe Judge on the Day of Judgement, He will be attended by the Virgin and St. John as the intercessors for humanity (Deesis groups). In addition, we find the concept of the teaching and blessing Christ who has descended to the world of man. The Madonna also leaves her majestic heavenly throne and turns towards the faithful, to whom, with the enchanting gesture of a young mother, she presents her Divine Son, who wants to play with her like any other child. Yet distance is preserved; the representatives of heaven remain above the people crowding at their feet.

Thirteenth-century art, monumental and universal, appeals to reason rather than the heart, to the congregation rather than the individual. Similarly, the Gothic sculpture of the cathedral is created for the mass of the believers, who are firmly rooted in a deep and unshakable faith. It radiates, not the loving tenderness of St. Francis, but the vigorous *bon sens*, the logical and rational spirit of St. Louis. 'The cathedral is the expression of man's gratitude to God: it presents to him Creation, turned Christian' (André Malraux).

*Building huts* The noblest competition went on between the French building huts, whose members strove constantly to raise higher and higher vaults about the bright and spacious naves. The work of other huts inspired artists to strive for ever nobler ideals. Undoubtedly, under the powerful impulses of the great architects, there was unanimity in the different workshops. Yet no artist ever copied the work of another; not a single example exists of identical

Fig. 34 – *A king. After Villard de Honnecourt*

figures, at Chartres no more than at Rouen or Amiens, in the Apostle series no more than among the prophets or kings.

The master-mason was in charge of the hut; he set the sculptors their tasks and saw to it that the iconographic programme, determined by the clergy of the cathedral, was carried out properly. The earliest surviving contracts date from the end of the fourteenth century, but things will harldy have been any different in the thirteenth. The whole programme was laid down at the beginning of the work, for the building itself as well as for the statues, which were carved either in the workshop or in the building hut. The place for each figure was clearly marked, as we know from existing records, particularly in the case of Rheims.

*Sculptors*

The master-mason supplies the sculptors working under his direction with drawings, sketches, and measurements. Sometimes he takes up mallet and chisel to make a few corrections, for he is himself a sculptor. He is as responsible for every detail of the sculpture programme as he is for the whole architectural scheme. The sculptor is also a stonemason; in the *Livre des Métiers* of 1268, by the dean of Paris, Etienne Boileau, he is often confused with him, for he is subject to the same severe discipline; he, too, has to pass through a long apprecticeship and must be thoroughly reliable in his work. In the thirteenth century the members of the building huts organized themselves according to trades; later, in the sixteenth and seventeenth centuries, they formed guilds. Sculptors at work in their hut with chisel, mallet and compasses were often portrayed in art, in the thirteenth century on the Saint-Chéron window in the north choir at Chartres, in the fourteenth on Giotto's campanile in Florence and at the Doge's palace in Venice, etc. These scenes show that the statues, usually completed in the workshop, were made for specific positions, to stand in a certain light.

*Technique*

A clear picture thus emerges of the work of the stonemason. The stone, from the best quarries of the region, arrives at the site already cut into rectangular blocks, usually of medium size. It is placed diagonally, almost in a horizontal position. As the material is chiselled away, a figure —Christ, the Madonna, a saint or a king —emerges from the rock. The sculptor, who wears gloves for his protection, first forms the arms, head and body with chisel and mallet, and then carves the hollows of the draperies with a special gouge. In the background are the drawing he works from, either on parchment or cut into wood, an angle measure and—rarely missing—a cup or glass from which to refresh himself when necessary; he does not use a model, nor a clay or plaster figure, which could have been transferred to the stone with the point and line method—a system apparently not adopted until the fifteenth and sixteenth centuries. During the great flowering of the building huts, the figure was carved directly from the instructions of the master-mason, in accordance with the programme laid down by the clergy. It must have taken several days to complete a boss or a bracket; to complete one of the archivolt sections with one or two figures about 4 ft. 6 in height will have needed six weeks, a large portal figure about three months. Obviously much depended on the hardness of the material. This technique also explains the preference for calm and restrained postures throughout the thirteenth century, for the precise and reserved gesture, which is governed by the character and shape of the block and thus corresponds so admirably to the clear upward movement of the architecture. Here the function of monumental sculpture is truly fulfilled. The figure preserves some of the block-like quality of the stone, some of its volume and strength. The tall statues on the towers of Rheims cathedral, nearly 14 ft. high, were carved from a series of superimposed stone blocks, each 2 ft. high, from Courville. Expression and gesture are of a restraint partly determined by the technique, but also governed by tradition. The broad faces, gay and self-assured, have none of the affectation that accompanies the realism of

*Colour in sculpture*

the end of the century. The gaze, like other features, is accentuated by colour, for colour was an integral part of sculpture and its setting. Face and hands were given their natural colours; mouth, nose and ears were slightly emphasized, the hair was gilded. Dresses were either covered in flowers or painted in vigorous colours; ornaments, buckles, and hems were highlighted by brilliant colours or even studded with polished stones or coloured glass. The whole portal looked like a page from an illuminated manuscript, enlarged on a vast scale.

Fig. 35 – *Sleeping Apostle, from an Agony in the Garden. After Villard de Honnecourt*

Old Testament figures on the central portal (right) of Chartres Cathedral. *C.* 1145–1155.
The two figures on the left, somewhat shorter and of greater plasticity, are slightly later than the two elongated figures on the right. Interpreted as pillars, they are part of the column and not — like later figures (cf. Plate p. 73) — placed in front of it. In the capitals the canopy, fully developed later on the south front of the cathedral, is already indicated. *Cf. p. 63*

Many contemporary records tell of the close relationship of sculpture and colour; undoubtedly, painting also served to some extent as a protection against the weather. The wicked angels at Santiago di Compostela are painted black, the good angels white. At Chartres the Madonna of the *porte royale* was gilded, as was the *Vierge Dorée* from the south transept porch at Amiens, of whose gilding some traces remain. The Armenian Bishop Marty who visited Paris in the fourteenth century, greatly admired the façade of Notre-Dame, which he compared to a miniature.

PLATE P. 83

Painting, too, followed strict rules. The *Livre des Métiers*, already mentioned in these pages, describes how the completed statue is to be impregnated with some kind of linseed oil and given an undercoat of white lead before it receives its final colours. The rule was '*que nulle sculpture de pierre séant à l'église ou ailleurs ne soit faite qu'elle ne soit imprimée*' — 'that not a single stone figure in the church, or anywhere else, was to be left "unprinted"', i.e. without its polychromatic decoration. The thirteenth century chose lively natural colours; in the fourteenth colours lose their radiance, and patterns, which now frequently cover the whole figure, become black, brown, or golden; some reports even speak of certain statues, like the Madonna of the Chapelle du Collège de Beauvais in Paris by Raymond du Temple, which were completed 'sans peinture' (without painting).

*Schools of sculpture*

The sculptors, chosen from the most capable stonemasons, are members of the building hut; every detail, the foliage of a capital or the tracery of a window, has to be carved with the same precision as a statue. They know the work of other huts, where they may even have worked themselves. This explains a certain resemblance between the sculpture of different schools, all of which, however, preserve their identity. No statue of Chartres can be confused with one of Paris or Amiens, any more than a work of the second half of the thirteenth century can be confused with one of the end of the century, for the evolution of Gothic sculpture is rapid and highly differentiated.

Though we can distinguish between the work of different hands in the same school, the identity of each group is clearly established. Undoubtedly, not every statue was made by the master-mason himself; many examples, even from famous workshops, are of indifferent execution. The architect has to reckon with such possibilities; in accepting them, he will try to give the best positions to the most beautiful figures, even where — as, apparently, at Rheims — they were not intended to be placed there.

*Local traditions*

Each hut preserves its own tradition. The calmest, most solemn monumental sculpture, steeped in the gentlest glow, appears at Chartres, though the sculpture of Paris shows greater elegance and a more aristocratic reserve, while the figures of Amiens are more natural and life-like, and those of Rheims, more carefully worked out, have a more graceful bearing and a sparkling vitality. The treatment of the draperies also emphasizes the distinction into schools and epochs. In Chartres the draperies fall in many thin parellel folds, like a soft flowing material; at Paris and Amiens they are deeper and more expressive, as if in a thick, heavy cloth; at Rheims they sometimes form thin folds (*mouillés*), in the tradition of Classic sculpture. In the fourteenth century these differences increase; folds become supple and generous and, draped around the figure, perhaps gathered over an arm, cascade down heavily, sometimes in a slightly monotonous flow.

No records are left of the great individual sculptors, although we know the names of the men in charge — Robert de Luzarche at Amiens, Gaucher de Reims and Bernard de Soissons at Rheims, Jean de Chelles at Notre-Dame in Paris. Yet none of the sculptors are mentioned personally and no text tells us anything about them. *Names of sculptors*

After Saint-Denis and Chartres with their *portes royales* from the middle and the second half of the twelfth century, after Senlis and Laon, Gothic sculpture attains its finest flowering in the great portal groups of the first half of the thirteenth century. The transept portals of Chartres, the result of nearly half a century's work, afford the best illustration of the path of Gothic sculpture from its early stages to the monumentalism of the middle and the second half of the thirteenth century and its last manifestations in the fourteenth; a distinct trend towards realism can be noted throughout.

After the cathedral of Chartres was burned down in 1194, it was decided to retain the old *porte royale* and the surviving towers on the west front. In consequence, the sculpture programme, displayed at other cathedrals on the west front, had to be distributed over the transept façades, which thus assumed greater significance than elsewhere. On the north front the central portal is dedicated to the Madonna, who, in the symbolism of the Middle Ages, is also the representative of the Church; the left portal displays scenes from the childhood of Jesus, and on the right are figures from the Old Testament. The south front illustrates the New Testament; the central portal tells the story of the Last Judgement, the left portal is surrounded by figures of the early martyrs, and the right by the confessors of the Church. This great sculpture programme, one of the most outstanding of the Gothic, took many years to complete. Work went on without interruption from 1200 to *c.* 1260; examination of the figures and of the decoration of the two porches, which were added later, will allow us to date the different portions. *Chartres*

The two central portals — the Madonna portal on the north transept and the Judgement portal to the south — are the earliest; in the author's view, the north portal was begun first. On both portals the jamb figures — the Patriarchs and Prophets on the north front, the Apostles on the south portals — are still stiff and elongated, like the figures on the *porte royale* on the west front. But the artist has imbued them with life; the proportions are already more natural, the heads turn in different directions. Yet the arms are still pressed to the body, the draperies are rigid and run parallel, and the pleats — a characteristic feature of the school of Chartres — are thin *PLATE. P. 61* and shallow. A gentle glow radiates from these figures, which are carved in the beautiful Senlis limestone.

*North portal* The north portal — as at Senlis and, above all, at Laon and Mantes — portrays Christ's ancestors, the Patriarchs and Prophets who spoke of His coming. On the left are David, Samuel, Moses, Abraham and Melchizedek, on the right Isaiah, Jeremiah, the aged Simeon, St. John the Baptist, and St. Peter, with the staff of Aaron on his breast. With their clarity of completely unbroken outline, their barely protruding eyes and their solemn astonished faces, these figures are among the finest of their kind in the Middle Ages. They inspired many similar groups — to name only the west front at Rheims — but remained unequalled until Claus Sluter, in the fountain in the Chartreuse at Champmol, re-awakened them to new life.

*South portal* The figures of the south portal are of the same type, although perhaps a little less rigid, with slightly more differentiated expressions. The finest, Christ at the central pillar, although clearly the work of a more experienced hand, bears some resemblance to the statues of the north portal, among others Jeremiah. The hollow eyes, the strong nose, the narrow lips, the protruding cheek bone have none of the serene yet simple grandeur of the

PLATE P. 67 *Beau Dieu* of Amiens, who rises above the crowd. The gentle and sensitive face, with the suggestion of pain and sorrow around the mouth, assumes more human features and seems to turn towards mankind. The figure of St. Anne with the Virgin on her arm, on the central pillar of the north portal, is probably the most recent of this group, since it cannot antedate the arrival of the head reliquary of St. Anne, hitherto preserved in Constantinople, in 1204 (the head is a modern replacement).

*Tympana* As at Senlis, the tympanum of the north portal tells the story of the Death, Ascension and Coronation of the Virgin; for the first time these scenes are told in the serene yet simple form that was to govern their representation throughout France in the thirteenth and fourteenth centuries.

The south portal portrays the Last Judgement. Here this subject, gradually evolved with more and more detail at Saint-Denis, Corbeil and Laon, is already presented in all its principal features — the Resurrection of the Dead, the weighing of the souls, and the separation into the blessed and the damned, with every kind of punishment and retribution. But the sculptor has not succeeded in giving unity to his composition; his work lacks the grandeur of the Last Judgement at Paris, Amiens, or Bourges. Almost the entire height of the tympanum is taken up by the figure of

PLATE P. 65 Christ, seated as the Judge of the World between Mary and St. John, and the angels with the instruments of the Passion. The women in the crowd of the blessed and the damned are already wearing on their heads the *touret* ('wheel'), of the time of St. Louis. The whole scene is framed by the Nine

*Side portals* Angel Choirs on the archivolts. The side portals were added gradually, more obviously so on the north transept. Of the earlier south portals, the Martyr's Gate on the left is the oldest: the three flanking figures on each

Chartres Cathedral. Figures of the damned from the right archivolt of the central south portal; the tympanum shows Christ pointing to his stigmata, flanked by the Virgin and St. John. Opposite the damned, in the left lower row of the archivolts, are scenes from Paradise; above, on both sides, are figures of the dead (partly shown in our illustration) rising from their graves. The figures from left to right depict a woman of fashion, a nun, and a merchant with his money-bag, all about to be taken by the devil, and a particularly hideous monster who is carrying off a nude young girl by the legs, her long hair trailing on the ground. *Cf. p. 64*

side, St. Stephen, St. Clement and St. Lawrence on the left and St. Vincent, St. Denis and St. Piat on the right, still represent the type of statue linked to the pillar, unlike the figures of St. George and St. Theodore, who, lively and natural, already stand firmly on their feet, and have become largely independent of the column.

In the six figures on the jambs of the Portal of the Church Fathers, though of the same type as those on the Martyr's Gate, the emancipation from the pillar, the transformation of the *statue colonne* into free-standing sculpture, has become complete. On the left are the Pope, an archbishop or a bishop and St. Leonard (or St. Sylvester), St. Ambrose and St. Nicholas. Tall, slim, of uniform bearing, looking straight ahead, perhaps slightly superior in their heavy robes, they have the reserve and dignity of princes of the Church. The three figures on the right are particularly interesting. St. Gregory, who radiates a strong inner life, listens to the dove who dictates the commands of the Holy Spirit to him; St. Jerome, the scholar and Bible translator, small, unassuming, almost timid, looks as if he were seeking the protection of St. Martin who stands next to him, an image of strength towering above the rest. Miracle-worker and Apostle, St. Martin had travelled across Gaul, seeking out demons, destroying pagan images, baptizing the crowds. Like St. Nicholas, St. Jerome stands on a horizontal base. Neither of them is any longer a pillar figure.

The tympanum of the left portal tells the story of St. Stephen, the first martyr; the tympanum of the Church Father portal shows scenes from the story of St. Nicholas and St. Martin.

The jamb figures on the side portals of the north front are sturdy and full of vitality. On the left are the Annunciation, with the Prophet Isaiah, and the Visitation, with the Prophet Daniel; on the right are Bileam, Solomon, and the Queen of Sheba. The left tympanum tells the story of the Nativity, the right illustrates the Judgement of Solomon and the sufferings of Job, framed by scenes from the story of Samson, Gideon, Judith and Esther on the archivolts.

*Porches*  The porches, added later, are covered with reliefs and statues of a more advanced style; they are like a premonition of the attractive statuettes of the former rood-loft, of which a few fragments survive.

*Chronology*  In the author's view, the different portions of this veritable '*summa*' can be dated with some degree of accuracy. The earliest part, in all probability, is the central portal of the north transept, whose sculpture dates from about 1200, possibly 1204, the year of the arrival of the relics of St. Anne. The statue at the centre pillar belongs, roughly, to the year 1210. At the same time, or slightly later, the jamb figures, the tympanum, and the archivolts on the south transept were begun. That of Christ teaching was undoubtedly completed by 1212, the date of the marriage of the probable donors, Pierre Mauclair and Alix de Thouars. The two southern side portals followed, first the left, *c.* 1215–1220, then the right, *c.* 1220–1225; work on the statues

Christ blessing, the so-called 'Beau Dieu' from the centre pier of the principal west portal of the Cathedral of Notre-Dame in Amiens. C. 1230. In bearing, gesture and attributes — the feet resting on a lion and a basilisk — this figure belongs to the tradition of the central south portal at Chartres, although the artist is clearly influenced by the school of Paris. The tympanum above the Christ figure displays the Last Judgement, with the resurrection of the dead, the division into the good and the wicked, and Christ as Judge of the World. *Cf. pp. 64, 70*

of St. Martin, St. Jerome and St. Gregory possibly went on until *c.* 1230. The northern side portals were not begun until 1220 or 1225; they were completed between 1230 and 1235, although work on the north porch, the archivolts and the jamb figures continued until the middle of the century. The four most recent jamb figures of the side portals date from *c.* 1230–1240, slightly earlier than the sculptured decoration of the porch. All these sections — and probably also the rood-loft — were completed when the cathedral was consecrated on 24th October, 1260.

The figures and reliefs of the west front of Notre-Dame, in Paris, date from the same time as the sculpture on the transept portals at Chartres. Their style is like a synthesis of Laon and the Chartres transepts on the one hand and the façade of Amiens on the other. Though less earnest than Chartres, Notre-Dame is also more elegant and formal than Amiens.

*Madonna portal*

The earliest part is the Madonna portal to the left of the central portal on the west front; its statues date from 1210–1220. Dedicated to the glorification of the Virgin in Paradise, it is the greatest song of praise to her to take form in the thirteenth century. The theme, established iconographically at Senlis in 1185, also appears at Mantes, Laon, Braisne, Chartres and, soon afterwards, at Longpont and Amiens. At Notre-Dame, it stands under a unique aspect. The traditional scenes, the Death of the Virgin, the Ascension, and the Coronation, with all the delightful and moving detail, had little appeal to the more rational and aristocratic mind that conceived the composition of the façade of Notre-Dame. Here the sculptor has shown the Death and Resurrection of the Virgin in a single scene; every statue takes its place within a vast scheme that is worthy of the architecture. The Madonna on the trumeau pier, the Saints on the jambs, the Apostle on the central portal, the figures on the right portal and the statues on the gallery of kings above are nineteenth-century work made in the studio of Geoffrey Dechaume, under the guidance of Viollet-le-Duc. The spandrils, however, as well as the archivolt figures and the numerous reliefs on the Madonna portal and on the central portal, are old and, in their composition and workmanship, of a remarkably high standard; their original gilding and polychrome decoration have unfortunately been lost.

At that stage the sculpture of Chartres has the character of high relief, although it still remains part of the building and therefore compels the artist to follow and respect the principal outlines of the architecture. At the same time a new feeling for nature becomes manifest in these portals, not only in the statuettes and in the different scenes, but also in the wealth of the characteristic plant motifs, derived from direct observation. But even here realism is still kept within the architectural context. Nature is experienced as Spring, precious, hesitant, though already full of promise, a promise that was to be shown in its fulfilment in the sometimes very pronounced realism of the fourteenth and, above all, the fifteenth centuries.

*Judgement portal*

The central portal with the Last Judgement was carved in *c.* 1220. Christ

The vice of cowardice: an armed man throwing away his sword and fleeing from a rabbit. From the cycle of the virtues and vices on the base of the central west portal of the cathedral of Notre-Dame in Amiens. *C.* 1320. Some authorities consider this cycle an early work of the Naumburg master. With the scenes of the months, the liberal arts and sciences, illustrations of works of mercy, and similar themes, they are part of the veritable encyclopedia of medieval life that unfolds on the façades of French cathedrals. *Cf. p. 72*

as the Judge of the World, surrounded by His heavenly retinue, dominates the Resurrection of the Dead and the Weighing of Souls, scenes destroyed in 1771 and replaced in the nineteenth century, partly with the help of fragments in the Musée Cluny. The reliefs on the base represent the virtues that guide the elect to Paradise and the vices leading the way to hell.

*St. Anne's portal*  On the right is the portal of St. Anne. Its tympanum, one of the lintels, the figures on the trumeau pier and the jambs, and some of the statuettes on the archivolts, from *c.* 1165–1170, had been intended for another portal in the manner of Saint-Denis and Chartres, but were re-used by the thirteenth-century architect. About 1225, to fit the composition in to the new façade, a second lintel was added with the story of Anne and Joachim and the marriage of Mary and Joseph. Their supple movements and more balanced proportions contrast with the severe, harsh draperies of the narrow, elongated figures in the scenes from the childhood of Jesus in the upper lintel. Above is the Virgin Enthroned — as at Chartres — attended by the founder of the cathedral, Bishop Maurice de Sully, the dean, and King Louis VII.

AMIENS  At Amiens, the three portals of the west front are in a remarkably good state of preservation; the tall jamb figures give some idea of the original portals of Notre-Dame. Though the proportions at Amiens are perhaps a little more slender and more elegant, the influence of Notre-Dame is unmistakable.

Nowhere has the iconographic programme of the theological, historical, moral and natural *summae* been realized more fully; in style and concept, the sculpture is of a unity unequalled elsewhere, for the whole work was carried out within a comparatively short time, between 1220/25 and 1236. Although different hands and different influences can be discerned throughout the Amiens workshop, there is, under the guidance of the master-mason of the cathedral, Robert de Luzarches, a unity, an intimacy that is considered a specific trait of the school of Picardy. In the jamb figures, on the tympanum reliefs and on the buttress piers it becomes the expression of a picturesque and gentle realism, of an art that aims to portray everything; even the mysteries of religion and its transcendental truths are told with great exactitude in a distinctly popular language.

The jambs on the three west portals are covered with statues and bas-reliefs.

PLATE P. 67  Christ, on the trumeau pier, the *Beau Dieu* of Amiens, surrounded by the Apostles and the four great Prophets, Isaiah, Jeremiah, Ezekiel and Daniel,

Amiens Cathedral. Madonna and Child, known as the 'Vierge Dorée' because of the original gilding, from the central pier of the south portal, 1255–1260. Immediately above are the Twelve Apostles, discoursing in pairs. In the arcading of the base are Prophets and sibyls (below) and saints (above). The Madonna and the Apostles clearly suggest the influence of the Rheims Joseph master; they are, without question, the finest example of his school. *Cf. p. 72*

PLATE P. 69

teaches under the archivolts that signify the heavenly spheres. The tympanum displays the Last Judgement, the base, within medallions, virtues and vices, —an almost exact repetition of the small bas-reliefs at Notre-Dame, in Paris— on the right portal are the Madonna and Child, at the sides large figures representing the Annunciation, the Visitation, the Presentation in the Temple, the Three Kings, Herod, Solomon, and the Queen of Sheba. The tympanum shows the Death, Ascension and Coronation of the Virgin. On the trumeau pier of the left portal are St. Firmin, first bishop of Amiens and patron saint of the cathedral, and his earliest successors. The translation of St. Firmin's remains is shown on the tympanum; on the base are the signs of the zodiac and the occupations of the months. The twelve Prophets, in four groups of three, stand on the buttress piers; below them, in quatrefoil medallions, are scenes illustrating their lives and their prophecies. The Gallery of Kings, with twenty-two figures, each measuring over 12 ft., occupies the rest of the façade.

The west front of Amiens thus combines scenes of the great events of both the Old and the New Testament.

South transept

A quarter of a century later, between 1260 and 1270, the sculptors of Amiens carved the figures of the Twelve Apostles and scenes from the life of St. Honoré above the south transept portal. At the trumeau stands the famous

PLATE P. 71

*Vierge Dorée*. The smiling face is turned towards the Christ Child. The beauty of her noble, yet relaxed, bearing, the magic of her expression, her restrained gesture and the natural fall of the draperies show that the impulse of Rheims has also reached Amiens.

RHEIMS

The sculpture of Rheims was not completed until the end of the thirteenth century. As at Chartres, Paris and Amiens, it allows us to trace the development of figure sculpture during one of the finest periods of French art.

Master-masons

The names of the successive master-masons are known to us: Jean d'Orbais and Jean le Loup, Gaucher de Reims and Bernard de Soissons.

North transept

The portals on the north transept at Rheims must be seen as three separate entities; the first leads into the sacristy, the second to the cloisters, and the third to the canons' court. The two great portals were made between 1220 and 1235 under Jean d'Orbais and Jean le Loup. At the central portal, the Sixtus gate, St. Sixtus is shown on the trumeau in his papal robes. On the jambs are the figures of Job, St. Remigius, an angel, St. Eutropius and St. Nicasius, and an angel from the first cathedral workshop.

The almost stunted proportions, the broad shoulders, the short legs, and the

Rheims Cathedral. The Visitation (of Mary and Elizabeth), from the central west portal (right). Before 1250. The 'Visitation Master' (cf. the Angel of the Annunciation, p. 77), who was obviously active in Rheims before the school of Amiens could exert its influence there, works in a distinctly Classic style, as can be seen from the draperies and the suggestion of the body underneath. The figures display the Classic counterpoise, their weight

resting on one leg, while the other stands at ease. The youthful head of the Virgin, the ideal portrait of a young girl (cf. Plate p. 75), faces the ideal portrait of an old woman. These figures were the direct inspiration of the German master who created the group of the Visitation at Bamberg which, like the French example, is one of the greatest triumphs of Gothic sculpture. *Cf. p. 74*

draperies that cover them in agitated, angular fall, already belong to a far more sophisticated art which, at the same time, is dominated by the influence of classical Antiquity, as can be seen from some of the most famous works on the west front. This change from one style to another is also strongly emphasized in the statues on the jambs of the adjoining Judgement Portal (1230–1235) and in the figures of St. Paul, St. James, St. John, St. Peter, St. Andrew and St. Bartholomew, as comparison with the six statues of Christ's forerunners and Christ's ancestors on the right jamb of the right portal on the west front will show. The tympanum of the Sixtus gate shows the martyrdom of St. Nicasius, Clovis' baptism, scenes from the life of St. Remigius, and Job among the ashes. On the Judgement Portal are the separation of the good and the wicked, figures of the virtues and vices, and a particularly charming scene of the elect whom angels are guiding to Paradise. Above is the Resurrection of the Dead, portrayed with great gusto and perfect realism by an artist who has shown the human body in innumerable positions with great anatomic accuracy.

*West front*

Though the west front of Rheims may lack the unity and the dogmatic and historical accuracy we admire at Chartres, Amiens, or Notre-Dame in Paris, the wealth and diversity of its sculpture have made it equally famous. Each portal has a window, surmounted by a tall gable, in place of a tympanum. The Madonna portal is flanked on one side by the Annunciation, the Visitation, Solomon, and the figure of a magician, on the other by the Presentation in the Temple, Isaiah, and the Queen of Sheba; in the gable is the Coronation of the Virgin. The left portal shows scenes from the life of Christ, the Passion and the Resurrection, distributed over the archivolts and the gable; it is also the portal of the diocesan saints, whose statues stand on the jambs. The archivolts, the outer buttress piers and the gable of the right portal are covered with scenes from the Apocalypse and the Last Judgement. The tall figures on the right jamb belong to an entirely different iconographic programme. They represent Christ's ancestors and Christ's forerunners, and were originally intended for a Madonna portal similar to that at Senlis. They were completed c. 1230.

PLATES PP. 73, 75

*Interior*

To quite an exceptional degree the sculpture programme unfolds within the cathedral and at the back of the portals. In rectangular niches, framed by foliage, the stories of St. John the Baptist, Abraham, Melchizedek, David, Anna and Joachim, and the Childhood of Jesus are told in a series of already highly realistic, meticulously worked figures.

*Buttress piers*

On the façade, flanking the rose window and on the buttress piers of the towers, are the witnesses of the Resurrection and of Christ's appearances after He had risen: St. Mary Magdalen, St. John, St. Peter, St. Thomas, St. Bartholomew, St. Paul and St. James the Less. Around the rose window are the story of David and Solomon and the series of Christ's ancestors, arranged in ten charming groups. On the upper portions of nave and transept, angels, kings and other figures of historical or symbolic significance

Rheims Cathedral. Head of the Madonna from the Visitation on the central west portal (detail from Plate on p. 73), No other figure in medieval sculpture exudes the spirit of classical Antiquity to quite the same degree. *Cf. p. 74*

complete the vast sculpture programme which has made Rheims famous.

Jean d'Orbais (1211–1231) and Jean le Loup (1231–1247) were in control of the Rheims building hut during the execution of the north transept portals between 1220 and 1235. According to the inscription in the labyrinth, mentioned earlier in these pages, Jean le Loup began the portals of the west front in 1235. His successor, Gaucher de Reims (1247–1255), who was probably more sculptor than architect, worked on the decoration of the three portals. Bernard de Soissons (1255–1290) 'ouvra à l'O', i.e. he worked on the rose window and supervised the artists who decorated the upper portions of the façade and the interior. Robert de Coucy completed the façade and the great towers of 1290–1311.

Two separate workshops must have been responsible for the sculpture began *c.* 1235; one of them, whose principal work is the Visitation, had consciously adopted Classic forms; the other, more traditional, is directly influenced by the Madonna portal at Amiens. A third, slightly later group asserted its influence under Gaucher de Reims (1247–1255) and remained active until the end of the century, long after production at the two other workshops had ceased.

This third group is the most original. Rich in all the experience accumulated during the first half of the century, under the guidance of a great innovator—undoubtedly Gaucher de Reims — freed from the Classic tradition and under the direct influence of the great building huts of the cathedrals, it creates around 1250 works both graceful and vigorous, among them the angel of the Annunciation, Mary and Joseph from the Presentation in the Temple, the angel of St. Nicasius, the unforgettable figures of the young David and the pretty Bathsheba on the great rose window, and many other outstanding examples that anticipate the art of the fourteenth century. The direct influence of this workshop, whose works rapidly became famous and were soon imitated everywhere, from Germany to Spain — even, according to Marguerite Falbord's discoveries in the Vatican archives, on the sculptured buttress piers at Orvieto — can also be felt throughout the art of the Rheims region, in the beautiful heads formerly in the Pol Neveux collection and now in the Louvre, or in the seated musicians formerly on the façade in the Rue de Tambour (Rheims Museum), as well as in the delightful figures of angels in gold, ivory or wood in the Louvre and in private collections. All these examples, undoubtedly created in the shadow of the art of the cathedral, have the elegant silhouette and the charming faces of their older brethren in stone.

Almost as soon as the transept portals at Chartres and the west fronts of Notre-Dame, in Paris, and Amiens were finished and while the workshops of Rheims were being formed, Jean de Challes began to create in a new spirit at Notre-Dame, in Paris. His figures on the transept portals come to life, their bearing is less rigid, the gestures become more varied and natural. The expression is accentuated by the eyes and, above all, in the lips, where a

Rheims Cathedral. Angel of the Annunciation. 1250–1260. From the central west portal (right). The work of the Annunciation master, this angel represents a further step in a development begun with the angel in the Amiens Annunciation. Probably intended originally as the companion figure to St. Nicasius, on the right, it was later incorporated in the Annunciation, while St. Nicasius was given a more sturdy-looking companion figure in the style of the earlier figures on the north portal. Like the angel to the right of St. Nicasius, more modern in style, the angel of the Annunciation shows the famous 'Sourire de Reims'. Both figures are considered the most beautiful of their kind in Christian art. Perfect examples of sculpture in the round, standing at counterpoise, they offer a variety of aspects. *Cf. p. 76*

smile seems to form; draperies fall in rich natural folds. This art, more melodious and realistic, lacks some of the ideal grandeur, of the serene nobility we admire on the west front; the composition no longer shows the same monumental unity. The scenes that succeed each other in the rows of the tympanum seem to form a continuous frieze; some of the medallions, treated like small pictures in stone, hardly belong any more to the unifying scheme of the architecture.

According to a fine inscription in the south transept, work was begun under Jean de Chelles on 12th February, 1258. The north portal, undoubtedly older, probably dates from *c.* 1250; the Madonna on the trumeau pier — though heavily damaged, the only surviving original statue of Notre-Dame — is of strikingly noble bearing. On the tympanum are scenes from the Childhood of Jesus and from the legend of Theophilos. The trumeau figure of St. Stephen on the south transept and the statues of the diocesan saints and the Apostles on the jambs are modern, although the story of St. Stephen survives in the tympanum in a composition which became so famous that it was copied at Meaux down to the last detail. The angels and saints of Paradise on the archivolts, of great charm — some of the angels seem to smile — are of a far more advanced style which foreshadows the art of the end of the thirteenth and the beginning of the fourteenth century. The small quatrefoil medallions on the base of the buttress piers contain scenes from the life of the students, told with great humour and lively realism. The same workshop, *c.* 1265–1270, was responsible for the decoration of the *porte rouge* on the north choir of Notre-Dame; it was then under the control of Pierre de Montreuil, who had succeeded Jean de Chelles. St. Louis and Marguerite de Provence kneel at the sides of the triumphant Madonna, who is framed by scenes from the life of St. Marcellus.

The south transept portal of St. Denis, also created under the guidance of Pierre de Montreuil, closely resembles the St. Stephen's portal in many respects. Here, too, were scenes from the Childhood of Jesus and probably also a Last Judgement. Its few remains recall the art of Notre-Dame, in Paris.

*Sainte-Chapelle*    The Apostle figures in the Sainte-Chapelle, consecrated 1248, also belong to the middle of the thirteenth century. Four of them are still in their original places; the others, damaged in the course of time, are in the Musée Cluny. Here, too, we meet the extraordinary versatility, the sophisticated and highly expressive art, of Pierre de Montreuil.

*End of cathedral art*    Cathedral art in the true sense, the art of innumerable anonymous sculptors working for the greater glory of God and thus in complete harmony with the world around them, comes to an end in the fourteenth century. Already in the last years of the thirteenth century the character of monumental sculpture begins to change; a tendency towards individualization appears, towards more dramatic calculated effects. Though work on some cathedrals continues, funds are often inadequate.

Bourges Cathedral. The Last Judgement, from the tympanum of the central west portal (1270–1280). The nudes, portrayed with an accuracy which reveals a degree of anatomical knowledge extremely unusual at that time, are clearly derived from the figures in the Last Judgement on the left north portal at Rheims. The angels guiding the elect, above, are stylistically also related to Rheims. Below the canopy on the left is Abraham, with souls safely 'in his bosom'. Above him are angels with crowns ready for the elect. *Cf. p. 30*

Kings, princes, bishops, and a few wealthy private patrons still commission statues for their palaces, chapels and tombs from the sculptors in their service, whose names are often known to us. Artists now try to reproduce the features of their patrons in their work. The individual portrait emerges rather more rapidly than the realistic figure; often, the draperies are still treated in the traditional manner, while the faces show close proximity to life. Sculpture becomes divorced from architecture. Frequently statues of the Virgin or of the Saints, in keeping with popular taste, sometimes without any great claims to artistic merit and unrelated to the façade, stand in churches and palaces, or in private and public chapels. One of the most important groups of this kind — now in the Bayonne Museum — was commissioned by Jean Tissendier, Bishop of Rieux (1324–1348), for his own tomb in the memorial chapel he had built in the Franciscan church of Toulouse after the model of St. Nazaire. It represents the Apostles, John the Baptist, and the Franciscan Saints with Christ and the Virgin. It cannot be related to the art of the north or the sculpture of Vienne and La Chaise-Dieu, but is a synthesis of severity and sophistication, almost a premonition of the art of Claus Sluter at Dijon, yet at the same time still rooted in the old ornamental tradition.

PLATE P. 83 Small reliefs, pictures in stone or marble, now emulate the intricacy and grace of the work of the miniaturist, the goldsmith and the ivory carver. The most famous figures of this type stand at the transept portals at Rouen, the façade of Lyon Cathedral, and the portal of the St. Clementine chapel in the palace of the popes at Avignon.

*Increasing realism* From the beginning of the fourteenth century onwards, in some regions already since the middle of the thirteenth, the treatment of decorative detail had been increasingly inspired by love of nature and a greater striving for realism. Iconographic interpretation changes, new subjects are chosen, movements, expression and composition pass through a metamorphosis.

St. Francis of Assisi and the Fioretti encouraged the sense of intimacy the faithful cultivated towards the Virgin and her Divine Son. The Apocrypha had already supplied further details about the childhood of Jesus, the life of the Holy Family in Nazareth, the Death and Ascension of the Virgin. The writings of the Pseudo-Bonaventura and St. Birgitta allow us to share in the life of the Holy Family. Brotherhoods are formed in commemoration of the Passion, and hymns, poems and tales are written about its mysteries. Sculptors are eager to invent new themes to meet the demand of a new piety, kindled by the weird realism of the descriptions of the Mystics. The Flagellation, the Crowning with Thorns, the Agony in the Garden, the Man of Sorrows, the Pietà and the Crucifixion all appear in the art of the time. The Crucifixion, in particular, from the beginning of the fourteenth PLATE P. 149 century onwards, is portrayed in all its agony in the art of the Rhineland (Plague Crucifix of 1304 in St. Maria im Capitol in Cologne), whence the famous Christ of Perpignan (1307) originates. The theme of the Entomb-

Bourges Cathedral. St. Michael weighing souls, from the same tympanum as the scene shown in the previous plate. At his left is an angel guiding souls to Paradise, at his right the devil, ready to receive the wicked. A boy in prayer, on whose head St. Michael has placed his hand in protection, awaits confidently his turn to be weighed. *Cf. p. 30*

ment, though already shown in the twelfth and thirteenth centuries — at the Porte Royale at Chartres already in 1150 — does not assume any great significance until the fifteenth and sixteenth.

The authors of many mystic visions are undoubtedly also responsible for the new intimacy between the saints and humanity, between Paradise and earth. Here, too, the mystics reproduce man's pious dreams and the more or less legendary reports that have been enriched from generation to generation. Sculptors translate these visions into stone; like all artists, they steep themselves in the new religious ecstacy, the *devotio moderna* that places men and animals, cities and countryside, crops and vineyards, under the patronage of the saints.

*End of monumental sculpture*

The tradition of the monumental sculpture of the thirteenth century undoubtedly lived on in the fourteenth at different places, for the decoration of many cathedrals and great churches still had to be completed. The figures of the virtues and the vices, and of the Wise and the Foolish Virgins, at Strasbourg date from that time, as do the large sculptures on the transept façade at Rouen. But proportions are rapidly reduced; statues become statuettes, stories told in high relie' n the tympanum and on the piers increase in number and variety. On the west front of Auxerre Cathedral the Judgement of Solomon, the story of John the Baptist and the Last Judgement unfold in dramatic scenes; the jambs of the right portal, in the style of Sens and in the finest Burgundian tradition, display David and Bathsheba and the liberal arts. On the central portal, in the manner of a wall-hanging, are scenes from the story of the Prodigal Son and from the Joseph legend, as well as small figures derived from the art of Antiquity. The left portal is covered with the famous scenes from Genesis dating from the beginning of the fourteenth century.

The sculpture within the church also becomes increasingly lavish. Roodscreens — as at Paris, Chartres and Bourges, to give but a few examples — are covered with reliefs of a remarkable artistry; statues of saints and the Virgin, as well as entire altars, still preserve the style and tradition of their particular region. The greatest artists of the age now create masterpieces in stone, marble, alabaster, wood, ivory and metal for their royal or noble patrons, less spectacular and more intimate works for the rising middle class, for the merchants and their wives, and, on a less ambitious scale though often modelled on the art of the great cathedrals, images for small chapels and poor village churches. Their work is without exception of interest to us, because of the types it represents no less than because of the emotions that have guided the artist's hand. Seated and standing Madonna statuettes, the Christ Child on the left arm, now occur frequently. They are mostly slightly elongated in their proportions, a little rigid, and with the curvature of the hip follow an earlier fashion, when the figure was still kept in balance by the classic counterpoise. Strong emphasis is placed on the flow of the draperies; the folds, gathered under the arm supporting the Christ Child, fall in thin, flat pleats. The Virgin Mary either looks straight at the beholder, or at her Child, her smiling features radiant with happiness, although at times her eyes may appear veiled in sadness. The most famous group of these fourteenth-century Madonnas was created in Paris; the best-known examples are at Magny-en-Vexin, Lisors, Ecouis, Beauficelle, Mainneville and at many other places in the Île-de-France. The famous statue of St. Louis in the church at Mainneville, created in 1304 for Enguerrand de Marigny, is distinguished by an unassuming yet noble realism.

*Madonna statuettes*

Notre-Dame, Paris. Adoration of the Kings. Painted sandstone relief on the northern choir-screen. 1325–1351.
Our illustration shows part of a continuous frieze. Christ's life, from His birth to the Passion, unrolls in the
manner of a miniature against the diapered gold background. Similarly, the reliefs on the south side opposite
show scenes of Christ's appearances after the Resurrection. The work is signed by the sculptors Jean Ravy and
Jean le Bouteiller. During the reign of Louis XIV many of the reliefs were severely mutilated in the course of
rebuilding. The colours were largely renewed on the basis of existing remains. *Cf. pp. 62, 80*

The theme of the standing Madonna, first adopted in Paris and in the Île-de-France, was soon taken up throughout the country, particularly in Normandy, the Champagne, Burgundy (the Iris Madonna at Beaune) and Lorraine (Morhange/Mörchingen, St. Dié, Maxéville and Bouxières near Nancy, Longuyon), where a specific type was evolved, whose influence was to extend towards the Rhine region.

*Tombs* In the fourteenth century sepulchral art attains a high degree of perfection; some of the greatest sculptors of the time of Charles V become veritable specialists as *faiseurs de tombes*, as creators of funeral monuments that show the deceased as a recumbent figure in high relief on the stone slab of the sarcophagus. The features, as life-like as possible, are often modelled from the death mask, which was taken from the body and used in the funeral rites. Already at the end of the thirteenth century the portraits of the dead are rendered with great realism. Queen Isabella of Aragon, who died in 1271 after a fall from her horse at Cosenza, in Calabria, on her return from a crusade to Tunis, is shown with a swollen face. Philippe III, the Bold, whose monument was created in 1298–1307 by Pierre de Chelles, the master of the Notre-Dame workshop, and his assistant Jean d'Arras, has a bony skull, protruding eyes, a powerful jaw, a large mouth, a fleshy nose and a receding chin — features that were to recur in the statues of Philippe le Bel and his three sons.

In 1311 the Comtesse d'Artois, one of the great patrons of her time, commissions her favourite sculptor, Jean Pépin de Huy of Belgium, *tombier et bourgeois de Paris*, with the execution of her husband's tomb and in the following year with that of the tombs of her father and her son, Robert d'Artois, who died in 1317 at the age of seventeen, and whose recumbent figure, worked with meticulous care down to the last detail, is preserved at Saint-Denis. The countess herself died in 1329.

Some — but by no means all — of these sculptors who, because of their favourite material, are also called alabaster carvers, came from the Meuse valley, whence the marble used for tomb stones and recumbent figures originates. They learned their trade close to the quarries, where they would quarry and cut the stone themselves. Pradel has noted that the sculptors working in Paris in the first half of the fourteenth century, contrary to a widely held belief, did not come from Flanders but were Frenchmen and Walloons, who had learned their trade at Mahout, in Artois, in Picardy, and in the region around Paris. In France, if not elsewhere — in England, until the end of the fifteenth century, even the most famous sculptors insisted on payment by the day — the sculptors of these sepulchral monuments were paid a pre-arranged sum. They differ from sculptors in stone in the care with which they reproduce the features of the deceased. Like portraitists, these sculptors in marble, who have established a personal reputation, are far better paid than other stone-carvers.

# IV. MONASTIC,
## MILITARY AND DOMESTIC ARCHITECTURE

The considerable influence of the monks in Merovingian and Carolingian times did not abate throughout the Romanesque and the Gothic; only the devastations of the monasteries in the Hundred Years' War and the attacks of robber bands were to prove a serious threat to conventual life in France. In the eleventh and twelfth centuries the Benedictines and Augustines, who already had numerous settlements in France, established many more foundations. New orders were founded throughout the country: the Cluniac order in 920, the Cistercians in 1098, the Grandmontains in 1076, the Carthusians in 1084, the Praemonstratensians in 1120, and the monks of Fontevrault in 1101.

The most important orders, the Cistercians and the Praemonstratensians, lost little of their influence during the Gothic, despite the rise of two new orders, connected with the new aims of the Church, in the thirteenth century: the mendicant order of St. Francis of Assisi (1208) and the predicant order of St. Dominic (1215).

Except for the two last-named orders, whose members strove for a close union with the life of the faithful, remote and isolated places were chosen for religious settlements. The Benedictines preferred the mountains, the Cistercians valleys.

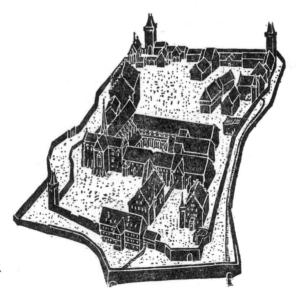

FIG. 36 – *Maulbronn Abbey (Germany). Cf. p. 86*

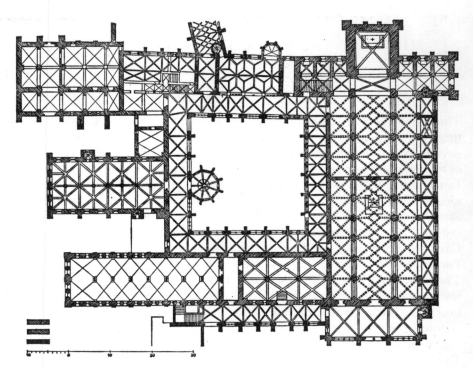

FIG. 37 – *Plan of Maulbronn (in our illustration, east is at the top of the page). To the north of the church are the cloisters with the octagonal fountain house and the canons' refectory beyond. To the east of the canons' refectory (upstairs) is the large dormitory, to the west are the lay brothers' quarters with a refectory and a work-room. At the eastern end, directly adjoining the church, is the chapter-house with a small oriel chapel*

PLATE P. 87
FIGS. 36, 37 The plan of the abbey usually follows the same scheme. At the centre is a square arcaded courtyard, the cloisters, flanked by the church and the living quarters. The whole settlement, reserved exclusively for the monks and complete with hospital, farmyard, artisans' houses, kitchens and lodge, lies within one vast enclosure.

The cloisters are a place for meditation, study and exercise. They link the different parts of the abbey where the life of the monks unfolds; depending on the situation, they lie to the north or south of the church. The church itself stands on high ground, while the living quarters are placed somewhat lower, near a river or an artificial canal, which acts as a water supply for kitchens and fountains and also feeds the drainage system. The arcading of

Mont-Saint-Michel. The abbey fortress of Mont-Saint-Michel, built between the 10th and 15th cent., lies on a granite rock just off the coast of Normandy. The nave of the cathedral was already completed in 1060, although most of the convent buildings and fortifications are of late 13th- or 14th- cent. origin. The tall choir, sur-

mounted only by the Norman spire, is visible for many miles. Though begun in 1446 and therefore a work of the Late Gothic, it follows the tripartite system of the 13th cent.; it is of the utmost austerity, despite the glazed triforium. The whole group is one of the most impressive examples of Norman-Gothic architecture.

the cloisters, with its more or less elaborate tracery according to its period of origin, opens towards an inner lawn; the ceilings, at first flat, are from the twelfth century onwards rib-vaulted, or even panelled as, in the thirteenth century, at Mont-Saint-Michel. Sometimes — as at La-Chaise-Dieu (Haute Loire), Ambronay (Ain), Maulbronn and Eberbach (Germany), to name a few examples — the cloisters support another storey. Normally they contain a fountain; at one side of the refectory is a lavatory with a fountain and a wide basin where the monks perform their daily ablutions.

Benedictine and Cluniac churches have an elaborate choir, often with an ambulatory and radiating chapels. In Cistercian churches — whose choir, of more modest dimensions, often has a flat termination — ambulatory and radiating chapels are adopted more generally in the thirteenth century, as at Royaumont (Seine-et-Oise) and Longpont (Aisne). Sometimes, as at Pontigny (Yonne), the radiating chapels are enclosed by a semi-circular wall. The churches of the Praemonstratensians and, in particular, of the Grandmontains, are of a much simpler layout. Like the Carthusians, the Grandmontains prefer a narrow unaisled nave, without transepts, terminated by a plain apse. Many Dominican churches, especially the earliest — like the Jacobin churches at Toulouse and Agen — have two naves, divided by a row of pillars, the first reserved for the monks, the second for the laity. In the earliest Jacobin church at Toulouse the monks' nave was narrower than the other.

To the east of the cloisters, in continuation of the transept, are the library, the sacristy and the square or rectangular chapter-hall, whose rib-vaulting is supported by piers or columns, which divide the room into several bays. From there a central door and two smaller side-openings, which must never be closed, lead to the cloisters.

On the other side are the *parlatorium*, or monks' parlour, the staircase leading to the *dormitorium*, the access to the garden and a large rib-vaulted hall, divided by a row of columns, where the monks assemble for work and study. The *dormitorium* with its low windows takes up a whole storey, usually the first floor to the east of the cloisters. The beds of the monks are placed in a row at a right angle to the wall. During the Gothic the *dormitorium* is usually rib-vaulted, with a central row of columns, as at Val (Seine-et-Oise) or Eberbach (Rhineland); at Poblet and Santa Creus, in Catalonia, the vaulting of the dormitory rests on transverse arches. Almost invariably, a staircase communicates directly with the church to allow the monks to attend Mass during the night (at Fontenay, Fountains Abbey, Eberbach, Maulbronn, etc.). In Cistercian monasteries the sacristan's sleeping place and the abbot's room were also on this floor.

The refectory lies at the side facing the church. Rib-vaulted — as at Bonport (Eure) — it is frequently divided by a row of columns (at Royaumont, Maulbronn, etc.). At Mont-Saint-Michel cloisters and refectory support a terrace facing the sea, *La Merveille*, built between 1203 and 1228 to the north of the abbey as a protection for the principal rooms which, because of lack of space, had to be arranged on different levels. The refectory was roofed in wood. At the narrow end was a prior's table; the monks' tables were arranged along the walls. During the meal a book was read aloud by one of the monks, for whom a small pulpit was reserved in a recess in the wall. Along the refectory were a stove with a chimney and the very simple kitchens, unless these formed a separate building with several compartments and a central chimney, as at Fontevrault.

On the western side of the cloisters were the store-rooms and, in the convents of the Cistercians, the refectory, kitchen and dormitory of the lay-brothers, separated from the cloisters by a narrow lane, the *ruelle des Convers*, to allow the lay-brothers to enter the church directly, without having to pass through the monks' section.

The infirmary for the sick and aged monks, no longer able to follow the rule of the order in all its severity, was a short distance away, generally to the east of the abbey. Other buildings within the enclosure were the forge and workshops, a bakery, a wine-press, a brewery, mills, the farmyard, granaries, the library, the cells of the scribes — sometimes, as at Citeaux and Clairvaux, these were grouped around a second set of cloisters — and, finally, the gate-house and the guests' quarters. In the convents of the Cluniac order, and in most others, the abbot's house formed a separate building.

The Carthusian convents, because of their specific rule, are planned differently. A characteristic feature is the grouping around two cloisters. The smaller cloisters are flanked by the church, chapter-hall and refectory, where the monks take some of their meals in common; around the large cloisters, which adjoin the first, are the small houses with their gardens where the monks live in complete isolation. At the centre of a lawn stands a fountain, often surmounted by a Calvary. One of the most famous of these schemes is the chartreuse at Pavia.

A bridge, a town hall, a castle or a dwelling-house were no more beyond the skill of the Gothic architect than the construction of a cathedral; the development of secular building closely follows that of church architecture, whose lead is universally acknowledged.

SECULAR ARCHITECTURE

The building of bridges, one of the most important public tasks, was sponsored by powerful associations, by the nobility, the bishops and archbishops. The records of Notre-Dame, in Paris, praise Maurice de Sully, Bishop of Paris and builder of the cathedral, for the construction of two new bridges. These rest on pointed arches of varying span, supported by buttress piers; a chapel was placed at the beginning of each arch or above the buttress. Sometimes, houses stood at the head of a drawbridge; the rent from them would contribute towards the upkeep of the bridge. Some bridges were fortified and had towers at the bridge-head, or in the middle, as at Cahors (Pont Valentré, 1308) and Orthez (Basses Pyrénées). Among the finest thirteenth- and fourteenth-century bridges are the Pont Saint-Esprit

*Bridges*

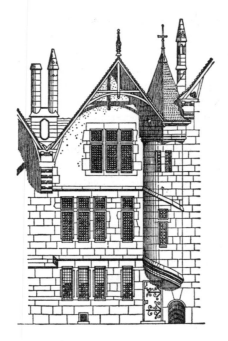

FIG. 38 – *Gothic house at Vitteaux, Burgundy, Cf. below*

across the Rhône (1265–1307), the bridge of Saint-Nicholas at Campagnac across the Gardon, the bridge at Limoges and the bridge at Montauban (1291–1355), the work of Mathieu de Verdun.

*Town halls*    With the growth of cities in the thirteenth and fourteenth centuries new tasks are presented to the Gothic architect. Most town halls are given an arcaded ground floor, with a council chamber and a chapel above. A large balcony or oriel served for speeches or important announcements to the people. At the side was the belfry, which contained the archives, the council treasure and the prison, as well as a look-out and the bells. In the fourteenth century the belfry is usually built apart from the town hall, an arrangement which becomes the rule in the fifteenth and sixteenth centuries. Magnificent examples outside France are at Ypres (Belgium) and Thorn (formerly part of the lands of the Teutonic order, then West Prussia, now Poland).

*Market halls*    Market halls occupy buildings of their own, with double roofs resting on wooden posts. Most big cities have one or several hospitals, which consist, basically, of a large, airy and well-lit chamber with rib-vaulting supported by pillars — as at Saint-Jean in Angers — or wooden barrel-vaulting (Tonnerre, 1296). Next to it, grouped around cloisters, are the buildings of the monks and nuns entrusted with the care of the sick.

*Houses*    The dwelling-houses of the Middle Ages — of which some fine examples survive, despite the vast destruction over the centuries — usually consist of a single building stretched out along the road or placed with the gable end against it to save space. Below, over the cross-vaulted cellars, and linked with them by a straight staircase, are the kitchen, a storage-room or a shop. A corridor leads from the street to the stairs communicating with the upper floors and a courtyard, with a well at the centre, which often contains a second building with a stable, a wash-house and the servant quarters. Next to the kitchen is a bakehouse. Surviving contemporary records fully support these descriptions.

On the first floor, reached by a straight staircase (more often by a spiral staircase, enclosed towards the courtyard by a turret or sometimes fitted into an oriel above the entrance) is the principal living room, with a painted

FIG. 39 – *Houses at Cluny from the 12th, 13th and 14th centuries (left to right). Cf. pp. 90 f.*

ceiling and well-lit by a series of windows towards street and courtyard. The large fireplace occupies a space between the windows or along the end wall. If the building is very large, it can be divided by curtains and tapestries; the rooms so formed are named according to the character of these hangings — the red room, the green room, the unicorn room, etc. Kings and nobles carried in their luggage large bales of fabrics which not merely served to decorate their travelling quarters, but also to divide the large rooms that cannot have been very comfortable to live in.

Some houses had two storeys above the ground floor, as well as a solar — which occupied part of the roof — and a granary extending the whole height of the roof-tree.

In German-speaking countries, as well as in the Auvergne and in Brittany, houses occasionally follow the arrangement of Antiquity, still customary in the fifteenth and sixteenth centuries; they are grouped around a court-yard, the rooms being reached from galleries linked by spiral staircases.

Houses built in stone, which survive in many towns, are generally con-structed of a shell of masonry, filled with rubble and mortar. At one side, often at the corner, is a small projecting tower with a 'pepper-pot' roof and containing a small room or a newel staircase leading to the solar and the granary.

Façades sometimes feature sculpture; in Germany, the famous Mainz 'Hausmadonnen', because of their great diversity, form an important group within this type of decoration. In France, outstanding examples include the *maison des musiciens* at Rheims (now destroyed, though fragments are pre-served in the Rheims museum) and the *maison du grand veneur* at Cordes, which is decorated in bas-relief. Almost everywhere coats-of-arms, mottos and shields have been carved into the façade, particularly in the fifteenth and sixteenth centuries, although the chief decoration are still the portals and windows that often occupy the whole width of the first two storeys. The windows terminate horizontally, as on *la Grange aux Dîmes* at Provins (western Champagne, 13th cent.), Najac (Aveyron) and Villeneuve-lès-Avignon (14th cent.). In Germany, rows of crow-stepped windows rising from the same base, with three or five openings, are not uncommon. Sometimes blind arches occur above the door or window jamb below a flat relieving arch, as on a thirteenth-century house at Chartres opposite the north tower of the cathedral. Elsewhere, following the example of ecclesiastical archi-tecture, windows may terminate in pointed or quatrefoil arches; the latter can be cut from the jamb or — as at Rodez and Chalon-sur-Saône in the fourteenth and fifteenth centuries — built in wedge stones. But all these openings are an anachronism below horizontal ceilings and present a considerable problem, for they are difficult to shut with solid or glazed doors or windows. From the middle of the thirteenth century onwards the round-headed window is therefore generally replaced by one of rectangular shape, below a jamb supported by a segmental arch, and decorated with a stone window cross whose transom bar bisects the vertical post in the upper third; early examples include the windows of the great hall in the castle of Boulogne (1231) at the palace of the counts of Provins (*c.* 1240) and at the *maison des musiciens* at Rheims (*c.* 1250). In the fourteenth century window crosses and transom bars are frequently decorated with patterns and ornamental borders.

Until the fourteenth century roofs are almost flat, with small dormers or lunettes to admit the light at the base. As roofs and gables become steeper, dormers and lunettes also increase in size.

Timber houses were built throughout the Middle Ages. They are solid carpenter's work, built in heart-wood which has been smoothed with the adze. In the thirteenth and fourteenth centuries these houses are built on frames, joined by dowelling. Each storey projects above the previous one. The framework surrounding the windows can be arranged vertically with horizontal cross-beams, diagonally, or in the shape of a St. Andrew's Cross. The in-filling is clay, plaster, brick, rubble, lath or timber. The sides most exposed to the rain are weather-boarded or faced with shingles.

Stone and wooden houses may show considerable regional variety, depending not least on the climate. In very hot or very cold districts, walls are thick and windows narrow; in temperate zones we find thinner walls with many large windows. In the south and in the mountains, windows are few and small; in central Europe and in the north, where sun and light are precious, the windows occupy almost the entire façade, reducing the solid wall to an indispensable framework. In the north, where snow and rain are frequent, roofs are invariably steep, in the south — to offer fewer points of attack to the severe storms — flat. Local characteristics are to some extent also reflected in the plan, in the arrangement of the rooms, the placing of the stair turrets and the decorative detail. In certain districts of France, northern Germany, Holland and Scandinavia, where stone is scarce, houses and even churches are frequently built in brick. We speak in this connection of the so-called brick Gothic.

In the fourteenth century, the domestic architecture of the towns attains a high degree of perfection. Many royal palaces, castles and mansions have perished in the course of time, although we can still gain some idea of their magnificent layout. The rooms, linked by corridors, often had antechambers and bathrooms. The main hall, with its beamed ceiling, was lavishly decorated: tall windows — as we can still see from illuminated manuscripts — let in the light; the huge fireplaces were decorated with statues and bas-reliefs. In the royal palace in the Cité in Paris, renewed by Philippe le Bel, the great lower hall with its cross-vaulted Gothic roof, supported on four rows of columns, and the original kitchens with their four stoves have survived until the present day. The great hall in the palace at Poitiers has an open timber roof; the vast fireplace is decorated with statues of Charles V and Queen Isabella, and of the Duc de Berry and his young wife, Jeanne

*Castles and palaces*

de Boulogne and Auvergne. Remains have also survived of the bishops' palaces at Angers, Meaux, Soissons, Noyon, Auxerre, Laon and Narbonne. Other examples can be quoted from Germany, Italy, the British Isles, Scandinavia, etc.

PLATE P. 95 The papal palace at Avignon had a double function: the original building, erected between 1336 and 1342 by Benedict XII, a former Cistercian monk, was both fortress and convent. On one side, in the *tour des anges* — a donjon PLATE P. 3 in the full sense — were the living quarters of the Pope, on the other, in the APPX. PL. 23 shadow of the cathedral of Notre-Dame-des-Doms, was the chapel. The cathedral itself rises from a parched rock above the Rhône valley; the buildings for the members of the papal court and the papal conclave are grouped around cloisters, all within a framework of high walls and towers. The new palace contains the large pillared audience chamber with, above, the Cappella Clementina, built in 1342–1352 by Jean de Loubières for Clement VI and completely covered with painting and sculpture. From within the whole vast complex appears like a palace, from the outside as an impenetrable fortress.

*Military architecture* Under the influence of Byzantine and Arab engineers, whose superior knowledge was fully appreciated by the crusaders, military architecture was perfected as never before in the twelfth century. By the end of the century the fortress-builders were constantly gaining new experience, for their structures had to withstand the new ramming machines invented by the engineers. As each church reflected the experiences gained in an earlier building, so each fortress and palace benefited from the innovations tried elsewhere. In the thirteenth century military architecture attained a stage where it was to remain until the invention of gun-powder demanded an altogether different system of protection. Until then the basic principle of an effective defence was passive resistance behind impenetrable walls; the need was for tall towers and thick stonework, square, round or battlemented watch-turrets, curtain walls and palisades.

In the times of the greatest unrest, at the end of the twelfth century and during the Hundred Years' War, many castles were built throughout Europe to guard frontiers, roads and rivers. At the same time cities raised walls for their protection; these walls also have towers, often of several storeys, are closed by heavy wooden gates, and frequently can only be approached by a drawbridge.

*Fortified towns* In France the best-preserved fortified towns of the thirteenth and the first half of the fourteenth century are Angers — a city still dominated by the towers of its castle — Carcassonne and Aigues-Mortes.

The wall of Carcassonne is, in part, still of Visigothic origin; its towers are closely grouped, the thick centre walls rise vertically. The whole construction recalls the Gallo-Roman epoch. The castle was built in 1130 by Roger Aton, who had renewed the Visigothic wall. In 1226 the fortress surrendered to the king of France; it subsequently became one of the strongpoints for

FIG. 40 – *The donjon at Vincennes, near Paris*

steepest; it is surrounded by two lines of curtain walls, which also guard the governor's quarters. A narrow door, reached after passing through the fortifications, affords the only access to the tower. The castle walls, which follow the contours of the mountain, form an irregular fortified square. In front, nearest the plateau and the only point open to attack, is a triangular bulwark with a sturdy tower. Château-Gaillard thus seemed to defy capture for ever. Yet on 6th March, 1204, it fell to the enemy, who had made extensive preparations, within six hours. One position after another was captured; the governor, Roger de Lascy, was killed at the threshold of the donjon, where he had tried to shelter with his retinue. Château-Gaillard passed into the hands of Philippe-Auguste; nothing could now stop the conquest of Normandy. The inadequacies of this fortress, hitherto thought impenetrable, became clear. Too many lines of defence within a narrow area had proved an advantage to the attacker; the territory had become too difficult to survey for a really effective defence. The donjon, still part of conventional defensive strategy in the eleventh and twelfth centuries, had become obsolete with the invention of new methods of warfare (cf. the relief with the siege of Toulouse on the *pierre du siège* (1218) in the cathedral of St. Nazaire, Carcassonne).

The aim was new a simpler system, with a strong line of defence at the weakest point; a new type of donjon, even taller and more extensive, rose at the spot where an enemy was likely to attack. The castle of Saint-Gobain, at the edge of a large forest, seems to have been based on this scheme, as was Coucy. In Palestine and Syria the Crusaders had learned the lesson of the importance of the donjon from Byzantine engineers and Arab fortress-builders. Paul Deschamps has given us some idea of the construction of most of these donjons, both in France and in the Near East, which — like the

97

Crac-des-Chevaliers — were built in the second quarter of the twelfth century. A tall square tower, at the most exposed place, was flanked by round turrets; it was further protected by a rectangular bailey, separated from the main building by a moat. The influence of the east proved fundamental to the design of fortresses and war machines; yet it needed the disaster of Château-Gaillard to open the eyes of the west to the inadequacy of the established tradition of defensive warfare.

Coucy is the creation of Enguerrand III, who at one time dreamed of supplanting the young Louis IX on the throne of France. The fortress, at the extreme end of the steep mountains dominating the town, was built in 1225–1240. It is surrounded by a system of walls and moats, which follows an irregular plan; towers rise at each of the four corners. Towards the plateau — and therefore in the direction of a likely attack — the round donjon, taller than the other towers, dominates the long line of the castle's defences and, above all, the main approach; a curtain wall acts as further protection. The layout is simple and of the utmost clarity. The donjon, 177 ft. high, has a diameter of 100 ft., its walls are over 24 ft. thick. With three stories, each occupied by a large hall with double floor, its terraces and its machicolated walls, it defied all enemies. In 1652, Métezeau tried to blow it up at the order of Mazarin, but only the ceilings fell in. Finally, the tower became a victim of the First World War.

A number of thirteenth-century castles have survived as ruins, many of them in the mountains, like Najac, built in 1253 by Alphonse de Poitiers; others, among them Mez-le-Maréchal near Nemours — with a rectangular wall, fortified by towers, the strongest of which served as donjon — and the castles of Braisne and Nesles in the Aisne region were situated in the plain. In central France, square donjons can still be found frequently, as at Uriel (Allier) and Castelnau de Bretenoux (Lot).

FIG. 40 The fourteenth century had a preference for rectangular towers. A famous example is the Tour des Anges in the Palais d'Avignon, a donjon in the true sense, above the Pope's apartments. At Vincennes, the castle begun by Philip VI of Valois and completed by Charles V in 1366, the tall square donjon, 170 ft. high, rises from the centre of the wall on the side most threatened, facing Paris.

Abbeys and episcopal palaces, even churches, were often fortified in the fourteenth century, particularly in the south, as at Béziers and, above all, Albi, the most outstanding brick cathedral of the time around 1300, similarly the Jacobin church at Toulouse, Les-Saintes-Maries-de-la-Mer in the Camargue, Royat in the Auvergne, and Saint-Victor in Marseilles. But fortified portals, belfries hard of access, and machicolated nave roofs and oriels also occur elsewhere in France, chiefly in Burgundy. It has been rightly pointed out that these fortified churches of the thirteenth and fourteenth centuries were only built in towns unprotected by wall or castle; in times of attack from armed bands they had to serve as places of refuge.

of Charlemagne. The same spirit, a synthesis of religious faith and patriotism, has produced this window at
Chartres, which not only illustrates episodes from the Roland song, but also elaborates the story of Charlemagne.
A total of twenty-two scenes tell of the adventures of the king in the East (where he had never been) and of his
fights against the Moors in Spain. The medallion in our illustration forms the upper termination, directly
below the pointed arch of the window. *Cf. p. 102*

become less elongated, draperies less clinging, proportions more natural. The nave windows are filled with tall figures of marked outline, standing within an arch; in the second half of the thirteenth century these are surmounted by small canopies. The medallions of the lower windows contain few figures, each of whom is clearly identified. Ornament, particularly in the border, loses in importance. The tall windows portray Christ, the Virgin, Christ's ancestors, the Prophets, the Apostles and the Saints of Paradise; the medallions of the smaller windows tell stories from the Old and the New Testament.

Numerous workshops existed for the making of stained glass. At least three are known in connection with the nave windows at Chartres, apart from individual masters responsible for windows in the choir, the choir ambulatory, various chapels, the transept clerestory — where St. Denis is shown presenting the oriflamme to Henri Clement of Metz — and the two great rose windows that seem to float above the pierced wall like glowing orbs. The development of the art of stained glass in the first half of the thirteenth century can be clearly followed at Chartres, whose influence extends to Bourges, Semur, Sens, Auxerre, Notre-Dame in Dijon, Lyon, Rheims and Troyes as well as to the great Norman cathedrals of Rouen and Coutances. But only a single signed example survives from

FIG. 41 – *The earlier of the two Madonna windows in the Elisabethkirche, Marburg. c. 1260*

that time in France: the window of the Patriarch Joseph at Rouen Cathedral, which is inscribed with the name of *Clément, verrier de Chartres*.

The second outstanding group are the Paris workshops where the windows of the Sainte-Chapelle were made. Here Biblical scenes are broken up into hundreds of medallions, from which even the miniaturists drew inspiration, as the *Bible Moralisée* of St. Louis proves. Yet despite the influence they exercised on the workshops of Mans, Tour, Angers, Amiens, Beauvais, Rheims and Strasbourg, they must be seen as the crowning culmination, as the end rather than a beginning.

Changes already inaugurated in the last third of the thirteenth century become more distinct in the fourteenth; colours lose some of their glow, pieces of white or matt glass become more numerous, while borders are more elaborate and architectural, to show off all the better the rhythm of the tracery. The window, whose considerable dimensions occupy the entire free space below the vaulting ribs, is divided by numerous vertical stone posts, which give discipline to the composition and draw the gaze upwards. The iron transom bars disappear, as do the medallions that would only divert the eye from the general upward movement of every line. Windows now contain a single scene, within a grisaille framework. Since the proportions

Evreux Cathedral. Nursing Madonna (Maria Lactans). Central group from the window of Charles the Bad, *c.* 1330. The complementary panel — not shown — portrays the kneeling donor. Part of an extensive series of windows, painted in colour and in grisaille, which were commissioned for the cathedral in the course of the fourteenth century by Count Louis of Evreux and the kings of Navarre. *Cf. p. 104*

of the figures cannot be adapted to fill the entire window, canopies and bases are introduced, linked by columns. The figure, now almost completely enclosed, in consequence gradually yields its importance to the painted architectural setting which, with leading gables, cornices, crockets, finials, parapets, bell-gables, keystones and buttress arches, becomes increasingly fantastic. All these features are accentuated with silver stain against a brightly coloured or pale background. Silver stain, used for the first time between 1310 and 1330 (Jean Plafond) in Normandy and in the Île-de-France, is obtained with the help of silver oxyde or silver nitrate; it fuses with the glass in firing, producing a yellow colour where it has been applied. These glowing colours make the architecture appear warmer again. The glass itself is now no longer grey or greenish but white.

Glass-painting thus becomes brighter and brighter, emphasizing the function of the windows more and more, a rich light now floods the interior. At the same time colour — here as in the other arts — turns increasingly sober, a development which attains its peak in the second half of the fourteenth century. The preponderance of white glass, the architectural settings and the lozenge-shaped panes reduce the importance of the colours to such a degree and create so brilliant a light that the figures become almost unrecognizable.

The drawing in these fourteenth-century windows is delicate and graceful, sometimes even a little mannered. Enchanting figures of angels, apostles, prophets and saints enliven the architectural detail, the damasks and the tapestries. Glass-painters now try to emulate the grace and precision of the miniaturists of the Paris school. In the middle of the fourteenth century perspective appears in the representation of buildings and interiors in painting, in the pavements and plinths no less than in ceilings. This brings a fundamental change in the general impression: windows lose their carpet-like quality and instead come to resemble panel paintings that no longer merge organically with the buildings but tend to isolate themselves from their surroundings.

This style, essentially of the fourteenth century, manifests itself already at the end of the thirteenth in the choir windows of Saint-Urbain, at Troyes. But nowhere can the development of glass-painting in the fourteenth PLATE P. 103 century be studied better than at Evreux Cathedral. The windows in the choir, by Jean-du-Prat and Geoffroi Faë, and by Guillaume d'Harcourt — who has shown his patron, Canon Raoul de Ferrière (d. 1330) at the feet of an enchanting nursing Madonna — can stand comparison with the finest miniatures and statues of the time. Stylistically, they recall the art of the glass-painters of Rouen (Cathedral and Saint-Ouen) and Paris, whose influence extends throughout the Loire valley and the Île-de-France as far as Mézière-en-Brenne (Indre). The relationship with the windows of Amiens and Beauvais, with the cathedral and Saint-Pière in Chartres, with the Mantes collegiate church, with La Trinité, Vendôme, and the cathedrals of Meaux,

Reliquary from a Limoges goldsmiths' workshop. Middle of 13th cent. Gold with cloisonné enamel. *Louvre, Paris (Gift of Martin Le Roy. Height* 10¹/₄ *in., width 5 in.*).
From the end of the 14th cent. onwards, the remains of martyrs or saints were displayed in precious shrines on the altar. In the Gothic, a place was often set aside for a cathedral's entire treasure of relics — usually preserved in one or several reliquaries — behind the altar or in the rood-loft. *Cf. p. 114*

takable in the head reliquary of St. Louis, formerly in the Sainte-Chapelle, of St. Martin, at Soudeilles (Corrèze) and St. Agapit, in Tauriac (Lot). Nor must we forget the statues of Madonnas, saints and angels, the most famous of which are the kneeling angels at Jaucourt (Aube) and the silver Madonna in the Louvre, presented to the Abbey of Saint-Denis in 1339 by Queen Jeanne d'Evreux, who was as great a champion of the arts as the Comtesse Mahaut d'Artois — patron of Jean Pepin de Huy (1302–1324), the master responsible for the marble tomb of Robert d'Artois (d. 1317) in St. Denis — before her.

With the art of the goldsmith, enamel-painting also attained a high degree of perfection, particularly in Paris, under the reign of Philippe le Bel, and in the twelfth- and thirteenth-century workshops of Limoges, whose productions were greatly esteemed throughout the Christian world. One of the greatest artists in this medium came from the workshops in the Meuse valley.

PLATE P. 111

PLATE P. 113

Prophet with a streamer from the Three Kings' shrine in Cologne Cathedral (Fig. 42). After the destruction of Milan by Frederick Barbarossa in 1162, the relics of the Three Kings were brought as booty to Cologne, where Archbishop Philipp von Heinsberg (d. 1191) commissioned a precious shrine, which was not completed until the early thirteenth century; it is the work of several masters, although the composition is attributed to Nicholas of Verdun. The shrine, constructed in oak and shaped like the nave of a basilica, is entirely covered in metal discs, decorated in enamel and filigree and studded with precious stones. The relief decoration at the sides — part of which is shown in our illustration — consisting of twenty-four Prophets, Kings and Apostles in beaten silver, fully gilt, is of outstanding importance. In almost full sculpture, these figures, with their animated gestures, life-like features and intense gaze, are far in advance of all contemporary sculpture. The figures at the narrow ends, from another hand, represent, in front, the Adoration of the Kings and Christ's baptism, with Christ enthroned between two angels above, and at the back the Flagellation and the Crucifixion, surmounted by Christ blessing St. Felix and St. Nabor, whose remains were also meant to be housed in the Three Kings' shrine. *Cf. p. 110*

This is Master Nicholas of Verdun, whose principal works are in the convent of Klosterneuburg, near Vienna (the Klosterneuburg Altar, dated 1181, is the most outstanding example of European enamel art; originally part of an ambo, it consists of fifty-six scenes on separate panels), in Tournai Cathedral (Madonna shrine of 1205), and in Cologne Cathedral (Three Kings' shrine, c. 1205–1220). The style of his figures, probably derived from Classic-Byzantine models (Hermann Schnitzler), indicates that the Classic phase of the Gothic, which finds its supreme fulfilment in the monumental sculpture of Chartres (porches and transept portals), is near.

PLATE P. 115

FIG. 42

*Techniques* The two principal techniques of the enamel-painter are champlevé and cloisonné. In the first, hollows cut into the copper ground with the burin are filled with a coloured enamel powder which, when fired at a high temperature, more or less fuses with the roughened ground. The drawing is formed by the remaining metal ridges, which are afterwards gilded. In cloisonné the outlines of the drawing are soldered to the flat ground in wire; the remaining spaces are again filled with coloured enamel powder. The relationship of colour and outline is similar to that in glass-painting, where the coloured panes are set in strips of lead, except that the drawing stands out more radiantly in gold.

*Brass* The workshop of Hugues d'Oignies, near Namur, achieved fame for its brass fonts, candelabras, lecterns, ewers and basins, which were exported all over Europe.

IVORY CARVINGS Another manifestation of Gothic court art are the numerous travel altars and statuettes in ivory, which can be studied in large numbers at the Louvre and the Musée Cluny. They are the reflection of a more intimate kind of piety, of an increasingly personal form of worship. The statuettes are often small copies of monumental figures or groups in stone, marble or wood, known to the faithful from the portals or interiors of the cathedral; they may include the Madonna and Child, the Coronation of the Virgin, the Crucifixion, or the Descent from the Cross. Diptychs, triptychs and polyptychs frequently show scenes from the Childhood of Jesus and the Passion. Here, too, Paris led in the late thirteenth and the early fourteenth century, although a vast export trade throughout Europe soon caused the establishment of many local workshops, whose style shows the influence of their particular region.

PLATE P. 109

FIG. 2 The more secular products of the minor arts must not be forgotten. Combs, minne caskets, brooches and dress ornaments, often decorated with charming scenes of the chase or from legends of chivalry, are executed with the same meticulous care as the delightful miniatures of this age.

# VI. THE TRIUMPH OF FRENCH GOTHIC

So great was the persuasive force of the art of the French cathedrals with their tall and radiant naves rising to the sky, of the powerfully fortified castles, of this inventive and vigorous art that personified all the longing of the High Middle Ages, that from the end of the twelfth and throughout the following century it triumphed throughout Christian Europe. Patrons, architects, bishops, and monks, and above all the Cistercians — who have therefore, not always quite accurately, been called the missionaries of the Gothic — carried this new art to the remotest regions, to Hungary and Bohemia, Sicily and England, Italy and Spain, even to the Holy Land itself. Later, their role passes to the Dominicans and Franciscans.

French princes, nobles and clerics living abroad commissioned French artists to re-create the works of their motherland. At the same time, foreign builders learned the basis of the new art in French workshops; here they became masters, and what they had learned they could transform into new achievements in their own countries through a synthesis with their indigenous tradition. It is due to them that the Gothic was not merely copied outside France but could grow into a truly European style as well as into a series of national variations. This demanded the specific developments described in the following pages.

England is one of the countries where the Gothic was to triumph at an early stage; here, we find the same Norman tradition that is the basis of French Gothic architecture. Yet very quickly a separate style evolved whose character is quite distinct from that of French art. ENGLAND

The political, economic and religious links between England and France continued after the Norman conquest. In the Norman period Norman architecture and art had spread throughout the country. The relationship became even closer after the accession of the Plantagenet kings. The influence of religious orders also made itself felt in the British Isles: St. Pancras of Lewes repeated in Sussex the plan of Cluny with its double transepts and an ambulatory with five radiating chapels; the plan of Clairvaux was followed in the Cistercian Fountains Abbey in Yorkshire.

The Cistercian abbey of Fontenay, in Burgundy, rose while St. Bernard was still alive; it was largely built by Ebrard, Bishop of Norwich, a member of a wealthy Arundel family, who in 1139 retired to Fontenay, where he also died. He is buried at the foot of the main altar of the new church. The Cistercian abbey of Pontigny, near Auxerre, is the burial-place of three English exiles, three Archbishops of Canterbury: Thomas Becket, Stephen Langton and Edmond Rich; the last-named died there in 1240 and was *Cistercian abbeys*

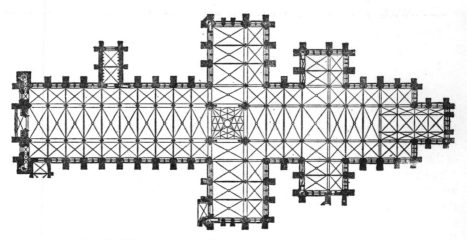

FIG. 43 – *Plan of Salisbury Cathedral. Cf. below*

canonized six years later. His tomb has since been visited by innumerable English pilgrims.

*Universities*  We have spoken elsewhere of the large number of students from England, Scotland and Ireland at the university of Paris, where the English had six colleges of theology alone: their greatest contemporary scholars, William of Occam, Roger Bacon and Duns Scotus (John of Malmesbury, also known as Scotus Erygena), were active there. Oxford and Cambridge are foundations based on the Paris model. From the Norman conquest onwards French was the official language of the court and the aristocracy, of Parliament, the law and public life. The Hundred Years' War took many Englishmen across the Channel, where they came to know and appreciate French culture.

*Beginnings of rib-vaulting*  It is therefore all the more remarkable that English Gothic art should have developed its own identity so quickly. Rib-vaulting was already known at a very early date in England, as Durham Cathedral (according to N. Pevsner already vaulted in the new technique *c.* 1104–1130), Peterborough,

FIG. 46  Winchester, and Gloucester prove. But its structural advantages were hardly exploited; the construction remains clumsy, the thick walls are still strengthened with great buttress piers, arches remain semi-circular. In the

*Norman tradition*  decoration the geometric stylized motifs of the Anglo-Norman tradition live on. But out of this very tradition English art develops forms unknown to the

*Characteristic plans*  French Gothic. One of the most notable differences lies in the plan, with the elongated choir already characteristic of pre-Gothic churches in England.

FIG. 43  At the crossing, above the extensive transepts, stands the great central tower, a typically English feature inherited from the previous Norman phase

FIG. 44  (Salisbury, Lincoln).

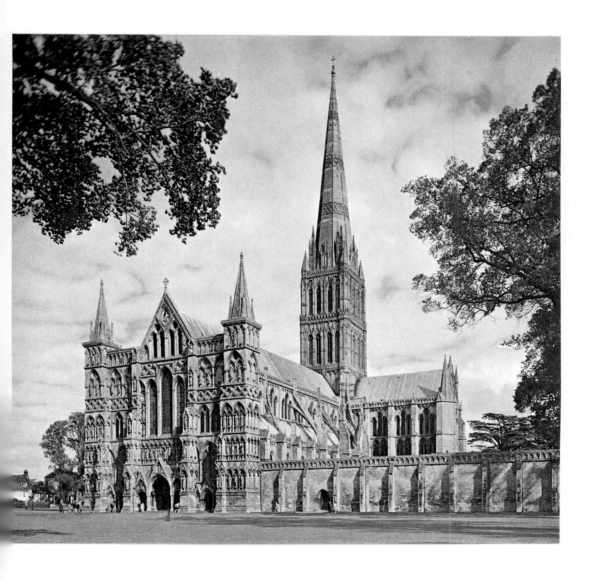

Salisbury Cathedral, from the south-west. Built 1220-c.1270, by Elias of Durham. The west front, like the slightly earlier façade of Wells, shows the characteristic English trend to create vast walls for the display of sculpture and to disguise structural components with decorative features. Like the rest of the façade, buttresses and piers have been covered with a network of niches, filled with the statues of former bishops, saints, angels, and martyrs. The central tower, 394 ft. high, was built c. 1330; it is the third-highest medieval church tower in Europe and the tallest in England. The south transept, which terminates in a straight wall, can be seen in our illustration. Like many English examples, the cathedral, in contrast to most continental churches, lies outside the city centre. Surrounded by vast expanses of lawn, it appears in full view. *Cf. pp. 120, 124*

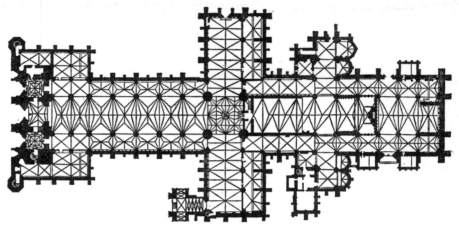

FIG. 44 – *Plan of Lincoln Cathedral. Cf. p. 118*

PLATES PP. 119, 123
*Retro-choir*

Beyond the transepts, the choir is intersected by a second, shorter group of transepts, the so-called retro-choir, which, at Lincoln and Canterbury, is divided into separate chapels, each serving a specific function. Unlike most of the Continental cathedrals, English cathedrals were originally abbey churches: this fact explains the great length of the choir, where large numbers of ordained monks had to be accommodated. Often the different sections are further divided by partitions reminiscent of rood-screens.

*Central tower*

Direction, too, is not as important as in French cathedrals, where the gaze is drawn from the entrance at the west front to the choir. In England the centre is in the space below the great tower at the crossing, a derivation of the Romanesque lantern tower. Since the whole interior is orientated towards this area, even from the choir, the apse is usually not polygonal but straight, pierced by a tall window. Nor is the general upward movement as distinct as in France; the emphasis tends to be more on the horizontal run of the different storeys, and even the clustered piers therefore do not rise from the ground floor but from the arcades or even the triforium. Within, decorative aspects count far more than in French cathedrals. Another

APPX. PL. 5

characteristic English feature is the horizontalism of the façade, which is merely one aspect of the horizontalism prevalent throughout English art in general.

*Early English*

In the second half of the twelfth century the influence of the Île-de-France asserts itself from time to time in connection with the Romanesque-Norman tradition. Of the churches that show distinct French traits, the most famous are the Cistercian abbey at Roche (Yorkshire) and Canterbury Cathedral, begun, according to Gervais of Canterbury, by a French architect, William

Tomb of Queen Eleanor of Castile. 1291–1293. *Westminster Abbey, London.*

After the death of the universally loved queen, the courtly art of southern England, whose manifestations can be seen throughout the southern and eastern parts of the country, passed through its greatest flowering. When Queen Eleanor died in 1290, her husband, Edward I, took the most elaborate measures to commemorate her. In the twelve resting places of the funeral cortège between Hardy, in Nottinghamshire, where the Queen had died, and Westminster Abbey, her final resting place, great memorial crosses were raised; their planning and execution recall similar crosses erected twenty years earlier in France in memory of St. Louis. At the same time, Edward I ordered a memorial chapel to be built in the royal palace at Westminster; this chapel, later dedicated to St. Stephen, is clearly inspired by the architecture of the Sainte-Chapelle in Paris. Like the church of Saint-Denis in France, it became the burial-place of kings and queens; in the wealth of its funeral monuments it is — after the ravages at St. Denis — unequalled in Europe. As the first monuments to be placed there, Edward I commissioned life-size figures of his father, Henry III, and of Eleanor of Castile from the London goldsmith William Torel, who cast the monuments by the *cire-perdue* (lost wax) method. The thickness of the bronze, unusual in a work of this kind, shows that the master had no previous experience in the casting of life-size bronze figures. A replica, also by Torel, is in Lincoln Cathedral, where the Queen was embalmed on her journey to Westminster and where her heart is buried. *Cf. p. 124*

FIG. 45 – *Lichfield Cathedral. Nave wall. Cf. p. 124*

Lincoln Cathedral. View from the south transept towards the angel choir, which has a straight eastern termination, pierced by a vast window. The High Gothic choir was built between 1255 and 1280 to replace an earlier choir from the first, Early Gothic, phase. Its name is derived from the thirty angel reliefs in the spandrils between the triforium arches, one of the principal works of English 13th-cent. sculpture. Building materials of different colours are used — dark Purbeck marble forms a contrast with the warm-toned light sandstone. Everywhere the walls are enriched with ornament. The trefoil dog-tooth pattern fills the spandrils between the arcades, just as the triforium spandrils display angel reliefs; the zone around the base is enlivened with blind arcading. Characteristic features are the staggered arches of the arcades, the short and slender vaulting shafts and the free-standing tracery in front of the clerestory windows. All these features — like the clustered piers, each consisting of a bundle of eight shafts held together with shaft rings — indicate a strong feeling for space that contrasts most markedly with the architecture of French Gothic cathedrals. *Cf. p. 120*

FIG. 45 of Sens, in 1175. William, a master of his craft, was a man of a lively mind and an outstanding reputation. An accident put an end to his career in 1178. Other important examples in this group are Chichester Cathedral, partly

PLATE P. 123 re-built after the fire of 1186, and the Angel Choir at Lincoln, begun in 1192. The piers, surrounded by columns joined within shaft rings, rise up to the ceiling; the buttress arches at the roof of the blind gallery are linked with the outer flying buttresses. The foliage of the capitals is clear evidence of the continued influence of the Île-de-France and the Champagne, which was finally to triumph in the choir of Westminster Abbey in the middle of the thirteenth century.

PLATE P. 119 The influence of Anjou is similarly reflected in the aisled chapel of Salisbury Cathedral, reminiscent of Saint-Serge at Angers, in the choir at Winchester and on the façades of Wells and Salisbury, whose blind arcades and corner turrets recall the façades of Notre-Dame de Puy, Candes, and Cunault.

*Decorated* But already in the middle of the thirteenth century, with the beginning of the High Gothic, English architecture gradually emancipates itself from foreign influence; buildings like Salisbury Cathedral (begun 1220), the choir and transepts of Beverley Minster, the transepts at York, and the choirs of Worcester, Ely and Wells display a grace and elegance that was to become even more marked in the second half of the thirteenth century, during the so-called decorated phase of the Gothic, which lasts until *c.* 1360.

*Curvilinear* The curvilinear style, in some of its features not unlike the much later flamboyant phase of the French Gothic, flowered from the end of the thirteenth to the middle of the fourteenth century; it is followed by the per-

*Perpendicular* pendicular style, which appears like a reaction against the Baroque exuberance of the decorated and curvilinear phases. One is almost tempted to describe it as a return to the severe, linear spirit of Celtic ornament.

*Sculpture* English sculpture, exactly like architecture, has a distinct character of its own. In the twelfth century the portal of Rochester Cathedral adopts to some extent the sculpture of the *porte royale* at Chartres — the Christ in Glory, the *statues colonnes*, representing King Solomon and the Queen of Sheba, on the jambs. In the fourteenth century English sculpture regains its independence. At Lincoln and Winchester, at Wells, Salisbury and Lichfield, the statues on the façade are arranged in tiers, in niches whose spandrils show small sculptured scenes. Though some comparison with Romanesque façades in the west of France is brought to mind, we must recall in this context the essentially monumental quality of English architecture. A

PLATE P. 121 remarkable trait distinguishes many seated and all recumbent figures, whether in wood, bronze, stone, Purbeck marble or alabaster: the legs are crossed, and the expression is of a vitality rarely found elsewhere. The enamel tomb figure by Guillaume de Valence in Westminster Abbey is a product of Limoges; many alabaster tumbas, however, come from Notting-

APPX. PL. 22 ham, as do the small, often somewhat harsh and angular, carved altars with small alabaster statuettes, which were exported throughout the

Christian world. Alabaster sculpture is found, above all, in Westphalian churches — the Mercy Seat in the Wiesenkirche, Soest — though it also occurs throughout Western France and Spain.

The art of Tournai, also strongly influenced by the art of the Île-de-France, profoundly affected the architecture of Flanders and the Escaut valley throughout the thirteenth century — to mention only Notre-Dame de Pamela at Oudenaarde and Saint-Nicolas, Ghent — and also left its mark on Zeeland. NETHERLANDS APPX. PL. 9, 17

At Orval, in the Belgian part of Luxemburg, at Aulne, in the Hainault, and at Villers-en-Brabant, the Cistercians departed from the erstwhile severity of their churches, which now mirror the elegance of the cathedrals of the Île-de-France and the Champagne. At Floreffe near Namur, at Bonne-Espérance in the Hainault and at Parc, near Louvain, the Prae-monstratensians introduce French Gothic, recognizable even in its later Baroque disguise. *Architecture*

In plan and composition, the choirs of Tournai and Sainte-Gudule, in Brussels, as well as the old cathedral of Cambrai, follow Soissons and Rheims. Saint-Martin, Ypres, has adopted the plan of Saint-Yved, Braisne. In Bruges, Notre-Dame and Saint-Sauveur are reminiscent of the architecture of Northern France, in Holland it is the choir of Utrecht cathedral. In the fourteenth century Notre-Dame de Huy, the churches of Breda and Dordrecht, the cathedrals of Malines, Antwerp and Haarlem suggest, in their simplicity and deliberate uniformity, the handsome choir of Saint-Ouen, Rouen. The Gothic of these regions, harsh and severe, shows a trend towards abstraction. The reaction against the simplicity and economy of these buildings takes the form of a love for — at times over-elaborate — movement and decoration towards the end of the fifteenth and the early sixteenth century.

Sculpture

In thirteenth- and fourteenth-century sculpture French influence is most notable in the art of Tournai, whose fonts and funeral monuments, carved in a little-known type of granite, were exported throughout Europe; famous examples are at Therouanne and Saint-Jean, Bruges. Notre-Dame de Huy bears witness to this vigorous, simple and down-to-earth mood that distinguishes the art of Flanders and the Walloon provinces no less than that of Artois and Picardy.

SWITZERLAND

Like Belgium, the French-speaking provinces of Switzerland stood entirely under the influence of French art; the cathedral of St. Pierre in Geneva, Lausanne Cathedral, the church of Volère in Sion (Valais) and the churches of Neuenburg and Freiburg in Saxony, recall the cathedrals of Lyon and Vienne and Notre-Dame in Dijon. The influence of Burgundian art lives on in the fifteenth century, in painting and sculpture as well as in architecture.

SCANDINAVIA

Despite the great distance, Sweden, Denmark and Norway are also touched by French art, undoubtedly because of the connection between French and Scandinavian monasteries during the twelfth and thirteenth centuries.

Denmark

Bishop Absalon of Roeskilde, the founder of Copenhagen, who had studied in Paris for two years, commissioned a Cistercian from Arras to build his cathedral. In 1162 he brought Cistercian monks to Soroe, near Copenhagen; the church has a choir with a straight apse and square chapels, which — as in many French Cistercian chapels — open towards the transepts. The large number of Limoges enamels and ivory carvings of the Paris school in churches and museums is proof of the love of French Gothic art in all its aspects throughout contemporary Denmark.

Sweden<br>APPX. PL. 20

The first apostle to the Swedes, the ninth-century monk Ansgar, came from Corbie, in Picardy; through him, a lasting link was established between France and Sweden. The second archbishop of Lund, Eskil, Primate of Sweden and friend of St. Bernard, visited Clairvaux and brought Cistercians to his country. Alvastra abbey was his foundation. The church has a choir with a straight termination and square chapels; the barrel-vaulting of the nave is supported by the transverse barrels of the aisles, following the Burgundian scheme of Fontenay. Stephen, Bishop of Uppsala, the first abbot of Alvastra, was the founder of Salby and Varnhem, whose plan recalls Clairvaux and Pontigny. On Gotland, French Cistercian influence is balanced by German and Byzantine. The Praemonstratensians, who came after the Cistercians, also displayed great activity. Saint-Gilles-du-Gard was no less important to the Swedes than to the Poles; from here pilgrims brought back their impressions of French architecture. Finally, the schools — and later the university — of Paris attracted students from all over northern

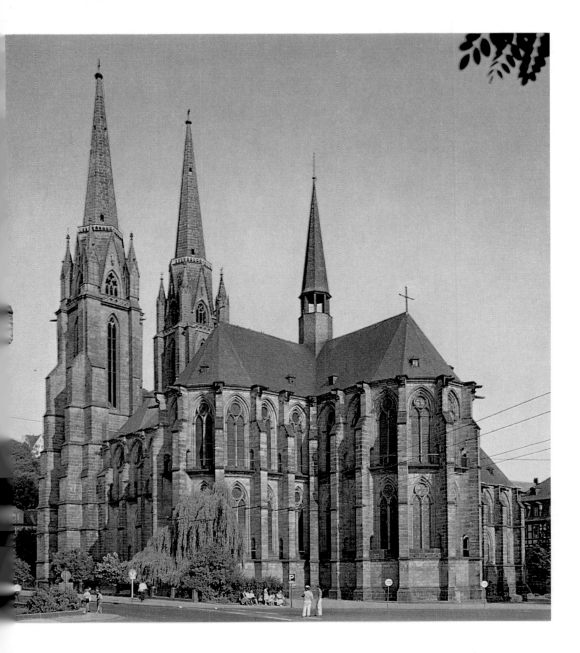

Elisabethkirche, Marburg. Built in 1235, four years after the death of St. Elisabeth (1231), the former Land-gravine, in her memory and as the church of the Teutonic Order. Though the church was consecrated in 1283, the towers were not completed until 1360. Our illustration shows the eastern triapsal arrangement which, as in the Rhineland, consists of three arms of equal length. The southern arm, clearly visible in the photograph, contains the so-called Landgrafenchor, where the rulers of the province are buried. The roof, which does not distinguish between nave and aisles, emphasizes the building's character as a hall church. *Cf. p. 136*

Europe, from Sweden, Denmark, Norway and even Finland; from 1385 onwards, the Scandinavian archbishops took their degrees at the university of Paris. The archbishop of Lund built a college for Danish students, the first of the foreign colleges on the hills of St. Geneviève. The Swedes followed suit and within a very short time had three colleges; later, the universities of Orléans and Montpellier were to become as important as Paris to Swedish students. It is known that the stonemason Etienne de Bonneuil, who had been active in Paris, was called to Uppsala in 1287 to take charge of the building hut of the new cathedral; he was probably a sculptor rather than an architect.

*Norway*  Close ties of friendship existed between the royal houses of Norway and France. In 1248 St. Louis sent Mathieu de Paris to King Haakon IV to persuade him to take part in the Crusades. Phillip the Bold presented Haakon's son, Prince Magnus Lagaboetir, with a piece from the Crown of Thorns, which was preserved in a chapel modelled on the Paris Sainte-Chapelle. At the same time, Norwegian Gothic was strongly under English influence. The nave of Trondhjem Cathedral, the most important stone-built church in the country, with its centralized tomb chapel of St. Olave to the east, resembles Lincoln, and Norwegian Cistercian abbeys are based on English models. Yet in sculpture and painting French and English influence often seem equally balanced.

*Sculpture*  In Sweden, the influence of French sculpture is particularly strong in the regions of Gotland and Uppsala at the end of the thirteenth and the beginning of the fourteenth century. It has already been pointed out that Etienne de Bonneuil, who came to Uppsala with his assistants from the Paris building huts, was more sculptor than architect; it would seem that the south transept was, in part, his work. The archivolts and quatrefoil medallions with the Six Days of Creation, as well as the statue of St. Lawrence on the trumeau, might easily have been created by a French master. Though Norwegian architecture is more markedly English in character, some of the monumental sculpture at Trondhjem Cathedral is strongly reminiscent of Rheims and of the Apostle figures at the Sainte-Chapelle, above all the statue of St. Dionysus, who is holding his head in his hands.

*Finland*  In Finland, where Christianity did not become established until the middle of the twelfth century, the most important Gothic monument is the granite-built cathedral of Abo, whose polygonal brick choir was added in the fourteenth century.

GERMANY  In Germany, as in England, the influence of French High Gothic is absorbed into an indigenous art, a specifically German Late Gothic. These processes lie only partly within the scope of this volume, and are therefore discussed at greater length elsewhere; they fall, on the one hand, within the realm of Late Romanesque and Early Gothic, and, on the other, belong to a development which culminates in the Late Gothic of the second half of the fourteenth century.

Chapter-house of the former Cistercian abbey at Maulbronn (Württemberg), looking towards the cloisters. First half of 14th cent. After Early Gothic beginnings, the work of travelling Cistercians, the mature Gothic unfolds in all its glory. The walls, pierced towards the cloisters with traceried windows, and the stellar vaulting — one of the earliest examples in south-western Germany — make this interior seem weightless and transparent. Maulbronn is one of the most complete surviving medieval monasteries in Europe. *Cf. p. 132*

| | |
|---|---|
| *Romanesque tradition* | Strong tradition-bound concepts of form at first allowed French influence to assert itself only very gradually in Germany. It will help towards an understanding of the situation if we recall that, around 1200, after a long preparation beginning about sixty years earlier, the great cathedrals of the French High Gothic were already rising, or even approaching completion — |
| APPX. PL. 2 | the west front of Notre-Dame *c.* 1215 — while the Romanesque was passing through one of its most decisive stages in Germany. At Worms, the cathedral with its elaborate west choir was re-built on its old plan; the Hohenstaufen west choir and the vaulting of the Romanesque nave date from 1200–1239, the extension of St. Aposteln, Cologne, with its great triapsal choir to the east, belongs to roughly the same period. Many more examples could be quoted. Yet we cannot really speak of German architecture being left behind, of a rather late joining-up with the mainstream of European development, for basically we are faced with two distinct national interpretations. |
| *National attitudes* | The French constructive approach corresponds to a German sense of plasticity, to a feeling for architectural grouping. In contrast to the emphasis on direction in French architecture, German as well as English cathedrals reflect a longing for a centrally-orientated composition, except that in Germany — unlike England, where the interior is centred on the tower above the crossing — the tendency is to seek a balance of equally important eastern and western sections. A façade as a frontal display and starting point, with the choir as the goal of a flow of movement, is basically alien to German cathedral-builders, who prefer to make the western entrance part of a group rather than a spectacular main front (Maursmünster/Marmoutier in Alsace, the west choirs of Worms, Mainz, Bamberg, Naumburg, etc.). |
| *Façade as westwork* | This different attitude persists even when the Gothic is firmly established in Germany. The single-tower façades of Freiburg, Strasbourg, Ulm and |
| APPX. PL. 6 | Berne and the twin-towered façade of Cologne Cathedral still have the massed effect of the old westwork as the balance of the choir. Even the buttressing is never reduced to the skeleton framework of French cathedrals, but remains subordinate to the general block-like grouping. |
| *Treament of the wall* | These differences are also reflected in the interior. German architecture strives, at least to begin with, for the preservation of the wall in its full thickness, for aesthetic no less than for structural reasons. In French Gothic, the vaulting system also determines the character of the wall, which is divided |

Freiburg Cathedral. View along the nave towards the choir. The nave was begun in 1235. The clustered piers and the large wall areas between the arcades and the window zone — unlike French cathedrals, without a triforium — are characteristic of the Gothic of the Upper Rhine. The area between the low triumphal arch and the vaulting is part of the tower which formerly rose far above the roof of the earlier Romanesque church. The Late Gothic choir, begun in 1359 by Johann Gmünd to replace a Romanesque choir, was not consecrated until 1510. *Cf. p. 142*

into load-bearing and screening components. In German architecture, instead of a break-up of the wall, we find an increasing emphasis on depth; the thickness of the walls is, if anything, accentuated. Thus the attached

PLATE P. 131

vaulting shafts, apart from their structural function, serve to emphasie plasticity. The triforium, too, has never become fully accepted in German architecture; the trend is rather to articulate the solid wall between the ground-floor arcades and the clerestory windows. Exceptions to this rule (Strasbourg, Cologne, Altenberg, Regensburg) always indicate some special link with France. Though Germany uses the devices of the French Gothic, she does so in her own manner.

*Links with France*   German art preserves its originality, despite the long and close connection between the King of France and the Emperor, or between the French clergy and the priesthood of the Rhineland, whose domains often overlapped; thus the dioceses of Metz, Toul and Verdun were under the jurisdiction of the Archbishop of Trier, whose territory bordered Rheims, and German students visited the schools of Laon, Chartres, and Paris.

*Monastic orders*   The main source of French influence in Germany were the monastic orders, at first the monks of Cluny, then the Cistercians, whose ascetic interpretation of architecture came closest to the German attitude. The Cistercians stressed the basic shape of the building, dispensing with articulation wherever possible. Their churches are without tribune, triforium or towers. Figure portals and stained glass with representations of figures were anathema. In place of decoration, the emphasis is on the function of every component and

PLATE P. 129

on extremely careful workmanship. The quality of the masonry at buildings like the western portion of Maulbronn — dated 1201 — has never been surpassed.

*Magdeburg*   The first church on a Gothic plan with ambulatory and radiating chapels

APPX. PL. 7

was built at Magdeburg, by Archbishop Albrecht, who had studied in Paris. It replaced the tenth-century cathedral of Otto the Great, which was burned down in 1207. The foundation-stone for the new church was laid

FIGS. 47, 48

in 1209, two years before Rheims. We find at Magdeburg stylistic traits characteristic of French buildings already in the middle of the twelfth century, though here combined with traditional features of German art; the plan of the choir is derived from Burgundy and the Upper Rhine, yet the three-storied composition, the traditional groined vault in place of rib-

Marienkirche, Lübeck. A church of the 13th and 14th cent. The choir was completed in 1291, although the west front with the towers was not begun until 1304. The Gothic *flèche* of the early 16th cent. was not replaced when the church was rebuilt after the second world war. With its simple forms, determined by the limitations of the material, the Lübeck Marienkirche is the prototype of the brick churches of the Baltic, which retain the Franco-Netherlandish type of choir with ambulatory and radiating chapels and flying buttresses, while dispensing with transepts. Severe and restrained, the Marienkirche is a characteristic monument of a Baltic merchant city. *Cf. p. 150*

133

vaulting and the thick, powerful piers are completely German in character. The ambulatory with its radiating chapels appears from the choir as if it were hollowed out of the stone, the more so because the chapels — unlike those of French Gothic churches — act as a dark foil behind the ground-floor arcades instead of drawing in the light through tall windows. Late Romanesque forms also predominate in the capitals.

APPX. PL. 15 The bishop's gallery above the choir ambulatory, originally a tribune storey which was omitted from the new nave, shows new stylistic features. It is undoubtedly the work of a group of Cistercian artisans, whose progress we can trace from Maulbronn (porch) via Walkenried and Ebrach, near Bamberg, to Magdeburg. One of the characteristics of their work are the round-headed vaulting arches above the irregular plan of the ambulatory, which make it necessary to place the bases for diagonal ribs and for transverse arches at different levels, causing the keystones to become 'displaced'. It is this impression of restlessness French architects had tried to overcome with the introduction of rib-vaulting. German art, with its 'old-fashioned' solution, had preserved the plasticity and dynamism of the articulation.

All the further building phases of Magdeburg Cathedral are governed by the changes in the responsible building huts and the subsequent alterations in the original plans. This situation is not only characteristic of Magdeburg, but of the whole development of German architecture, which is primarily determined not by established building huts, but by the the need to engage groups of journeymen-artisans.

Shortly before 1250 the project of a tribune for the nave is finally abandoned; at the same time the piers are raised, the transepts widened and some of the supports removed. Very wide, low aisles contrast with a tall nave. A unique solution is achieved in the treatment of the nave wall: the number of bays

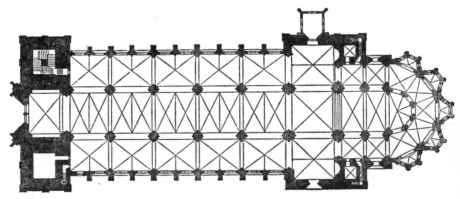

FIG. 47 – *Plan of Magdeburg Cathedral. Cf. p. 132*

Fig. 48 – *Magdeburg Cathedral. Longitudinal section. Cf. p. 132*

is doubled in the clerestory region, following the system of the articulation of the aisles. The relationship between supports and openings in the window zone is entirely un-French; here the windows are interpreted as breaches made in the wall and not as a network between piers. The vaulting shafts appear as a way of articulating the wall rather than as supporting elements. Flying buttresses are accordingly dispensed with, the building relying for support entirely on the thickness of the walls.

Similar examples could be listed throughout Germany; at Bamberg and Bonn the articulation of the inner wall is Gothic, yet the vaulting still rests on thick, typically Romanesque walls. For a considerable time apses and radiating chapels continue to be roofed with half-domes, while the aisles are given groined vaulting, as in the Martinskirche in Worms and in many Cistercian churches, including Arnsburg (Hesse), Otterberg (Palatinate), Ebrach (Franconia) and Lehnin (Brandenburg), to list but a few early thirteenth-century examples.

Romanesque architecture in the Rhine region did not yield to the Gothic until long after its adoption in France, in the first decades of the thirteenth century, when stylistic elements evolved in the Île-de-France, in the Champagne and in Burgundy, reached the Rhineland, where they combined with the indigenous tradition into the so-called Rhenish transitional style. This development — part of the whole problem of Late Romanesque and

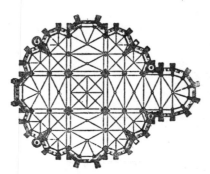

FIG. 49 – *Trier, Liebfrauenkirche. The plan is carved into the wall of a spiral staircase of the church; it was clearly considered an unusual and particularly successful example, rich in symbolism, already in the Middle Ages. Among the Gothic central churches, the Liebfrauenkirche in Trier is one of the largest and most important. Cf. p. below*

Early Gothic — is particularly marked in the Cologne churches of Gross-St.-Martin, St. Aposteln and St. Cunibert, and, to a lesser degree, in the Chapel of the Teutonic Order at Ramersdorf (Bonn), Andernach parish church, and the cathedrals of Limburg and Worms. In all these buildings we find French forms employed in a typically German spirit.

*Liebfrauenkirche, Trier*
APPX. PL. 18
FIG. 49

Germany did not produce a Gothic architecture in the true sense until the middle of the thirteenth century. The Liebfrauenkirche in Trier, built on a central plan with a slight emphasis on the choir axis, was begun in 1235/40. The light and graceful interior clearly shows French inspiration. The window tracery recalls Rheims, the plan is like an enlarged version of the choir of St. Yved, Braisne, whose semi-circle, with its radiating chapels, has been completed. But there is no suggestion of Braisne in the interior. The very scheme of a central plan is typically German, as is, to an even greater extent, the two-storied nave wall, without gallery of triforium, but with alternating supports that emphasize plasticity; the crossing rests on round piers with superimposed vaulting shafts which, again, add to the impression of volume. Everywhere within, we find a contradiction of the unifying tendency of the French Gothic. The result of dispensing with flying buttresses and using instead a system of solid buttress piers is less fortunate: the clerestory windows had to be partly walled up, for they would otherwise have opened the view into the roof-space of the aisles. Yet, altogether, the general composition is of a crystalline clarity.

*Elisabethkirche, Marburg*
PLATE P. 127

The Marburg Elisabethkirche, inspired by Rheims and Soissons, represents the same stage of the German Gothic. It served a double function as church of the Teutonic Order and as the sepulchral church of St. Elisabeth, the former Landgravine, who died in 1231 and was canonized four years later. The foundation-stone was laid in the year of her death, and the consecration ceremony took place in 1283. The Landgrafenchoir in the south transept is of outstanding importance in the history of German sculpture.

The plan reflects the original intention to create a centralized church on the model of the Cologne triapsal scheme, realized at St. Aposteln, St. Maria im

FIG. 50 – *Marburg-on-Lahn, Elisabethkirche. Cross-section. Cf. p. 140*

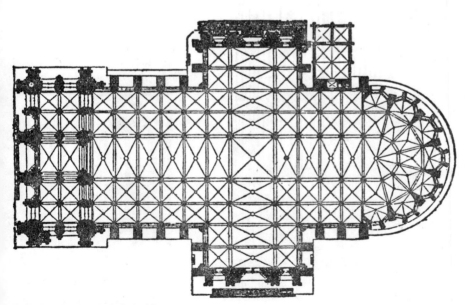

FIG. 51 – *Cologne Cathedral. Cf. p. 142*

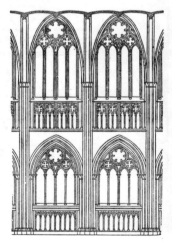

FIG. 52 – *Strasbourg. Cathedral of Notre-Dame. Cf. p. 144*

FIG. 53 – *Strasbourg Cathedral. Nave wall, with view to the aisle windows. Cf. p. 142*

Chorin. West front of the Cistercian abbey. With its carefully balanced proportions and the masterful articulation of the façade, Chorin is the most outstanding example of eastern German brick Gothic. The abbey was begun with the choir C. 1273 and was completed C. 1300 with the famous west front, one of the first examples of brick architecture in its own right. The basilica was not consecrated until 1334. The aisles are lower than the tall flanking gables suggest, the aisle roofs hide flying buttresses. There is no triforium, although the vaulting rests on alternating supports. The graceful rib-vaulting was gradually lost after the secularization of the abbey in the 16th cent. *Cf. p. 156*

Kapitol and Gross-St.-Martin, as well as in the church of the Teutonic Order at Tartlau in Transylvania. But to provide more space this scheme was abandoned in 1249, when a nave with aisles of the same height — in the manner of a hall church, though in the plan following the basilica type — was added. Within, the effect is largely determined by the play of the light on the closely spaced nave piers with their superimposed clustered piers. The influence of the Marburg Elisabethkirche throughout Hesse was considerable (e.g., Friedberg).

French cathedral Gothic had its first real triumphs in Germany at Cologne and on the Upper Rhine. In 1248, the foundation-stone is laid; at the same time, Master Gerhard of Amiens is placed in charge of the building hut. The choir (consecrated in 1322) — the only part completed during the Middle Ages — is like the *summae* of French architecture; ambulatory and radiating chapels presuppose the experience of the master of Amiens, the system of double aisles follows Bourges and Troyes, the glazed triforium the nave of St. Denis. On the outside, the system of flying buttresses is used for the first time in all its diversity on German soil. Yet, here too, the German sense of form is unmistakable in the use of French elements; the sturdy base of the towers recalls the westwork of Romanesque churches, just as the arrangement of the buttressing on the choir reflects a sense of mass and volume, while

Fig. 54 – *Freiburg in Breisgau. Cathedral. West front. Cf. p. 142*

Synagogue, from the south portal of
Strasbourg Cathedral. By the Master
of the Judgement Pillar. Sandstone.
After 1230. *Frauenhaus Museum, Strasbourg. Height 5 ft. 11 in.*
Ecclesia and Synagogue, as the per-
sonifications of the Old and the New
Testament, flank the twin portal of
the south transept of Strasbourg
Cathedral, at whose centre pillar
Solomon is enthroned as the Just
Judge. Only a few portions survive of
the original decoration of this portal,
where the secular courts used to sit
in former times. The two figures of
Ecclesia and Synagogue have been
replaced by copies on the Cathedral.
The originals, with the tympanum
group of the Death of the Virgin on
the same portal (Appx. Pl. 21),
belong to the most outstanding examples of the sculpture of the
Hohenstaufen period. The master,
possibly trained at Sens, may also
have worked on the transept sculptures at Chartres. Here in Strasbourg
he has translated the statuesque
principle of French sculpture into a
dynamism that expresses drama and
inner agitation. With the Synagogue,
the artist has portrayed the serene
beauty of the female form, idolized in
the contemporary epics of chivalry.
She 'represents no people, but a
stage in the story of Salvation. Universally human in her defeat, she is
yet a full equal seen through the eyes
of a truly noble and generous victor'
(W. Pinder). With the Bamberg
group, this is the earliest representation in sculpture of the theme of the
true Messiah, already prepared in
literature by a dissertation wrongly
attributed to St. Augustine and interpreted in the sculpture of Strasbourg throughout many stages.

APPX. PL. 6
APPX. PL. 14
FIG. 51 the relationship of both is expressive of the German concept of the balance of east and west. The interior, thanks to the narrow canyon of the nave and the general upward movement of all vertical components, seems like an accentuation of Amiens and Beauvais, an impression even further heightened by the use of clustered piers (in contrast to the cylindrical piers with their four attached columns at Amiens) and the absence of horizontal interruptions such as capitals or cornices. Another essentially German feature are the Apostles on the arcade piers of the choir and, later, the nave. In the Paris Sainte-Chapelle — as in the Naumburg west choir — they were placed against the attached piers of the wall.

It is significant that the German Romantic movement, with a renewed awareness of this sense of space, should have completed the work abandoned in the Late Middle Ages; work on the nave and towers was begun in 1842.

*Strasbourg* While Master Gerhard was active in Cologne, Master Rudolf was building the nave of Strasbourg, following the French scheme of St. Denis. Here, too, we find a three-storied nave wall with a glazed triforium, although — unlike St. Denis and Cologne — the Strasbourg triforium, instead of being linked with the tracery of the clerestory, is isolated above and below by a slightly projecting cornice. The plan is largely governed by the dimensions of the original Ottonian buildings whose foundations had to be used for the new cathedral; in consequence, the nave is of an 'un-Gothic' width. As in the nave at Magdeburg and in the church of the Berlin Franciscans, the nave arcades have an exceptionally large span.

FIG. 53 Strasbourg also leads with a new type of nave pier. The piers, originally with four attached shafts, are now so closely surrounded with vaulting shafts that the core becomes invisible. The resultant clustered piers, on a quatrefoil *Clustered piers* base, again emphasize the three-dimensional nature of the relationship between wall and support. This is even more noticeable in the slightly later PLATE P. 131
FIG. 54 Freiburg Cathedral where, the triforium having been omitted, the clustered piers form an impressive contrast against the plain nave wall. At the same time Freiburg carries this development even further: the general impression is no longer merely one of projecting piers but of an interplay of solids and hollows.

---

Madonna and Child, the so-called Milan Madonna. *C.* 1320. Painted wood. *Cologne Cathedral (Sakramentskapelle). Height nearly 7 ft.*
The figure has been re-painted; crown, sceptre and wreath are Baroque additions. The name is based on a confusion in the cathedral records with a Madonna bought in 1164 by Archbishop Rainald in Milan. The work is contemporary with the colossal Apostle figures which were placed on the choir piers shortly before 1322. 'These statues are the most outstanding products of the anti-naturalistic Mannerism of the age' (G. Dehio). The figure, unrelated to any natural movement and hidden by the cascading draperies, the remote expression, the idealized features, and the curve on the left — which extends from head to foot as if drawn between two points on a vertical line which, running parallel with the line of the pier, restores a greater tectonic order — are characteristic of Mannerist art.

FIG. 55 – *Oppenheim, Katha-rinenkirche. South windows, 1320–1340*

*Strasbourg west front*
**FIG. 52**

The façade of Strasbourg, one of the most important monuments of Gothic art in Germany, was not completed until the Late Gothic. The original scheme, supposedly by Master Erwin ('von Steinbach') and known as section B (the master's name was added on the plan over an erased name) could not be carried out in all its perfection. It was only followed up to the zone of the rose window, which was already placed somewhat lower than in the drawing. The revolutionary aspect of this design — whose monumental-ity, despite the Gothic twin-towered façade, once more recalls the westwork — lies in its verticality, in the determination to treat the horizontals merely as obstacles to be overcome. A wealth of decorative systems was created to screen and thus dissolve the wall. French Gothic would only have used such a screen if it could have served some structural function.

The Holy Sepulchre in the St. Maurice rotunda in the cloisters at Constance Cathedral (Lake Constance). *C.* 1300, *height 17 ft. 3 in., diameter 10 ft., height of figures 2 ft. 3 in to 2 ft. 8 in.*
The liberation of the Holy Sepulchre in Jerusalem was the aim of the Crusades, although Christ's tomb had already been the goal of many pilgrimages for several centuries. The rotunda raised above the Holy Sepulchre by Constantine the Great between 326 and 344 became a monument to the Christian faith and was copied on a smaller scale — usually as a chapel (Crusaders' Chapel) in gratitude and as witness to their piety by returning pilgrims. Three times Konrad von Altdorf, bishop of Constance and a descendant of the Guelphs, made the journey to Jerusalem; in 960 he commissioned the small rotunda north-east of the cathedral, modelled on the Holy Sepulchre and dedicated to St. Maurice. After his death in 975 the bishop was buried along the western outer wall of the chapel according to his wish. In 1283 the rotunda, with the chapel built above the bishop's grave, was replaced in its present form. At its centre stands the shrine shown in our illustration, a Gothic interpretation of the Holy Sepulchre, unique in the history of architecture.
Exterior and interior of this twelve-sided structure are decorated with sculpture. On the outside, the twelve figures in the lower row tell the story of Christ's childhood from Annunciation, Visitation and Nativity to the Adoration of the Kings. Above, between the steep, pointed gables, are the Twelve Apostles. The figure of Isaiah on the crocketed finial is a Baroque addition. At the corners inside the polygon are ten half-columns, which again support figures: the three Marys, shown twice, buying ointment from Hippokras and, with the angel of the Resurrection, on their way to the tomb on the Easter morning; the two scenes are separated by the three sleeping tomb guardians. Originally, the centre of the building contained a sarcophagus, probably with a recumbent wooden figure of the dead Christ, replaced by the present coffin in 1552.

The events shown, which are not told in scenes, but represented through figures, must be seen in the context of the mystery plays of the Church which begin to assume increasing importance in the Good Friday and Easter liturgy of the time; all the figures have theatrical, almost exaggerated gestures. There is no agreement about the master or school of sculpture responsible for this work. Links with the Regensburg Erminold Master, as well as with Strasbourg, Basle, and even Mainz, have been suggested. At a time when sculpture was already to some extent assuming a different, more narrative character, these figures must be considered as a last powerful assertion of the Classic art of the thirteenth century.

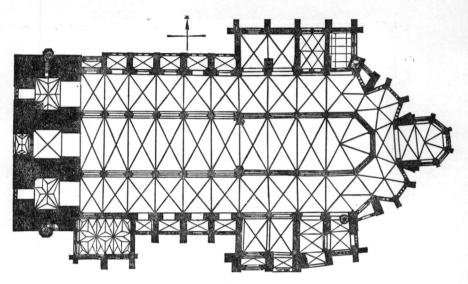

FIG. 56 – *Plan of the Marienkirche, Lübeck. Cf. pp. 133, 147*

Unlike Strasbourg, which was planned as a church with twin towers and only achieved its present asymmetric façade in the course of time, Freiburg represented from the very beginning the typically German scheme of a single-tower church, reminiscent of Romanesque central towers above the west front, not unlike the former western section — now destroyed — of the Vinzenzkirche in Metz. The deep porch of the Freiburg tower also shared some of the functions of the Romanesque westwork, for it served as a court room, as the programme of the portal sculpture emphasizes. It is the portal that makes the whole composition so unique. Even later changes of plan did not affect the uniformity of the concept. The square base, powerfully buttressed, is transformed into an octagon above the clock storey. The transition is

Group of Christ and St. John from the Nazareth orphanage, Sigmaringen (Baden-Württemberg); probably the work of a Constance master. *C.* 1320. Oak, painted and gilt. *Ehem. Kaiser-Friedrich-Museum, Berlin. Height* 35¼ *in. Cf. p. 162*

After 1280 German sculpture acquires a strong mystic quality. New types of devotional picture, rich in emotion, with few figures, appear. The Christ and St. John groups, of which barely twenty survive, belong to a comparatively narrow region of south-western Germany. They are, in the strict sense, portraits of St. John, of 'the disciple whom Jesus loved', who was allowed to partake of Divine mysteries at the breast of the Lord. The theme originated as an illustration to St. John's Gospel in book illumination (*c.* 1200), and was only translated into sculpture with the growth of a devotional literature — chiefly in the Dominican and Franciscan nunneries — based on the mystic concept of man's union with the Divine. The merging of the two figures into one outline, the linked hands, the expression of the youthful Apostle completely devoted to his Master, the line of the red

hem of the mantle over the knees of both figures and the identical dress are like symbols of complete unity. The earliest of these groups, immediate forerunners of the Sigmaringen group, come from the chapel of the Schülzburg (Cleveland/Ohio Museum), from the Katherinental convent near Dissenhofen, in Switzerland (Antwerp, Museum Mayer van den Bergh) and from the Cistercian church in Heiligkreuztal, Upper Swabia.

achieved through triangular finials that accompany the octagon from the beginning and terminate in lace-like filigree near the windows, thus achieving in the lower portion of the octagon the impression of a square, from which the pierced upper part — completed in the middle of the four-teenth century–seems to emerge gradually. The south tower of Chartres shows a similar combination of an octagon with a buttressing system, though on a very much smaller scale and without a pierced spire. Freiburg therefore has no equal in France; its only succession is in Germany. The last of the pierced towers occur at Burgos Cathedral — the work of Johann of Cologne — in Spain (*c.* 1450) and at the Late Gothic cathedrals of Berne, Ulm, Strasbourg and Thann.

*French influence*     In Germany, as elsewhere, the leading exponents of the Gothic are the Cistercians, who carry it from Burgundy to Germany and Austria, to Altenberg, Arnsburg, Bebenhausen, Ebernach, Ebrach, Heiligenkreuz, Lilienfeld, Marienstadt, Maulbron, Otterberg, Salem, Waldsassen, Walken-ried and to St. Agnes in Prague, as far as to the gates of Cracow, in Poland. The powerful logical spirit of these great and noble buildings gradually determines the face of the whole region. In the last quarter of the thirteenth century the collegiate church at Wimpfen on the Neckar was built — according to contemporary records — *opere francigeno*, in the French manner, probably by a master trained in Paris and Strasbourg. Like the Marburg Elisabethkirche, the cathedrals of Osnabrück, Münster and Regensburg are inspired by the Champagne; the Sebalduskirche at Nuremberg, on the other hand, reflects Burgundian influence. The influence of Soissons and Rheims is no less noticeable in the Lübeck Marienkirche, or Stralsund and Rostock, than at Tournai, while the cathedrals of Limburg-an-der-Lahn and Magdeburg, the façade of Halberstadt and the towers of Nuremberg and Bamberg recall the forms of Laon. Xanten is remiscent of Braisne, Paderborn Cathedral, built as a hall church, is almost a copy of Poitiers. The choir of Halberstadt Cathedral, begun in 1334, was based on the plan of St. Germain, Auxerre.

Forked Crucifix, according to an early, well-authenticated inscription (now lost) dating from 1304 (so-called Pestkreuz, i.e. 'Plague Cross'). *Cologne, Santa Maria im Kapitol. Height 4 ft. 11 in. Cf. pp. 80, 158, 162*
The image of the crucified Christ undergoes a transformation at the turn of the 13th to the 14th cent. The early 13th cent. had placed the Crucifix as the symbol of triumph high up on the triumphal arch between nave and choir (Halberstadt, Wechselburg, Freiberg). Slightly later, the Naumburg Master had portrayed a more human, less hieratic Christ on the rood-screen, dying, the crown of thorns on His head, His features rent with pain (Appx. Pl. 1). At the end of the 13th cent. all restraint is abandoned. Christ's sufferings are now portrayed mercilessly, demanding compassion; for this reason, this type of Crucifix is also known as 'Erbärmdekreuz', or 'Compassion Cross'. The body is distorted by pain to the point of hideousness. Heinrich Seuse, one of the great poets of the Mystic, has described the Crucifixion in a similar manner with a wealth of horrifying detail, though the purpose in his case is the condensation of emotions rather than mere realism. The cross, based on the living tree, has been known in this form since the bronze gates of Bernward von Hildesheim; it is based on the *arbor*

*vitae*, the Tree of Life, thus placing the figure of the Crucified within the context of the story of man's salvation. 'The significance, the lyric aspect, of the Cologne work and of the numerous forked and branched crosses as devotional pictures does not lie in the Crucifixion, but in the concentration of the whole story of the Passion into a single figure' (W. Pinder).

149

| | |
|---|---|
| *Hall churches* | The hall churches of Westphalia, Saxony and the Netherlands are inspired by the buildings of the Angevin school, whose naves and aisles are of equal height. They have no clerestory, buttress arches, transepts or ambulatory; their vaulting system, with ridge ribs rising from a square base, later gives way to the lierne vault, a more or less elaborate arrangement adopted in the fourteenth and fifteenth century throughout Central and Northern Europe as far as Scandinavia. With their emphasis on one vast single room, these hall churches form the strongest possible contrast to the cathedral of the basilica type; yet they reflect an attitude that was to determine — above all in Germany — the future development of the Gothic church. |
| *Brick Gothic*<br><br>PLATE P. 133<br><br><br><br><br>FIG. 56 | Conditions in eastern and northern Germany, as well as in the south of France, account for the so-called brick Gothic. Brick does not demand the same forms as stone. The Lübeck Marienkirche was to be decisive for the architecture of the whole Baltic region. Here, the source of inspiration is not so much the art of the Île-de-France as Breton and, above all, Norman building (Quimper, Coutances). Façade and plan follow the conventional scheme of the Gothic basilica with oblong vaulting bays, an ambulatory with radiating chapels and a system of exposed buttressing on the outside. The articulation of the nave wall, however, is confined to two stories, a passage in front of the windows replacing the triforium. Yet the absence of a triforium cannot exactly be considered tantamount with its complete rejection. Some churches — all of which have rendered walls within — had a painted triforium between the arcades and the window zone (e.g. the Cistercian church at Doberan/Mecklenburg). |
| *Hanseatic League*<br><br>PLATE P. 133 | The North German brick Gothic had several important centres. Lübeck as the outpost of the Hanseatic League, with its cathedral and the Marienkirche, ranks foremost in the Baltic. The so-called Wendische Quartier — the southern coast of the Baltic from Schleswig-Holstein to Pomerania, including many inland ports and trading centres — exercised considerable influence on the architecture of the Scandianavian countries and the Baltic. The great parish churches and cathedrals between Bremen, Hamburg and Lübeck on the one hand, and Danzig, Riga and Reval on the other, as well as many churches and secular buildings of the thirteenth and fourteenth centuries as far as Aarhus, in Denmark, and Gotland (Sweden), all reflect this common impulse. |

Vesper group from Scheuerberg, Thuringia. *C.* 1320. *Veste Coburg. Height 5 ft. 9 in. Cf. p. 162*
The mourning Madonna with the dead Christ in her lap is already known in Byzantine art; as an isolated devotional picture, this group is a creation of the German Mystic. The term 'Vesperbild', customary in German-speaking countries, is derived from the evening devotions (*ad vesperam*) associated with this theme. The Coburg group, of vast dimensions, is the earliest surviving example. The subject is not derived from the Bible but — as Schwietering has proved — from a profane hero epic by Chrétien de Troyes, in whose poem 'Iwain' Sigune holds the body of her dead lover, whom she has driven to his fate, on her lap. In the course of time this theme

was adopted in religious poetry and devotional literature. The dimensions, no less than the mood of this group, suggest the influence of Hohenstaufen sculpture (the Bamberg Elizabeth and the Naumburg Madonna). From Thuringia and Franconia this motif spreads throughout Germany to Italy, where it takes form in the Pietà. In contrast to the stark monumentality of the Coburg group, the Vesper pictures of the following years aim to arouse the mystic *compassio* (Vesper groups in the Erfurt Ursuline convent and the so-called Pietà Röttgen in the Bonn Landesmuseum, both *c.* 1330).

*Teutonic Order*   From about 1260 onwards, the Teutonic Order assumes increasing importance in the region between eastern Pomerania and the Russian border near Narva. It produces its own type of brick Gothic throughout the territories where, at the period of its greatest flowering in the fourteenth century, it establishes a firm military system of government; the most characteristic examples of this architecture are great fortified castles, the most important

*Marienburg*   amongst them the residence of the Grand Master, the Marienburg on the river Nogat, a tributary of the Vistula. After the fall of Acre (1271), when the Order temporarily settled first at Cyprus and then in Venice (1309), the principal centre was established at Marienburg, in the region that was now the heartland of the mission of the Teutonic Knights. The Marienburg was begun in 1280; in the course of the Order's building activities, lasting over 130 years, it grew into one of Europe's largest castles. The main building, in the manner of the Order's early castles, can be considered the archetype of a fortified convent. Four buildings of several stories enclosed a rectangular courtyard; two-storied arcaded galleries linked the different rooms such as chapel, chapter-hall, dormitories, armories, kitchens, etc. Towards the outside, the four wings, whose derivation from individual houses was indicated by gables, formed a compact brick cube, decorated with large-scale designs in glazed brick.

At the corners of these castles usually stood square towers, of which one was developed as a belfry; along the roof zone was a rampart walk with battlements. Careful workmanship and well-chosen proportions make these castles works of considerable architectural merit. The interiors, with stellar or conoidal vaulting supported on slender granite piers cut from single blocks, were often of outstanding beauty. Apart from the Marienburg, the castles at Königsberg, Thorn, Reden and Mewe, as well as the Bishop's castles at Heilsberg and Marienwerder, are amongst the Order's most

St. John the Evangelist. Detail from a triptych in the Wiesenkirche, Soest. Tempera on oak. *Ehem. Staatliche Museen, Berlin. Overall size 2 ft. 4 ins.* × *3 ft.* 11¹/₄ *in.*
The triptych is divided into three arcades of equal width, resting on half-columns. The central arcade shows the Trinity, while in the left arcade — opposite the St. John in our illustration — the Madonna, as a supplicant, her arms opened and her hands stretched out, turns towards the centre. Unlike her, the figure of St. John is almost frontal, only slightly turned towards the left. The draperies are in the so-called zigzag style, which was widespread throughout the Lower Rhine region between Hildesheim and Cologne; it is to some degree a transformation of impulses evident in Late Byzantine painting. The folds of the upper garment, unlike 12th-cent. draperies, no longer follow the lines of the body but, their natural fall broken, cut across and terminate in sharp points. The gestures of the hands and the position of the feet show a similar agitation, probably based on the intention to project the space needed by the figure into the plane.
This work belongs to the earliest examples of German panel-painting. It was created by an unknown master of the Cologne or Westphalian school shortly before the middle of the 13th cent. Although it comes from the Wiesenkirche in Soest, it was most likely painted for an earlier church, probably by the same artist as the frescos in the Soest Nikolaikirche. Stylistic criteria also suggest links with a fresco of the Crucifixion in St. Cunibert, Cologne (*c.* 1247), whose St. John resembles in some respects the figure in our panel picture.

152

*Marienwerder*  outstanding monuments. Marienwerder, castle and fortified cathedral in one,
FIGS. 25, 26, 27  is unique of its kind, except possibly for Albi, in southern France. The dates
of origin of these two supreme examples of brick architecture are the same,
yet problems of form have been approached very differently in each case. At
Albi, with its round piers and towers, the curve predominates, while Marienwerder and the Marienburg, governed by the right angle, recall the forma-
tive force of the crystalline rock.

Outside the realm of French, English and central German military architecture and the castles of the Crusaders, the buildings of the Teutonic Order
in former Prussia (the former provinces of West and East Prussia, as well as
Estonia and Latvia) are the most important examples of European fortified
PLATE P. 163  castles, apart from the Hohenstaufen buildings in Apulia (Castel del Monte).
The same spirit is manifest in the architecture of other orders and of the
cities of Prussia, among them the Cistercian abbeys of Oliva, near Danzig,
and, above all, Pelplin (formerly West Prussia), with their severe steeply
rising brick façades, flanked by polygonal stair-towers as if by the shafts of
lances. The plan of these basilica churches, however, recalls the churches of
the Hanseatic towns. The nave and transepts of Pelplin bring to mind
another great brick church of the period round 1300, the Cistercian abbey
*Doberan*  of Doberan, in Mecklenburg. Doberan, the most outstanding example of
Cistercian High Gothic on the southern Baltic, instead of following the
traditional plan of the churches of the order throughout Europe, is based
on the scheme of the great Hanseatic brick churches in Lübeck, Schwerin
and Rostock which, in turn, derive their ambulatories and radiating chapels
from the churches of the region around Tournai and Utrecht.

*Danzig*  Another example of the synthesis of elements derived from the architecture
of the Teutonic Order and the Hanseatic towns is Danzig's principal
church, the Marienkirche, one of the largest brick churches in Europe.

The Earthly Paradise. Fresco in the eastern vaulting bay of the western rood-loft in Gurk Cathedral (Carinthia,
Austria). 1220–1260.
The western rood-loft, an episcopal chapel of two cross-vaulted bays, lies above the porch of the elaborate west
front of the cathedral, between the two towers. On each side of the altar on the east wall are three arcades
of coupled pillars which open the view towards the nave and the choir. Theological concepts, painting, and
architecture, are in complete harmony. The Earthly Paradise on the eastern vaulting bay corresponds to the
Heavenly Jerusalem on the western; the altar wall — which opens towards the church — below the Paradise
scene displays a fresco of the Virgin enthroned, surrounded by Saints; opposite, on the western wall, below the
heavenly Jerusalem, is the Transfiguration. Scenes from the story of man's salvation and medallions of Prophets,
Apostles and Saints cover the remaining walls. The frescos were painted in 1214, after the death of the donor,
Bishop Otto. Badly damaged by fire, they were restored under Bishop Dietrich II shortly after 1260. Both
bishops are shown on the eastern wall. To what extent the frescos belong to the first and to the second period
has never been established. Despite the strong emphasis on colour — in the eastern bay predominantly greens
and blues — line is of considerable importance in these paintings, chiefly because of the combined fresco and
fresco secco technique. With a surprisingly sure hand, the master has sketched the preliminary ochre drawing
and later the undercoat into the wet ground, letting them dry together. He then applied the colours on the dry

ground, finishing with the black outlines. Today, little remains beyond the underpainting and the drawing; we can thus gain a particularly good insight into the artist's characteristic manner. The figure of Christ, whose robe (probably one of the earliest examples of the zigzag style north of the Alps) is broken in a zigzag fall, contrasts with the figures of Adam and Eve, drawn in continuous lines. The trees, in the Byzantine tradition, are formulae rather than naturalistic representations.

Begun in 1343, it is virtually the culmination of the entire brick architecture of the Baltic; it inaugurates a development of the Gothic that was to achieve its greatest flowering in these regions.

*Territory Brandenburg*   A third important area of the north German brick Gothic is Brandenburg, the territory between the Elbe and the Oder, formed by the Ascanian Margraves in the twelfth and thirteenth centuries. These vigorous and enterprising rulers called first Praemonstratensians, then Cistercians, and finally the Mendicant orders into their country, founded many monasteries and towns and cultivated lands rich in forests and streams, though badly neglected by their original Wendish inhabitants. The mature Gothic of the Ascanian phase

*Chorin*
PLATE P. 139   culminates in the Cistercian buildings at Chorin (near Eberswalde, north of Berlin). Church and abbey presuppose a century-old tradition of indigenous brick architecture; the new forms of western Gothic art have undoubtedly come by way of central Germany, above all via the Cistercians at Pforta, in Thuringia. Chorin was begun in 1274. The cruciform basilica shows the reduced system, without a triforium and with hidden buttress arches under the aisle roofs (as at Doberan and, slightly later, Salem/Baden). Chorin is also the first example of a tall polygonal choir, realized in Thuringia at Pforta and, earlier, in the famous west choir at Naumburg, both modelled on the hall-like choirs of French cathedrals, whose finest example is the Sainte-Chapelle in Paris. An interesting feature at Chorin are the clustered piers, which follow the rhythm of the Romanesque 'tied' system, while the delicate rib-vaulting in the nave is over small bays. The form of the piers at Chorin is probably derived from the earlier Franciscan church in Berlin.

PLATE P. 139   The façade is one of the finest of its kind in the Middle Ages. Here the ban on towers in Cistercian architecture inspired, for the first time, a solution dominated by gables that rise beyond the outline of the roofs. The flat, lively relief, achieved with the help of the slender buttress piers, blind arcading and tall windows, in complete contrast to the style of the Teutonic Order and the Hanseatic towns, is the symbol of a sophistication attained only in the marches under the Ascanian rulers, whose principal foundation was Chorin.

---

Annunciation. By an unknown Cologne master, *c.* 1320–1325. Tempera on oak. *Wallraf-Richartz Museum, Cologne. Height 1 ft. 4*$^1$/$_2$ *in., width 13*$^5$/$_8$ *in.*
With a Presentation in the Temple, of the same size and also in the Wallraf-Richartz Museum, this panel was probably part of an altar. Around the time of the consecration of Cologne Cathedral (1322), the Cologne school of panel-painting passed through its first great flowering; like contemporary architecture, it was an art orientated towards the west, towards Burgundy and northern France as well as the southern Netherlands and England. The emphasis on detail, reminiscent of the art of the Paris school of ivory-carving and of the miniaturist (Arundel Psalter, London, British Museum), gives the pictures a quality well suited to the mystic-lyrical piety of the age. The figures, of a courtly elegance and grace and almost bodiless, seem to float against the incised gold background. Though gestures and bearing show a close similarity with the same scene in the *Somme-le-Roi* by the Dominican Laurentius in the Bibliothèque Mazarin in Paris, courtly mannerism has given

way to greater freedom and sensitivity. Other important examples of this school, apart from the panel in our illustration, are an altar with the Crucifixion in the same museum, a diptych with a Crucifixion and the Madonna in the Deutsches Museum in Berlin, and the Clarenaltar and the choir-screens of Cologne Cathedral. With these works panel-painting assumes increasing importance in the 14th cent.

| | |
|---|---|
| *Silesia* | The influence of Brandenburg's brick Gothic extended deep into Poland, where its manifestations frequently appear like a synthesis of the architecture of the Teutonic Order and of a specific Silesian Gothic, whose principal monuments are Breslau Cathedral — probably built by Cistercians — and the Cistercian churches of Heinrichau and Trebnitz. |
| *Sculpture* APPX. PL. 21 *Naumburg Master* | Gothic sculpture follows the same path as architecture in Germany, although the absence of a powerful indigenous tradition meant that French influence could assert itself very much more quickly. The development of the Naumburg Master can be traced from France, via the building huts of Amiens, Chartres, Noyons and Metz to Mainz (rood-screen) and Naumburg where, *c.* 1250–1270, he created the founders' figures of the west choir, which are interpreted as individual portraits. Outstanding amongst them are the shy and reserved Uta, in the strongest possible contrast to her proud and martial husband Ekkehard, the forceful and aware Reglindis, and the aged Gepa. Uta's whole bearing is expressed in the heavy mantle that seems to hide her from the world. Around 1260 the same master created the rood-screen at the west choir, with a Crucifixion and reliefs of the Passion, full of a dramatic, yet hidden tension. The features of the Christ are expressive and realistic; |
| APPX. PL. I PLATE P. 149 | the mood is like an anticipation of the mystic plague crosses of the early fourteenth century (Santa Maria im Kapitol, Cologne, 1304, Perpignan, 1307). |
| *New sense of space* | Though there can be no doubt whatever about the French training of the Naumburg Master, his art illustrates all the characteristics of German sculpture. Here the connection with the architecture is never as marked as in France; instead of making the figures part of the façade, the artist creates round them a space of action. The Naumburg figures in the west choir stand in front of the piers, opposite each other; the impression thus arises of some central event, of some relationship between them. Similarly, Ecclesia and Synagogue on the Strasbourg south portal become divorced from their architectural background and, across the central figure of Solomon, assume the character of two actors in a dialogue. The angel pier — where, as in the figures of the south portal, elements derived from the monumental sculpture of the Île-de-France (above all, as W. Sauerländer |

Konrad von Altstetten, miniature from the Manessa MS., *c.* 1320. *University Library, Heidelberg.*
Religious and secular mysticism merge in the poetry of the Minnesingers of the 13th and the early 14th cent. and find their most eloquent expressions in a series of illuminated manuscripts, of which the most famous is the Manessa MS. The poetry of the Minnesingers, in no way spontaneous and naive, unfolds in the images and formulae of courtly convention: knight and lady play their part according to fixed rules which were evolved in the south, in Arabic Spain, and passed through further elaboration and sophistication in southern France. The hero and lover always plays the helpless serf who looks longingly to his unattainable mistress, thirsting to dedicate his life to her, though his desires never find fulfilment because the subject of his songs is no woman of flesh and blood but some remote ideal image. Yet the Minnesinger, within the clearly defined rules of the game, runs the whole gamut of emotions, from fire to tenderness, from brilliant wit to art.

The Manessa MS. contains the songs of 140 Minnesingers and 138 miniatures, each bearing the coat-of-arms of the singer. Other, less sumptuous, manuscripts are at Stuttgart and Weingarten. Their common source is probably a collection of individual songs formed — according to the poet Hadlaub — by the Zurich senator Rüdiger Manesse (d. 1304) and his son Johannes (d. 1297). Stylistically, the Manessa MS., written and illustrated after the death of the two collectors, is obviously influenced by the French school of minature-painting, although the illustrations have a distinct originality.

159

has pointed out, from Sens Cathedral) have been transformed — is placed into an entirely un-French relationship with its surroundings; it is truly the centre, the focal point, of the surrounding space.

*Freiberg (Saxony)* The same tendency towards a central orientation of the sculpture groups is characteristic of the porch of Freiburg Cathedral, of the portal figures at Magdeburg and of the Freiberg (Saxony) Golden Gate with the tall and sturdy *statues colonnes* and the Adoration of the Kings on the tympanum. Here, too, despite the comparatively 'French' arrangement of the jamb figures, we find the German tendency towards synthesis, reflected in a sculpture programme compressed into a single portal cycle, instead of the customary French scheme of three portals. The staggering of the portal — in its forms still Romanesque — is another way of emphasizing the central aspect of the whole composition.

*Bamberg* Other important groups include the portals of Paderborn and, above all, the Bamberg sculpture — the Adam's Gate and the Princes' Portal, whose figures are of a beauty reminiscent of Rheims and Strasbourg, the famous horseman who appears the quintessence of a Hohenstaufen knight, the Visitation group, and the Ecclesia and Synagogue, the last-named of considerable grace and firmness under robes that seem swelled by a rounded youthful body. In all these figures, of which few are still in their original places, the orientation towards some focal point is clearly recogniable.

*Sculpture in the* As in France, the trend in the fourteenth century is towards a more intimate
*14th century* and anecdotal character, towards greater realism and emphasis on the bourgeois every-day qualities, combined with a strong expressive power that is the mark of fourteenth- and fifteenth-century German sculpture. Famous examples include the portals of the Sebalduskirche and the Lorenzkirche in Nuremberg, as well as the cathedrals in Nuremberg, Worms and Erfurt, and the Apostles in the choir of Cologne Cathedral.

Niccolò Pisano (*c.* 1225–before 1287), Marble pulpit in Siena Cathedral.
In the 13th cent., with the increasing importance of the sermon in the services of the mendicant orders, the pulpit gradually replaces the ambo. The earliest pulpits are found in Italy, where they owe their origin to the influence of the Franciscans and the Dominicans; in the north pulpits as a rule do not appear until the 15th cent. The pulpit, decorated with sculpture, becomes the vehicle of a scholastic programme, not unlike the sculpture cycle of the cathedrals. Niccolò Pisano, whose work on the cathedral and the baptistry at Pisa leaves little doubt that he must have had considerable knowledge of architecture, also gave the pulpit architectural forms. About six years earlier he had created the Pisa baptistry, giving it the shape of a hexagon — more in accord with Gothic feeling — instead of the traditional rectangle. The Siena pulpit, though similar in composition, is far more elaborate. The octagon, in place of the hexagonal plan, demands more reliefs and more corner figures. In contrast to Pisa, the Siena pulpit stands on a profiled marble base; in the north Italian tradition, every second column rests on a lion which stands over its prey. Above the eight foliated Gothic capitals are Sibyls, in the spandrils above the trefoil arches Prophets and Evangelists. The centre column, on which the floor of the pulpit rests, has at its base the seated figures of the Seven Liberal Arts and Philosophy. The seven reliefs on the parapet show scenes from the life of Christ and the Last Judgement, separated by the corner figures of the Seven Virtues and the Virgin. An eagle supports the lectern.

Since Vasari, Niccolò Pisano has been considered a master of the proto-Renaissance. Yet his work shows no anticipation of a rebirth of Antiquity, but is part of the conscious succession of Classic art striven for by Frederick II in Apulia, the province where Niccolò seems to have originated. The master's knowledge of Roman Antiquity is reflected in the sturdy figures; his reliefs are clearly a resumption of the many-figured high relief style of Roman sarcophagi. Yet, although a number of actual copies of Classic examples can be traced in Niccolò's work, these are placed into a Gothic context, in the sense of a meeting between Antiquity and the new spirit coming from France, as the Siena pulpit so convincingly demonstrates. In his last work — and, even more so, in the art of his son, Giovanni — the Gothic finally comes to full flower in Italy. *Cf. p. 176*

At the same time, the Mystic, chiefly in Germany, creates new types of the devotional picture — the Pietà, the Man of Sorrows, the Plague Crucifix, the Christ and St. John group. Cologne becomes the centre of this new development in sculpture which brings the dematerialization of the solid block through deeply incised furrows in face and body and through the unnatural elongation of the limbs, and culminates in the middle of the fourteenth century in the tombs of Bishop Otto von Wolfskehl (d. 1345) in Würzburg Cathedral and Bishop Friedrich von Hohenlohe (d. 1352) at Bamberg. The so-called Parler art, after the middle of the century, came as a reaction against this negation of the human form.

EASTERN EUROPE  The influence of the French Gothic extended as far as eastern Europe, carried above all by the Cistercians to Bohemia and Poland, to Hungary and present-day Yugoslavia. Some famous masters, also undertook the long journey to eastern Europe. Villard de Honnecourt, whose sketch-books survive, travelled to Hungary from northern France via Rheims and Lausanne and Matthias of Arras went to Prague to take charge of the building hut of the new cathedral, founded by the German Emperor Charles IV (1334).

Towards the end of the fourteenth century, Paris, as the great centre of the arts, was supplanted by the new seat of the Papacy, Avignon, where many Flemings went to study the art of the Italian Trecento, and, later still, during the Late Gothic, by Dijon, where Swiss and Swabian masters formed *Bohemia* an indelible impression of the lively realism of Sluter and his school. Bohemia, converted to Christianity in the thirteenth century, opted for the west during the schism and abandoned Byzantine art. In the thirteenth century King Ottokar, who had received a thorn from the Crown of Thorns from St. Louis, built the convent of the Holy Crown, on the plan of the Cistercian abbey of Fontenay, in Burgundy, to house this precious relic. French influence predominated for some time amongst the Kings of Luxemburg. John of Bohemia, who was educated in Paris, where he had met the poet and musician Guillaume de Machaut whom he brought back to Prague, died at Crécy with the flower of the French nobility.

His son Charles IV, the future head of the Holy Roman Empire, visited Paris and Avignon; surviving records speak of his admiration for French archi-*Prague* tecture. It was he who brought Matthias of Arras to Prague in 1334 to build the cathedral of St. Vitus, on the model of Narbonne Cathedral, within the area of his castle, furnished by him in the manner of French royal palaces. After the death of the French master in 1352 the work was continued almost to its completion by Peter Parler of Schwäbisch Gmünd, who made many changes to the original scheme, which gradually hardened into a Gothic formalism.

*Hungary* Hungary had always had links with France and French art, not merely after the fourteenth century, when the House of Anjou ascended the throne of Hungary, but already in the eleventh, when the closest ties of friendship

Castel del Monte, the hunting-lodge of the Hohenstaufen Emperor Frederick II in Apulia, built *c.* 1240, 'a synthesis of Roman, Eastern and Gothic elements' (N. Pevsner). An octagon with an octagonal courtyard and, at the corners, octagonal watch-towers, linked by staircases with the upper storey and the roof. The portal, surmounted by a simple triangular gable and the only access to the interior, is an eloquent witness to the emperor's conscious affirmation of the Classic tradition. Every outer wall is pierced with a small Gothic window. Towards the courtyard the façade, opening into arcades and loggias, loses all its severity; the rooms, probably due to Cistercian influence, are rib-vaulted. *Cf. p. 154, 178*

existed between St. Stephen and St. Odilon of Cluny, and a Hungarian, St. Ladislas, founded the abbey of St. Gilles (1091), which was a perfect replica of Saint-Gilles-du-Gard. In the twelfth century Bela III, a brother-in-law of Philippe-Auguste — he was married to Margaret of France, the daughter of Louis VII — asked the Cistercians to build convents on the Burgundian pattern on Hungarian soil. The Templars and the Knights of the Order of St. John followed the Cistercians around the middle of the thirteenth century. Villard de Honnecourt tells us how he was invited to Hungary, probably by the Cistercians, with whom he was on friendly terms. He was undoubtedly connected with the building of the cathedral of

Estergom and St. Elizabeth in Kaschau, where we can find many French features; the arcading of the castle chapel at Estergom shows a remarkable similarity with that of the choir tower at Saint-Germain-des-Prés. In 1287 Jean de Saint-Dié, a French architect from the Vosges, was in charge of several churches under construction in Transylvania.

*Poland*   Poland — like Bohemia converted to Christianity in the twelfth century — similarly accepted the authority of the Church of Rome and the art of the west. Again the Cistercians came as the bearers of French art. The abbey of Suleiov (1232) is the first manifestation of Gothic forms. We find the same influence in the Dominican and Franciscan churches of the fourteenth century — even in Cracow Cathedral — though with certain specifically German modifications: the choir is longer, the brick construction follows the north German technique and buttress arches are missing.

The church of Jak illustrates the influence of French art on the Hungarian sculpture of the twelfth and thirteenth centuries. The Christ figure and the Twelve Apostles, of *c.* 1256, are derived from the statues at Saint-Gilles-du-Gard, though some of the detail also recalls the work of Benedetto Antelami in northern Italy, and Vézelay.

A group of the Madonna and Child Enthroned brings to mind a similar group on the *porte royale* and on the west front of Notre-Dame, Paris.

SPAIN   Close links existed between France and Spain. After the Arab conquest the country was gradually re-taken with the help of French knights. From 1033 onwards veritable crusades, organized from Cluny and encouraged by the Papacy, swept across the Pyrénées; nobles and clergy from Aquitaine, Gascony, Poitou, Limousin, the Champagne, the Île-de-France, Normandy and Burgundy took part in them. In the course of time the whole of Spain was re-conquered; the Roman liturgy, introduced by French monks, displaced the Mozarab, French writing Visigothic.

*Mudejar and*   But this French predominance must not allow us to forget the great civilia-
*Mozarab art*   tion produced by the contact between Christians and Moslems at centres like Toledo, Cordoba and Seville. Spanish and Mudejar art — the art of Moslems under Christian rule — as well as Mozarab art, which is the art of Christians under Moorish influence, bear the stamp of an Arab culture

Siena Cathedral. View from the south transept towards the polygonal crossing and the choir. Begun in the first quarter of the 13th cent. The nave was completed *c.* 1259, the crossing with the dome, over an octagonal plan, *c.* 1264. It has been proved that building workers from the Cistercian abbey at San Galgano, in the Maremma, were active in Siena while the cathedral was rising; the general disposition of the plan was probably influenced by them to some degree. The bands of black and white marble and the elaborately sculptured capitals and cornices below the clerestory produce a startling effect. In our illustration the portrait busts of popes, part of a vast series of papal portraits, can be seen on the cornice of the nave wall. The façade, dispensing with flying buttresses, emphasizes the homogeneous character of the building; it is clearly influenced by Orvieto Cathedral (Appx. Pl. 4). *Cf. p. 176*

that was at one time spread over the entire country from Gibraltar to the Pyrénées' a memory of past events that has been preserved forever.

*Pilgrims' Road*
The Pilgrims' Road to Santiago da Compostela, the path taken by the pilgrims to the grave of the Apostle, is called in Spain the *chemin français*. It was the gateway to French art into northern Spain and to Hispano-Mauresque influence into the south of France.

Catalonia, at one time part of the Carolingian empire, is a virtual outpost of French culture. United with Rousillon, it acknowledged until 1258 the supremacy of the kings of France and maintained close links with the counts of Toulouse. Until 1091, the date of the foundation of the archbishopric of APPX. PL. 8 Tarragona, the Catalan bishops were under the authority of the archbishop of Narbonne. The connection across the Pyrénées was never completely broken; the counts of Catalonia and of Cardagne were amongst the most generous benefactors of Saint-Nazaire de Carcassonne, Saint-Gilles-du-Gard, Saint-Victor of Marseille, and Cluny. All these facts help to explain the relationship between the art of the Languedoc and Rousillon, between Burgundy, Poitou and northern Spain, Saint-Sernin de Toulouse and Saint-Foy de Conques, Santiago de Compostela and San Domingo de Silos.

*Cistercian foundations*
Here, too, Gothic art was introduced by the Cistercians, who, in the second half of the twelfth century, enjoyed the same favour as the Cluniac monks before them. In 1131 St. Bernard sent the first monks to Alphonso VII; in the same year he founded Moruela, near Zamorra. In 1147 the king's sister, Sancha, settled Cistercians at Espina, in the diocese of Palencia. L'Escale-Dieu, in the diocese of Tarbes, established sister foundations at Oliva in Navarre, at Fitero and Monsalud in Castile, and at Veruela in Aragon. Other foundations followed: Valbuena and Santa Maria de la Huerta in Castile, through Berdoues of Auch; Poblet, the 'Saint-Denis' of the kings of Aragon, was founded in 1149 by the monks of Fontfroide, the neighbour abbey of Narbonne. In 1187 Alphonso VIII called Cistercians to Las Huelgas, near Burgos.

*Carthusian and Praemonstratensian foundations*
Nor did the Carthusians and Praemonstratensians remain inactive. Their abbeys, too, without exception show French influence. Burgundian and southern French Gothic dominates Spanish abbey churches as much as convent buildings, as E. Lambert, P. Lavedan, G. Gaillard, P. Deschamps and Torres Balbas have shown. At Las Huelgas, Angevin art comes to life again in the church and the chapter-hall, one of the most magnificent buildings of its kind in Spain. Saint-Vincent and the cathedral of Avila show the influence of Vézelay, the old cathedral of Sigüenza recalls Notre-Dame, Poitiers; Narbonne and Fontfroide inspired the churches and abbeys of Catalonia, Barcelona Cathedral and the nave of Gerona — begun in 1316 FIG. 57 APPX. PL. 16 by Master Henri de Narbonne and completed in 1397 by Maître Pierre de Saint-Jean of Picardy — no less than Saint-Marie-de-la-Mer in Barcelona and the cathedral of Palma de Mallorca, where a hall type of interior, characteristic of northern Catalonia and south-western France, has been developed.

Resurrection of the Dead. Detail from the relief of the Last Judgement on the right pier of the west front of Orvieto Cathedral (Umbria).

After 1310, by an unknown — probably Sienese — sculptor, perhaps Lorenzo Maitani, who was cathedral architect at Orvieto from 1310 onwards. Part of the relief is attributed to Niccolò di Nuto, who held Lorenzo Maitani's office after 1330. In view of the uniform character of the relief, the contribution of any of the other sculptors active at Orvieto seems unlikely.

The sculptures on the lower zone of the four piers on the west front at Orvieto, the most extensive example of a sculpture programme in Italy, are a powerful manifestation of the spirit of the scholastic Gothic. The cycle begins with Genesis, on the first pier on the left, while the first pier on the right, in antithesis, displays the Last Judgement, of which a section is shown in our illustration. The two inner piers, next to the main portal, show — also in antithesis — scenes from the Old Testament, with Prophets, a sibyl and the Tree of Jesse on the left, and scenes from the New Testament on the right. The Resurrection of the Dead, though interpreted in a more Classic spirit (not unlike Niccolò Pisano's treatment of the same subject at Pisa), leaves no doubt that the master had seen the cathedrals of Rheims, Amiens and Bourges. Not only has the relief been given great depth, in the manner of Late Classic sarcophagi reliefs, nor is it only a question of portraying nudes of a Classic anatomy; the artist has gone much further by illustrating Late Classic and early Christian sarcophagi in every detail.

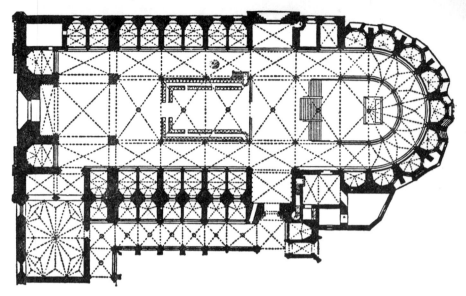

FIG. 57 – *Plan of Barcelona Cathedral. Cf. p. 166*

*Toledo, Burges,*
*Léon*

FIGS. 58, 59

FIGS. 60, 61

More than anywhere else the influence of the great cathedrals of the Île-de-France can be noted in the Spanish cathedrals of the thirteenth century, perhaps the work of French architects employed by prelates who had spent many years in France. Toledo, with its double aisles of varying height and transepts that do not project, brings to mind Bourges and the choirs of Le Mans and Notre-Dame, Paris. Burgos was rebuilt from 1221 onwards as a Gothic church in the manner of Bourges and Coutances. At Léon, plan, piers and foliated capitals recall Rheims, the three portals on the east front the transept portals at Chartres. The impulse of Burgos and Léon is taken up at Palencia and Lugo, in Castile. Many of the parish churches and abbeys of the end of the thirteenth and of the fourteenth centuries belong to the type met most frequently in southern France: an unaisled nave with chapels between inner buttress piers, a transept into which the chapels open, and a polygonal choir.

*Islamic tradition*

But despite the persuasive power of the French Gothic, the Islamic tradition retained a firm grip on Spanish architecture and gave Spanish churches their specific character. The tall bell-towers with pierced walls resemble minarets, the lantern domes above the crossing might be taken from mosques; the horse-shoe arch lives on, as do decoration in plaster and glazed pottery, whose linear, almost filigree-like patterns are distinctly Islamic. All these traditions prove particularly strong in the south, as at Cordoba, where Gothic churches, chapels, and houses, built in the fourteenth century, are

168

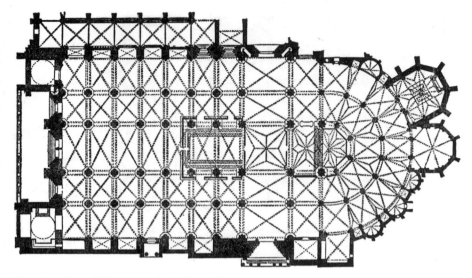

Fig. 58 – *Plan of Toledo Cathedral. Cf. p. 168*

Fig. 59 – *Toledo Cathedral. Cross-section. Cf. p. 168*

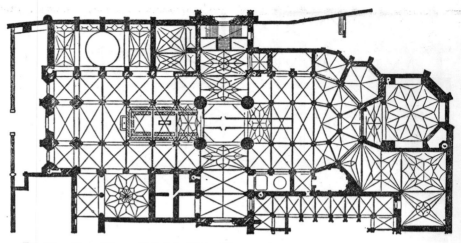

FIG. 60 – *Plan of Burgos Cathedral. Cf. p. 168*

*Characteristics of Spanish sculpture*

covered in Islamic ornament, entirely in keeping with a fashion that was to survive for almost another hundred years.

French Gothic also influenced the style of Spanish sculpture until the fifteenth century, when Flemish and German elements begin to assert themselves. Yet sculpture retains its Spanish character to a greater extent than architecture. The west portal of Santiago de Compostela, the work of Master Matthias, dated 1183, is clearly derived from French portals of the

Giotto di Bondone (*c.* 1266–1337). Christ's Capture. Fresco in the Arena Chapel, Padua. *C.* 1305. *Approx. 28 × 30 in. Cf. p. 110*

Giotto's frescos in the Arena Chapel in Padua consist — apart from the Last Judgement on the west wall and the Annunciation on the Triumphal Arch — of a cycle of thirty-seven scenes from the life of Christ and the Madonna, distributed over the nave walls. Though only a fragment survives of Giotto's work, it can clearly be seen that these frescos form the culmination of his whole development; through them, he has created a canon of form that was to dominate the painting of the Trecento. To the whole of western painting his new vision is of decisive importance. In contrast to earlier fresco painters, Giotto places his many-figured scenes within a rectangular frame, whose lines also determine the run of the composition. He thus becomes the creator of the picture in its own right as we know it today. Within the frame, Giotto sees the scene from a central viewpoint, Systematically, the whole setting, free of all superfluous detail, is orientated towards the central event, the Judas kiss. Christ's earnest and yet mild gaze transfixes the eyes of the deceitful Apostle with the sly and bloated face who is about to implant the treacherous kiss. Everything culminates in the expression of the two profiles, dramatically high-lighted by Judas' yellow mantle, the strongest colouristic accent of the picture. At the sides are the Roman soldiers with staves and torches; Peter, cutting off Malchus' ear, can be seen on the left. Though the scene is crowded and does not occupy a very large area, the effect, through the broad modelling of the sturdy backs and the powerful profiles, is of a monumentality characteristic of this particular stage of Giotto's development. Though suggestions of space appear, the plane is nowhere transcended. Without the mathematical calculations of the slightly later invention of linear perspective, the beholder's relationship to the picture remains entirely optic and spiritual. The conditions have been created for the rise of panel-painting.

Fig. 61 – *Burgos Cathedral. Transept window.*
*Cf. p. 168*

same period, as is the portal sculpture of Saint-Vincent, Avila. Yet both examples surpass their French archetypes, at Avila through the generosity of the composition and the expressive gestures, at Compostela through the monumental and dramatic character. This distinct trait of Spanish sculpture from the thirteenth century to the end of the Middle Ages is in no way affected by the interrelationship of northern Spain and southern France in the realm of architecture. In the thirteenth century, the Kings of Navarre — related by marriage to the Capet and the Counts of the Champagne — preferred French artists and bought works of the Paris school: their court was entirely French in its tastes. The miraculous Madonna of Saragossa can be likened to the Madonna statues of the Île-de-France; the portals of

Duccio di Buoninsegna (*c.* 1255–1318/19). Maestà. Completed 1311. *Siena, Domopera.*
In 1506, Duccio's Maestà was replaced by Vecchietta's bronze tabernacle, in 1771 the picture was sawn apart. Since 1878, the principal portions have been preserved in the Domopera at Siena, the remaining fragments are in various European museums (Berlin, London etc.).
In gratitude for the victory of Montaperti, the city of Siena dedicated itself to the Virgin, in whose honour a great cathedral was raised. In 1308 Duccio was commissioned to paint the altar-piece for this new building; three years later, amidst the sound of drums and trumpets, his picture was carried in a solemn procession, resembling a triumphal march, from the artist's workshop to the cathedral. It is Duccio's last dated work. On the recto, of which the centre portion is shown in our illustration, the Virgin Enthroned appears surrounded by angels, Apostles and Saints. The predella, in front, tells the story of the Nativity and Christ's early childhood; the whole composition is surmounted with scenes from the life of the Virgin. The verso was originally divided into small separate scenes, arranged in four rows, of Christ's life, Passion and Resurrection. The whole work consisted of nearly a hundred pictures of different size.
Duccio's Madonna was created when Giotto's frescos in the Arena Chapel were already finished. This fact illustrates strikingly the difference between the schools of Florence and Siena. Duccio did not create a new image of the visible world; he is a preserver, not an innovator. His figures have none of the individuality of Giotto's; throughout his life, the master adhered to the *maniera greca*, although he imbues Byzantine stylistic elements with feeling and subtlety. 'His Madonna paintings are filled with the melancholy and mature alien beauty of the Graeco-Oriental world' (Oertel). His deliberate acceptance of tradition is fundamental to the entire Sienese school, which, until well into the 16th cent., differs in this respect from all the other Italian schools.

Burgos and Léon follow Chartres exactly, as do the portal of Sarmental and the entrance to the cloisters at Burgos, as well as the south transept portal and the three portal-group on the west front at Léon, where the central portal, dedicated to the Last Judgement, is interpreted in the same manner as Burgos, whose statues, in their graceful animation, recall the angel figure with the famous *sourire de Reims*.

PLATE P. 77

The portal with scenes from the Childhood of Jesus is also clearly inspired by Chartres, while the composition of the Madonna portal repeats the theme of Notre-Dame, in Paris, down to the last detail. Yet the *genius loci* loses none of its vigour: the beautiful Madonna figure on the trumeau pier, Notre-Dame-la-Blanche, remains distinctly Spanish.

APPX. PL. 8

Here, too, Romanesque and Moorish elements are apt to linger on, as at Tudela and Tarragona. In the fourteenth century Italian sculptors in marble introduced the style of Pisa in Catalonia and Aragon; but they find few followers and the French tradition effectively resists all new influence, both in Pamplona and in Toledo, in monumental sculpture no less than in recumbent tomb figures.

PORTUGAL

In Portugal, too, the memory of Islamic art was not entirely displaced with the coming of the Gothic. Like Spain, Portugal had many close ties with France; from the end of the eleventh to the end of the fourteenth century the country was ruled by a Burgundian dynasty. In 1095 Alphonso of Castile had bequeathed Portugal to his son-in-law Henry of Burgundy, who had helped him greatly in his struggle against the Moors. In 1139 Henry's son, Alphonso I, assumed the title of King of Portugal; his descendants ruled the country until 1383. Here, too, cathedrals and abbeys were built, first by the Benedictines, who mostly came from Moissac, then by the Cistercians; a Benedictine, St. Géraud de Moissac, called to Portugal by the archbishop of Toledo, Bernard de Sédirac, became archbishop of Braga. The bishop of Coimbra, Bernard, was also French. After his victory over the Moors, Alphonso I founded Alcobaça, the great Cistercian abbey, with the help of monks sent by St. Bernard.

*Lisbon*

Lisbon cathedral, which — like the old cathedral of Coimbra — is modelled on St. Fides of Conques and the churches on the Pilgrim's Road, was re-built in the Gothic manner. The cloisters, like those of Porto Cathedral, follow the example of Fontfroide, outside Narbonne. The church of Alco-

*Alcobaça*

baça, built between 1153 and the first years of the thirteenth century and one of the largest of the order, recalls in its plan, the articulation of the wall, the heavy rib-vaulting and the absence of decoration the second church of Clairvaux as it must have looked at the time of St. Bernard's death in 1153.

ITALY

In northern Italy, we find several preliminaries to Gothic rib-vaulting, although none of them were brought to their logical conclusion. From the end of the eleventh century onwards and in the first half of the twelfth, Italian architects, particularly in the north — as at San Ambrogio, Milan — used round-headed arches as a purely decorative feature on groined vaulting

Pietro Cavallini (d. *c.* 1334). Four Apostles from the Last Judgement in the church of St. Cecilia in Rome. 1293.

In Rome, Cavallini took the decisive step from Byzantine to Gothic painting; his work inaugurates the entirely fruitful meeting of the *maniera greca* and the style from north of the Alps. In their arrangement the seated Apostles follow Byzantine examples, yet the repetition of a specific motif — draperies, a book, etc. — customary in the Byzantine school, has been avoided. Everything is differentiated in Cavallini's work — from the turn of the head and the direction of the gaze to the hair styles and even the age of the Apostles. Every attribute is entirely individual. As in the sculpture of the Gothic cathedral, every figure is seen by itself, without any gesture that may link it with its neighbour, yet it participates fully in the central event. Under the influence of Gothic sculpture, the figures become more substantial and three-dimensional, an impression further increased through the fall of the light. Only fragments survive of the paintings elsewhere in the nave, though even there the influence of the French Gothic is unmistakable, particularly in the tall figures of Prophets below painted canopies, surmounted with crocketed gables, in the window zone.

175

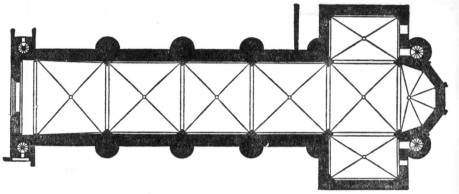

Fig. 62 – *Plan of San Francesco, Assisi. Cf. p. 177*

compartments made entirely of mortar and without any keystones. C. Enlart has shown how the Gothic of the Île-de-France reached Italy at the end of the twelfth and the beginning of the thirteenth centuries; it was, again, introduced by the Cistercians, first in central Italy, in their abbeys at Fossanova, near Terracina, in the Pontine marshes (1197–1208), at Casamari, in the south of the province of Rome (1217), at San Galgano, near Siena (1218–1310), San Martino, near Viterbo, Santa Maria of Arbona in the Abruzzi (1208), Chiaravalle, near Milan and Chiaravalle, near Piacenca. The influence of Burgundian art, whose instrument were the Cistercians, is also evident in Siena Cathedral, begun by monks from San Galgano. Here, too, the pilgrims' roads to Rome, to St. Nicholas of Bari and, later, to the Santo of Padua, are an important factor in the growing contacts between France and Italy.

PLATE P. 165

At the same time, Gothic architecture in Italy springs from a firm native tradition that tends to act as a barrier rather than a gateway to French influence. Where Gothic forms are taken up, a new, specifically Italian manner evolves. Italian churches lack, above all, the French type of twin-towered façade, for the tower, in Italy, had been treated as a separate entity, the free-standing campanile, since the early Middle Ages: at Florence, Giotto's campanile rises next to the cathedral. Nor is the façade interpreted three-dimensionally; instead, the emphasis is usually on the plane, with articulation into smaller areas through painting or mosaic (as at Orvieto Cathedral, *c.* 1310).

APPX. PL. 4

The Gothic interior, too, is treated differently in Italy; closely spaced, ecstatically ascending clustered shafts mean little to a tradition that favours light and spacious halls, with widely-spaced piers and barely pierced walls, decorated with paintings. The nave walls are usually two-storied, often with a projecting cornice dividing the arcades from the window zone (Florence Cathedral and Santa Croce; Siena Cathedral). Frequently, the character

PLATE P. 161

of the hall church is emphasized by having small, instead of large, windows in the nave wall, placed high against the ceiling (e.g. Santa Maria Novella, in Florence, and SS. Giovanni e Paolo in Venice).

FIG. 65

S. Andrea, at Vercelli in Piedmont, is chiefly influenced by Paris and Laon. The church was built in 1209-1221, by Thomas le Français, canon of Saint-Victor, Paris. Towards the end of the fourteenth century several French masters — later also Germans — were active at Milan Cathedral. Genoa Cathedral, whose composition recalls Rouen with its *risalit* windows *Genoa* and the three portals, displays some Norman features, attributable perhaps to the trade links between the two cities.

Some Italian churches follow simpler types of French interiors, among them *Assisi* the great Franciscan church at Assisi, built between 1236 and 1259. It was FIG. 62 formerly thought to have been modelled on Angers Cathedral, from which it differs, however, in the emphasis on large, unbroken wall areas; indeed, it might well be equally indebted to the chapels of royal and episcopal palaces (Rheims, Saint-Germain-en-Laye, Sainte-Chapelle, Paris). The Franciscan church at Todi would seem to be inspired by Poitiers Cathedral.

In the kingdom of the Two Sicilies, French influence appears at its strongest. *Sicily* It came with the monastic orders and was greatly encouraged by the Hohenstaufen rulers, who wanted to surround themselves with the finest achievements of the architecture of the west. The Norman dynasty raised churches in the Norman and Burgundian manner, as those at Venosa, Bari, Barletta and, in Sicily, Cefalu and Monreale; yet all these are pre-Gothic Norman buildings of a distinctly Byzantine cast. The Hohenstaufen rulers, above all Frederick II, remained loyal to French art; Frederick's favourite architect was Philippe Chinard, a French master, who apparently came from the

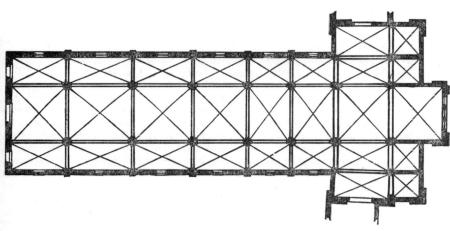

FIG. 63 – *Plan of Santa Maria Novella, Florence*

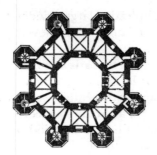

FIG. 64 – *Plan of Castel del Monte. Cf. p. 163*

PLATE P. 163

FIG. 64

Champagne and whom Frederick had brought with him from Cyprus. In Lucca Cathedral, in the castles of Trani and Syracuse, and, even more, at Cosenza Cathedral and Castel del Monte, built by Frederick in the midst of the Apulian forests, the art of the Champagne and the Île-de-France comes to life once more, albeit transformed by the southern tradition. The regular octagonal plan of Castel del Monte may have been suggested by Frederick himself.

With the brother of St. Louis, Charles of Anjou, who was crowned in Rome on 6th January, 1266, the influence of French art is further strengthened in the kingdom of the Two Sicilies. French architects active there include Pierre d'Angicourt from the Beauvais region, Geoffroy de Bois-Guillaume from Normandy, Pierre de Chaulnes from Picardy, and another Pierre, who had worked at Saint-Maximin in Provence. Churches and castles rise in the style of the Île-de-France, the west of France and Provence — Lucera Cathedral, St. Lawrence, St. Eligio and St. Dominic in Naples, S. Francesco in Messina. Castel del Nuovo in Naples, with tall towers reminiscent of the castle of Angers, was built in 1279 by Pierre d'Angicourt. In commemora-

Simone Martini (*c.* 1284–1344). Entombment. Tempera on poplar. *Ehem. Staatliche Museen, Berlin.* 8³/₄ × 6 *in.* After Giotto, Simone Martini is the most important painter of the Trecento. Like Duccio, whose pupil he probably was, he worked chiefly in Siena. In 1339, he was called by the Pope to Avignon. The small picture shown in our illustration probably belongs to this late phase; it is the centre of a triptych whose wings are in the Antwerp Museum and in the National Gallery in London. The original gold ground was later overpainted with the landscape and the sky, which gradually darkens towards the top of the picture. Duccio's strength lies in his mastery of the human face — here accentuated under Giotto's influence into the vehicle of ecstacy and despair, in sharp contrast to the gentle, contemplative mood of his work before his call to Avignon. Giottesque is, above all, the rounded plasticity of the Apostle figures, particularly in the case of the Apostle in the foreground. The weightlessness of the dead Christ, by contrast, is characteristic of the school of Siena. The artist has portrayed the transition of suffering through all its stages, from sorrow to despair. Mary places her arm around the body of her Son in disciplined grief; one woman on the left is tearing out her hair, another, in a gesture found in Byzantine painting though here rich in drama and expression rather than part of an iconographic scheme, throws up her arms. On the right, St. John, weeping into his mantle, turns away from the scene. This ecstacy of pain and surrender to sorrow correspond to the new spirit of the mystic.

Fig. 65 – *Florence, Sante Maria Novella. Nave wall. Cf. p. 177*

tion of his victory at Benevento over Conradin, the last Hohenstaufen Emperor, Charles I of Anjou commissioned two entirely French abbeys, Santa-Maria della Vittoria in the Abruzzi, and Santa-Maria in Realvalle, near Pompeii; the last-named church was built in 1274–1283 *à la manière des abbayes cisterciennes de France* by three French architects, Henri and Gauthier d'Assonne and Thibaud de Saumur. On the other hand, the great Sienese painter Simone Martini, who was working for King Robert of Anjou in Naples in 1317, was invited to decorate the papal palace and the cathedral of Notre-Dame-des-Doms in Avignon.

But despite the foundations of French orders on Italian soil, despite the outstanding example of French architecture and despite the beauty of buildings like the cathedrals of Orvieto and Siena, where the legacy of Burgundy and the Languedoc was translated into an Italian idiom, French art could not gain a permanent foothold in Italy, for it could not prevail against the influence of Byzantine art in the south and of the Romanesque in the north — as René Jullian has shown recently — or against the legacy of the Classic style in Tuscany.

Already at an early stage the sense for calm and regular forms, for a slightly monotonous harmony, inspired works that are apt to follow a certain canon; throughout — as at Giotto's campanile in Florence, to name but one example — the proportions are of a beauty we cannot admire sufficiently. The love for unaisled naves and vast rooms with bare, unarticulated walls that almost demand to be decorated with frescos triumphs over mystic longing and upward-striving, over the search for light and radiance. From the beginning of the Trecento the Renaissance begins to supplant the Gothic in Italy.

*Sculpture*   The situation in the other arts is exactly the same: the influence of French sculpture had begun to penetrate to Italy at the end of the twelfth century.

The portal figures of Vezzolano di Albugnano, and the tympanum with the
Madonna surrounded by angels, recall Chartres and Paris, the rood-screen
with the figures of Mary's ancestors and scenes of her Death, Ascension and
Coronation is a faithful copy of the rood-screen at Senlis. In the thirteenth
and fourteenth centuries it is the influence of French bas-reliefs and ivory
carvings rather than monumental sculpture that can be traced in Italian
art. The tomb of the consort of Philippe the Bold, Isabella of Aragon, who
was killed in an accident, is the work of a French sculptor and also one of the
earliest examples of a cast taken from the dead body, a method frequently
employed in the fourteenth century. The medallions from the west front
of Lyon Cathedral were much copied south of the Alps. Andrea Pisano
translated the grace and delicacy of the ivory carvings of the Paris school into
stone at the Florence Baptistry. Some of the most remarkable reliefs occur
on the buttress piers of Orvieto Cathedral, where between 1310 and 1330
scenes from the story of mankind, from Genesis to the Resurrection of the
Dead and the Last Judgement, were carved in marble under the guidance
of Lorenzo Maitani. These bas-reliefs, full of vitality and grace, are undoubtedly influenced by the school of Rheims, as some of the scenes from
Genesis and the Resurrection of the Dead clearly show. M. Falbord, of
Columbia University, on the basis of hitherto unpublished records of pay-
ments, has established for Orvieto the existence of a sculptor *venu d'Outre-*     *Orvieto*
*Monts* who came from France and was trained in the best French tradition.
After the middle of the century the new spirit of the coming Renaissance,
already manifest in painting through Giotto, also gradually asserts itself in
sculpture.

The pulpit of the Pisa baptistry, begun in 1260 by Niccolò Pisano, a native
of Apulia, marks a break with the Gothic tradition. Niccolò, who made a
close study of Classic portrait busts and Christian sarcophagi, regained the
measured grace of Antiquity; a wealth of forms long forgotten and a new
interpretation of perspective in the relief are some of the characteristics of
his art. His work at the pulpits of Santa Andrea, Pistoia, at Pisa and in
Siena is continued by his son Giovanni in a more agitated style. Giovanni
had undoubtedly visited France — as Herbert von Einem has proved —
where he saw the reliefs with the Death, Ascension and Coronation of the
Virgin at Senlis, Paris, Chartres and Amiens, for he appears to have been
inspired by these compositions in some of his work (1270-1275). Later
generations of the Pisano and their pupils spread the new style throughout
Italy, each of them, however, in his own way: for example, Andrea Pisano
with his pulpit at Verona, or Nino Pisano, whose tall statues, often carved
in wood, have a freshness, clarity and calm far removed from the manner
of Niccolò and Giovanni.

No survey of the Gothic would be complete without some reference to the     NEAR EAST
emanations of French Gothic art throughout the Mediterranean, above all
in twelfth-century Syria and Palestine, where the Crusaders had founded

Frankish colonies, which lingered on throughout the thirteenth century, when the Crusades came to a sudden end in 1291; nor must we forget Cyprus, the final refuge of the Christian settlers in the Middle East.

*Jerusalem*    In the kingdom of Jerusalem it is the art of south-western and southern France whose traces appear on the portal, the apse and the campanile of the church built by the Crusaders at the Holy Sepulchre in Jerusalem, or at Notre-Dame in Tortosa, at the cathedral of Sebaste, on the portals of Gaza and Naplouse and, finally, at the cathedral of St. John at Acre, of which a single portal — moved to Cairo by Sultan Kelaoun — survives. At Nazareth five figure capitals with scenes from the lives of the Apostles St. James-the-Greater, St. Matthew and St. Thomas, undoubtedly intended for a portal which was never executed, are clearly modelled on Burgundian capitals, in particular a capital at Plaimpied/Cher (casts in the Musée des Monuments Français, Paris).

*Cyprus*    In Cyprus French monuments survive throughout the former — entirely French — kingdom of the Lusignans; here the dominant influence is that of the Île-de-France and the Champagne. The cathedral of Nicosia — begun in 1209 by Archbishop Thierry, the former archdeacon of Troyes and brother of the precentor of Notre-Dame, Paris — recalls in its plan Notre-Dame and in its articulation the churches of the Champagne and Burgundy; the foundation-stone was laid by Queen Alix de Champagne. One of the portals may well have been designed by Eudes de Montreuil, a member of the same famous family of sculptors and architects as Pierre and Raoul de Montreuil and the companion of St. Louis during his stay in the Île-de-France in 1247. The apse of Famagusta Cathedral, from the beginning of the fourteenth century — the period when Cyprus was passing through its greatest prosperity and had become the centre of a highly evolved civilization — is influenced by Saint-Urbain, in Troyes, the façade is modelled on Rheims. The abbey of Lapais, in a picturesque setting on the rocks above the sea, takes up the Gothic of southern France, similarly Sainte-Marie, Nicosia, Sainte-Anne, Famagusta, and the castle in the same city, while the castle of Saint Hilarion is reminiscent of the Gothic of the French north.

*Rhodes*    At Rhodes, conquered in 1305 and subsequently transformed into a fortress, the Knights of St. John built a vast palace around a cloistered courtyard, of distinctly southern character, along a street consisting of the houses of different nations, all prepared to defend the same faith and the same ideal. From the twelfth to the fourteenth centuries many fortified castles were built in Syria, Palestine and Cyprus by the Crusaders, by kings and nobles, bishops and monastic clergy anxious to protect their properties and to ensure free access to the Holy Places for all pilgrims. Today their ruins still rise from the desert and from mountains and crags above the sea, as powerful witnesses to courage, resolution and strength. Famagusta and Cérines were inland castles in the plain, with a rectangular Byzantine plan and corner turrets, surmounted by a tall square donjon. At Saint Hilarion, Kantara and

Buffavent mountain strongholds were built in almost inaccessible settlements, with double enclosures that could be surveyed from a donjon which protected the chapel and the living quarters and blocked the only point where an enemy could attack.

Crac-des-Chevaliers, the Château de Saône, and Kérak de Moab — of which Paul Deschamps has made a thorough study — built according to a clearly-laid down programme, are masterpieces of engineering that astonish us even today. The knights' chamber and its portico at the top of the Crac, in Syria, recall in their detail the sculpture of the Paris Sainte-Chapelle and of some of the finest buildings from the time of St. Louis.

In conclusion we might remember that French architects even travelled further, to the Far East: when Guillaume de Ruysbroeck, sent as ambassador to the Great Khan in 1253, arrived at the Tartar court, he met there the French master Pierre Bourchier.

## CHRONOLOGY

The chronology on the following pages embraces the period from the middle of the twelfth to the middle of the fourteenth century, i.e. the years whose art is the subject of this volume. The reader will undoubtedly be aware that the beginning of the High Gothic in France partly overlaps with the Romanesque art of adjoining countries, while its close is contemporary with the beginning of the Early Renaissance in Italy; dates of origin alone have been considered in compiling our chronology.

Where place-names only are given, these refer to cathedral churches.

| | FRANCE | ENGLAND | GERMANY |
|---|---|---|---|
| First half 12th cent. | 1134–1155 Chartres: north tower, west portals and window zone<br>1137–1140 St. Denis: west front and choir<br>1140–1164 Sens | 1133 Durham: nave | 1118–1135 Mainz: nave, eas choir, St. Gotthard chapel<br>1135 Königslutter |
| Second half 12th cent. | 1150 Noyon<br>1153–1191 Senlis<br>1160 Pontigny, Cistercian church (until early 13th cent.)<br>Poitiers Cathedral<br>1163–1182 Paris: choir<br>1170–1190 Laon (western nave bays and choir extension until 1210)<br>1172–1218 Bourges<br>1180–1200 Soissons<br>1190 Paris: nave<br>1190–1200 Nantes<br>Chars<br>1195–1200 Chartres: nave and choir | c. 1150 Lincoln: towers and lower portions of the west front<br>Norwich: central tower<br>1175 Canterbury rebuilt by William of Sens<br>c. 1175 Ely: south transept<br>1180–1239 Wells: nave<br>1180 Ely: nave completed<br>1184 Canterbury: choir, Trinity Chapel and corona completed<br>1190 Peterborough: nave completed<br>1192–1233 Lincoln Cathedral begun | 1151 Schwarzrheindorf<br>1166 Bonn: east choir vault<br>1173–1195 Brunswick<br>1176 Strasbourg begun<br>1178 Maulbronn vaulted<br>1185 Basle Cathedral begun<br>1186 Eberbach<br>1192–1219 Cologne, St. Ape teln n.p., Worms (end 12th early 13th cent.) |
| First half 13th cent. | 1200 Caen, St. Etienne: choir<br>1200–1216 Braisne, St. Ived: choir and transepts<br>1200–1300 Bayeux<br>1210–1241 Rheims: choir and transepts<br>1217–1254 Le Mans<br>1218–1275 Coutances<br>1220 Chartres: transept façades completed<br>1220–1236 Amiens: west front, nave<br>1225–1240 Dijon, Notre-Dame<br>1230 Chartres: porches<br>1231–1281 St. Denis: nave<br>1243–1248 Paris: Ste. Chapelle (J. de Chelles and Pierre de Montreuil)<br>1247–1275 Beauvais: choir (intermediate piers after collapse of 1284) | 1201–1222 Peterborough: west front<br>1217–1226 Durham: west towers<br>1218 Worcester: choir roofed<br>1220–1270 Salisbury Cathedral and Lady Chapel<br>1220–1230 Lincoln: Early Gothic portions of west front<br>1235 Ely: eastern portion completed<br>1242–1280 Durham: east choir (completed 1300)<br>1245–1260 London, Westminster Abbey: choir | 1200–1205 Basle completed<br>Gelnhausen<br>1200–1220 Andernach<br>1200–1239 Mainz: west ch<br>1209–Magdeburg begun (c<br>1219 Cologne, St. Gereon<br>1220 Magdeburg: Bishop's gallery<br>1220–1230 Maria Laach: p<br>1220–1230 Maulbronn: clo<br>1230–1280 Paderborn<br>1235 Limburg/Lahn vaulte<br>1235–1253 Magdeburg: na and transepts<br>1235–1283 Marburg/Lahn<br>1243–1253 Trier, Liebfrau kirche<br>1248–1322 Cologne Cathe |

| LY | REST OF EUROPE | EUROPEAN HISTORY | |
|---|---|---|---|
| e Piacenza begun<br>g–1139 Verona, San Zeno<br>–1140 Palermo, Cappella<br>tina<br>–1150 Parma Cathedral<br>● Florence, San Miniato | Netherlands: 1140 Tournai,<br>nave begun<br>Spain: 1142 Foundation of<br>S. Maria de la Huerta | *Germany:* 1106–1125 Henry V<br>1122 Concordat of Worms<br>1138–1152 Conrad II<br>1147–1149 Second Crusade | First half<br>12th cent. |
| –1180 Florence, baptistry<br>cathedral (12th and 13th<br>)<br>Pisa, baptistry (until end<br>cent.)<br>:a, cathedral (12th and 13th<br>)<br>Cremona, baptistry<br>oleted<br>–1214 Parma, baptistry<br>elami)<br>e, cloisters of San Paolo and<br>Giovanni | Portugal: 1154 Foundation of<br>Alcobaça<br>Spain: 1160–1190 Cistercian<br>abbeys of Poblet, St. Crues,<br>Santiago de Compostela and<br>Morerula<br>Denmark: 1191 Foundation of<br>Roskilde | *France:* the entire west passes<br>into English possession through<br>Eleanor of Aquitaine, consort of<br>Henry II Plantagenet<br>1180–1223 Philippe-Auguste II<br>*England:* 1154–1189 House of<br>Anjou-Plantagenet. 1154–1189<br>Henry II. 1164 Constitution of<br>Clarendon. 1170 Murder of<br>Thomas à Becket. 1189–1199<br>Richard I (Coeur-de-Lion).<br>1199–1216 King John<br>*Germany:* 1152–1190 Frederick I<br>(Barbarossa). 1190–1197<br>Henry VI. 1192–1194 War with<br>Henry the Lion, Duke of<br>Saxony and Bavaria. 1189–1193<br>Third Crusade. 1189–1215<br>Philip of Swabia and Otto IV<br>(until 1208)<br>*Italy:* Innocent III 1198–1216.<br>Height of papal power | Second half<br>12th cent. |
| –1217 Casamari, Cistercian<br>:h<br>●San Martino nr. Viterbo,<br>rcian church begun<br>San Galgano, Cistercian<br>:h<br>–1253 Assisi, San Francesco<br>–1323 Pisa, S. Maria della<br>●<br>Padua, Santo: nave (choir<br>● 1267)<br>Bologna, San Francesco<br>●<br>Florence, Santa Maria<br>lla begun<br>●Castel del Monte<br>●Venice, SS. Giovanni e<br>begun | Spain: Early 13th cent.<br>Tarragona, Sigüenza<br>1200 Avila (Castile)<br>1221 Burgos begun<br>1227 Toledo begun by Masters<br>Martin and Pedro Pèrez<br>Netherlands: 1234 Utrecht<br>begun<br>Netherlands: 1242 Tournai,<br>choir begun | *France:* 1209–1229 Albigensian<br>wars. 1226–1270 St. Louis.<br>Provence and Toulouse annexed<br>*England:* 1215 Magna Carta<br>1216–1272 Henry III<br>*Germany:* 1202–1204 Fourth<br>Crusade. 1215–1250 Frederick II<br>Conquests of Genghis Khan<br>(1206–1227). 1241 Battle of<br>Liegnitz. 1228–1229 Fifth<br>Crusade. 1248–1254 Sixth<br>Crusade<br>*Italy:* Lateran synod 1215 | First half<br>13th cent. |

| FRANCE | ENGLAND | GERMANY |
|---|---|---|
| **Second half 13th cent.** | | |
| 1250 Amiens: south transept | 1256–1280 Lincoln: Angel Choir | 1250 Strasbourg: choir and |
| 1250 Troyes (until 1506) | Lichfield (second half 13th | transepts completed, nave be |
| 1255–1290 Rheims: façade (rose | cent.) | Naumburg: nave and east |
| window 1285) | 1270–1300 Exeter: choir | transept first half 13th cent., |
| 1258–1269 Amiens: choir | 1272 Norwich: cloisters (until | west choir and towers after |
| 1282 Albi (until end of 14th | 1430) | 1250, east choir after 1280 |
| cent.) | 1280–1350 Exeter: west window | 1255 Altenberg (until second |
| 1290–1330 Paris: choir chapels | 1291–1360 York: nave | half 14th cent.) |
| 1292 Toulouse, Jacobin church | | 1260–Freiburg/Breisgau: na |
| | | begun |
| | | 1270–1350 Freiburg/Breisga |
| | | tower |
| | | 1273–1300 Chorin |
| | | 1274–1363 Magdeburg: faça |
| | | 1275–1325 Regensburg |
| | | 1276 Strasbourg: façade beg |
| | | 1291 Lübeck, Marienkirche |
| | | choir completed |
| | | End 13th cent. to 1368: Do |
| | | ran, Cistercian church |
| **First half 14th cent.** | | |
| 1318 Rouen, St. Quentin | 1300–1340 Wells: east choir | 1300 Lübeck, Marienkirche |
| 1334–1342 Avignon, Papal | 1307–1311 Lincoln: central | nave begun |
| palace | tower completed | 1304–1340 Vienna: choir |
| 1311 Rheims: nave completed, | 1317–1349 Worcester: nave | 1310 Freiburg/Breisgau: to |
| tympanum windows | 1318–1329 Gloucester: Norman | octagon |
| | aisles rebuilt | 1320 Oppenheim (tracery) |
| | 1321–1349 Ely: Lady Chapel | 1322 Cologne, choir vaulte |
| | 1325 Hereford: central tower | 1334 Chorin, Cistercian ch |
| | begun | vaulted |
| | 1330–1340 Lichfield: choir | 1343–Zwettl begun |
| | completed | 1343–Soest/Westphalia beg |
| | 1338 Wells: crossing | 1344 Prague Cathedral beg |
| | 1342 Ely: stellar vaulting and | (Matthias of Arras) |
| | crossing completed | |
| | 1346–1375 Exeter: west front | |
| | completed | |
| | 1350 Winchester: nave | |

| LY | REST OF EUROPE | EUROPEAN HISTORY | |
|---|---|---|---|
| –1326 Siena, San Francesco Siena, cathedral: nave ꞏleted Arezzo, cathedral begun –Orvieto, cathedral begun –1309 Siena, Palazzo ꞏco Florence, Santa Croce ꞏ a Florence, cathedral begun –1301 Florence, Palazzo ꞏhio | Netherlands: 13th–14th cent. Brussels; Ghent; St. Martin/ Ypres; Maastricht, Dominican church Sweden: c. 1260 Linköpping 1270–1315 Uppsala Spain: 1298 Barcelona begun, end 13th cent. Palma de Mallorca | *France:* 1284–1314 Philippe IV le Bel; height of French power in the Middle Ages *England:* 1258–1265 Rising of the barons. 1272–1307 Edward I *Germany:* 1250–1254 Conrad IV 1258 Conradin executed. 1256–1273 Interregnum, dissolution of Germany into small principalities. 1273–1291 Rudolf of Hapsburg. 1292–1298 Adolf of Nassau. 1298–1308 Albrecht I. *Italy:* 1266–1284 Charles of Anjou governs southern Italy from Naples. 1282 Sicilian Vespers. 1294–1303 Pope Boniface VIII. Institution of the Holy Years. After the Hohenstaufen period, Italy, gradually breaking up into separate small states, is impoverished by the wars between the Ghibellines and Guelphs. | Second half 13th cent. |
| –1404 Venice, Doges' ꞏe Florence, campanile begun | Netherlands: 1306 Amsterdam, Oude Kerk vaulted (completed early 16th cent.), early 14th cent. Brouwershaven, Grote Kerk 1312 Antwerp begun by Jean Appelmans (completed early 16th cent.) Netherlands: Kampen, St. Nicholas church Spain: 1312 Gerona, choir begun, 1328–1383 Barcelona, S. Maria del Mar | *France:* 1303 Imprisonment of Pope Boniface VIII. 1309–1377 Papacy at Avignon. 1328–1498 House of Valois. 1330 Beginning of Hundred Years' War 1342–1404 Philip the Bold of Burgundy. 1346 Defeated by the English at Crécy. *England:* 1307–1327 Edward II. 1327–1377 Edward III. 1346 and 1356 Victories of Crécy and Poitiers. 1349–1350 England struck by the Plague. Peace of Paris between England and France *Germany:* 1347–1378 Charles IV *Italy:* 1347–1354 Cola di Rienzo in Rome | First half 14th cent. |

| | FRANCE | | ENGLAND | |
|---|---|---|---|---|
| | Sculpture | Painting | Sculpture | Painting |

| | | | | |
|---|---|---|---|---|
| 12th cent. | 1135 St. Denis, central portal (without figures) 1145–1155 Chartres, west portals (centre: principal master right: St. Denis master left: Corbie master) 1163 Paris, St. Anne's portal (old tympanum) 1170/80 St. Denis north portal | | Chichester, reliefs (Raising of Lazarus, Christ w. Mary and Martha at Bethany) Lincoln, west portal reliefs Malmesbury, south portal reliefs Ely, Barfreston, Rochester (Maiestas reliefs) Rochester (earliest portal sculpture) ivory sculptures (Adoration of the Kings, V & A Museum, London) | Ill. MSS. of the sch of St. Albans (St. Alban's Psalter, Hildesheim) Vita S. Edmundi (Morgan Lib., N.Y. Great Lambeth Bib (Lambeth Palace, London) |
| First half 13th cent. | 1200 Senlis, portal figures 1200–1210 Chartres/ north, St. Anne's portal 1210–1220 Paris, Madonna portal 1212–1220 Chartres, south portals 1220–1230 Rheims/north, Sixtus portal 1212 Amiens, tomb of Evrard de Fouilloy 1225–1230 Paris, Judgement portal 1230–1240 Paris, Porte Ste. Anne 1230 Chartres/north: right portal, Solomon master and Master of the Royal Heads 1230 Amiens, west portals 1230–1250 Rheims, west portals 1236 Amiens, tomb of Geoffroy d'Eu | Pre-1223 Psalter of St. Louis and Blanche de Castile (Bibl. de l'Arsénal, Paris) | 1200–1210 York, St. Mary's Abbey, Prophets and Apostles Wells, tomb of Bishop Levericus 1225–1230 Worcester, tomb of King John 1230–1235 Wells, sculpture of the west front 1230–1240 Salisbury, tomb of William Long-spee | 1230 Apocalypse o Albans (Trinity Co Cambridge) |

| IANY | | ITALY | | |
| ture | Painting | Sculpture | Painting | |
| --- | --- | --- | --- | --- |
| Quedlinburg, stones of abbesses; screen relief from rf (Bonn) Freudenstadt, n Magdeburg, tablet nb of Frederick of n o Abbot's throne gburg, Cologne Trier, choir-screens Brunswick, lion Basle, Gallus Gate Hildesheim, St. el: choir-screen Magdeburg, tablet nb of Archbishop nann ne, St. Maria im ol: tombstone of ude (end of 12th rstadt, Liebfrauen- : choir-screens o) | 1159 Missal of Presbyter Ratmann (Hildesheim) 1170 Prüffening nr. Regensburg 1170–1185 Hymn of the Holy Cross, from St. Emmeran/Regensburg (Staatsbibl., Munich) Hortus deliciarum by by Herrad of Landsberg 1175– prayer-book of St. Hildegard (Staatsbibl., Munich) Liber Scivias of St. Hildegard (Landesbibl., Wiesbaden) 1196 Evangelistary from Speyer Cathedral (Landesbibl., Karslruhe) | 1135 Master Nicholas (Verona, Ferrara) 1162 Guglielmus (Pisano, cathedral pulpits) Pistoia, San Giovanni Fuorcivitas, jambs; S. Andrea, jambs 1170 Barisanus of Trani bronze gates at Trani and Ravello 1175–1200 Benedetto Antelami (Fidenza, Parma) 1180–1186 Bonanus (bronze gates at Monreale and Pisa) c. 1200 Verona, San Zeno: bronze gates | 1138 Sarzana, cathedral: Crucifixion | 12th cent. |
| Sonnenburg, Crucifixion ne) 225 Hildesheim, 1220 Halberstadt, auenkirche: x reiberg/Saxony: x and Golden Gate Vechselburg, x Halberstadt, auenkirche: Madonna Strasbourg dral: angel piers, tion and Death Virgin (tympana, a and Synagogue) | 1200– Strasbourg, stained-glass windows of German emperors and kings 1200–1225 Matins book of Abbot Conrad of Scheyarn (Staatsbibl., Munich) 1200–1230: Missal of Abbot Berthold Weingartner MS. (Morgan Collection, New York) 1211–1213 Psalter of Landgrave Hermann of Thuringia (Staatsbibl., Stuttgart) 1220–1230 Cologne, St. Cunibert: stained glass 1225 Carmina Burana (Staatsbibl., Munich) 1225 Hildesheim, St. Michael's: wooden ceiling | 1200– Benevento (bronze gate) 1225– Lucca, cathedral (St. Martin relief) 1233–1240 Capua: triumphal arch of Frederick II (demolished) 1225–1287 Niccolò Pisano of Apulia 1260 Pisa, baptistry: pulpit 1265–1269 Siena, pulpit 1278 Perugia, fountain 1240–1302 Arnolfo di Cambio 1276 Rome, Lateran: tomb of Annibaldi della Molara 1282 Orvieto, S. Domenico: tomb of Guillaume de Braye 1284– Florence, reliefs on façade of cathedral | 1225–1271 Florence baptistry: mosaics 1228 Subiaco, Sacro Speco: frescos First half 13th cent. Berlinghiero Berlinghieri | First half 13th cent. |

| | FRANCE | | ENGLAND | |
|---|---|---|---|---|
| | Sculpture | Painting | Sculpture | Painting |

First half
13th cent.

**FRANCE — Sculpture**

1240 Rheims: Joseph Master
1240–1250 Chartres, rood-screen (fragment)

---

Second half
13th cent.

**FRANCE — Sculpture**

1250 Paris, Ste. Chapelle: Apostle figures
1250 St. Matthew relief (Louvre)
1255–1260 and later: Rheims, inner west wall
1238 Amiens, Vierge Dorée
1270 Paris, Porte Rouge: Coronation of the Virgin
1275 Rheims, Maison des Musiciens
St. Denis, tombs of Robert the Pious and Constance of Arles
1290–1300 Fontenay, abbey church: Madonna

**FRANCE — Painting**

c. 1250 Vie de St. Denis (Bibl. Nat., Paris)
1253–1270 Psalter of St. Louis (Bibl. Nat., Paris)
1260 Ste. Chapelle Evangeliary (Brit. Mus., London)
c. 1295 Breviary of Philip the Fair, by Master Honoré (Bibl. Nat., Paris)

**ENGLAND — Sculpture**

1260–1265 Lincoln, Ecclesia and Synagogue
1282–1284 Hereford, tomb of Thomas de Cantilupe
1290–1300 London, Westminster Abbey: tomb of William de Valence.
1291–1293 tomb of Eleanor of Castile (by W. Torel)
1295–1300 tomb of Edmund Crouchback

**ENGLAND — Painting**

1250 Salisbury Psa[...] (All Souls, Oxford[...]
Evesham Psalter ([...] Mus.)
Missal of Henry o[...] Chichester
Historia Anglorum[...] Matthew Paris (B[...] Mus.)

| MANY | | ITALY | | |
| --- | --- | --- | --- | --- |
| pture | Painting | Sculpture | Painting | |
| ⁙ Münster, Paradise al | 1225 Soest, St. Maria zur Höhe (the Virgin in Glory) | | | First half 13th cent. |
| ⁙–1240 Bamberg: r-screens, Visitation m's gate, Princes' al (Ecclesia, Syna- ⁙e), Bamberg ⁙eman, Clement's b | 1227 Cologne, St. Gereon: baptismal chapel Cologne, St. Cunibert (Crucifixion) | | | |
| ⁙–1240 Mainz: rood- ⁙n, Bassenheim horse- | 1230–1240 Goslar Evangeliary | | | |
| ⁙ Brunswick, tomb of ⁙ry the Lion ⁙ Magdeburg, ⁙dise gate ⁙ Mainz, tomb of ⁙ried von Eppstein | 1240 Heisterbach Bible (Staatsbibl., Berlin) 1240–1260 Gurk: gallery frescos 1240 Soest Antependium (Berlin) | | | |
| ⁙50 Magdeburg ⁙man | 1250 Tristan and Isolde (Staatsbibl., Munich) | c. 1250 to post-1314 Giovanni Pisano | c. 1250 Giunta Pisano: Crucifixion panels in | Second half 13th cent. |
| ⁙ Paderborn, Paradise ⁙l | Retable from Quedlin- burg (Berlin) | 1278 Perugia, fountain 1284–1299 Pisa: | in Bologna (San Domenico), Assisi (S. | |
| ⁙ Mainz, 'Fust- ⁙enmadonna' | 1250–1260 Cologne, St. Maria Lyskirchen | baptistry 1301 Pistoia, | Maria degli Angeli) and other places | |
| ⁙–1270 Naumburg: ⁙ders' figures and ⁙ screen. Crucifixion ⁙ (1260) | (legend of St. Nicholas) | St. Andrea: pulpit 1302–1312 Pisa, cathedral: pulpit | 1266–1337 Giotto di Bondone 1272 Cimabue in Rome | |
| ⁙1270 Meissen, late ⁙s of the workshop ⁙e Naumburg Master | | | 1296 in Assisi 1278 Duccio di Buon- insegna mentioned in | |
| ⁙ Strasbourg, west ⁙ls: tympana and ⁙s | | | Siena (d. 1319) | |
| ⁙–1300 Regensburg: ⁙nold Master | | | | |

| | FRANCE | | ENGLAND | |
|---|---|---|---|---|
| | Sculpture | Painting | Sculpture | Painting |

| | | | | |
|---|---|---|---|---|
| 14th cent. | 1300– Beauvais (Museum), St. James Pre-1314 Bordeaux, St. André: north portal 1300–1325 Mantes, collegiate church: queens and saints 1319–1327 Paris, St. Jacques: Apostle (Cluny Museum) 1325– Amiens, Annunciation in the choir Rieux (statues in Toulouse Museum) 1325–1351 Paris, choir-screen reliefs by J. Ravy and J. le Bouteiller 1330 Paris, Madonna from St. Aignan, in Notre-Dame 1339 Silver Madonna of Jeanne d'Evreux<br><br>First half 14th cent.: ivory carvings of the Paris School, incl. numerous statuettes, travelling altars, Bishop's croziers, Minne caskets, etc. | 1300– Somme-le-Roi (Brit. Mus., London) 1316–1322 Vie de St. Denis (Bibl. Nat., Paris) 1325–1328 Book of Hours of Jeanne d'Evreux (Cloisters Coll., N.Y.) 1327–1343 Bréviaire de Belleville by Jean Pucelle (Bibl. Nat., Paris) | 1330–1335 Gloucester, cathedral: tomb of Edward II 1340 London, West-minster Abbey: tomb of John of Eltham 1348–1350 Oxford, tomb of Elizabeth Montagu<br><br>First half 14th cent.: alabaster reliefs | c. 1300 Master Tho Peterborough Psalte (Bibl. Royale, Bruss Ramsey Abbey Psal (Pierpont Morgan I N.Y.) Post-1300 Queen M Psalter (Brit. Mus.) Arundel Psalter (Br Mus.) 1308 Book of Hours (Fitzwilliam Mus., Cambridge) 1310–1325 Ormesby Psalter (Oxford) 1326/1327 Treatise Walter de Milemete (Oxford) Holkham Bible Pic Book 1330 St. Omer Psal (Brit. Mus.) 1330–1340 Psalter Robert de Lisle (Br Mus.) |

| MANY | | ITALY | | |
|---|---|---|---|---|
| pture | Painting | Sculpture | Painting | |

| | | | | 14th cent. |
|---|---|---|---|---|
| ;oo Constance, Holy ulchre | 1300– Cologne School (Crucifixion altar, Annunciation and Presentation in the Temple, 1320–1325) | 1275–1330 Lorenzo Maitani | 1305–1307 Giotto: frescos in the Arena chapel, Padua | |
| – Freiburg/Breisgau, Ionna from the ral portal, figures the porch | | 1310– Orvieto: pier reliefs *c.* 1285–1337 Tino da Camaino | 1308–1311 Duccio: Maesta in Siena | |
| st and St. John ps in south Germany 1, Feste Coburg ensburg Madonna | 1320 Manessa MS. 1322 Cologne Cathedral paintings on choir-screens | 1312 Pisa, Ranieri chapel 1315 Pisa, tomb of Henry VII | 1284–1344 Simone Martini 1315 Siena, Maesta 1322–1326 Assisi, | |
| r. Nat. Mus., iich) terneuburg, onna | 1324–1329 Neuburg convent, verso of the Verdun altar *c.* 1335 Solomon's | 1323 Naples, S. Maria Donna Regina: tomb of Queen Maria 1286 Pistoia, silver | St. Martin's chapel 1328 Siena, Guidoriccio *c.* 1300 Assisi, Upper Church: legend of St. | |
| Augsburg, bronze figure of Wolfhart Roth | throne, from Bebenhausen (Stuttgart) 1340 Hohenfurth, | paliotto of Andrea di Jacopo Ognabene (completed 1486) | Francis *c.* 1300–1334 Pietro Cavallini | |
| Cologne, St. Maria apitol: forked fix | convent church: altarpiece 1350 Glatz Madonna (Berlin) | 1343–1377 Andrea Orcagna active in Florence | 1291 frescos in S. Maria in Trastevere 1293 frescos in S. Cecilia | |
| Überlingen, inciation Freiburg/Breisgau, | Erfurt Museum, altar from the Augustiner-Kirche | Tabernacle at Or San Michele 1290–1348/9 Andrea | 1316–1334 façade mosaic of St. Paolo fuori le mura 1306–1345 Pietro Loren- | |
| Sepulchre –1340 Oberwesel, ent church: winged -piece | | Pisano 1330–1336 Florence baptistry, bronze gates 1347– Orvieto, upper | zetti in Siena 1320 Arezzo, altar in S. Maria della Pieve 1334/5 Siena, frescos in | |
| –1350 Pietà Röttgen n) veil, Lorenzkapelle: hets | | portion of façade | S. Francesco 1342 Siena, Birth of the Virgin (Opera del Duomo) | |
| Würzburg, tomb of von Wolfskehl Bamberg, tomb of rich von Hohenlohe | | | 1342– Assisi, frescos in S. Francesco 1317–1347 Lippo Memmi 1317–1350 Bernardo Daddi | |
| | | | Taddeo Gaddi, d. 1366 1338 Florence, S. Croce: Baroncelli chapel 1350–1360 Pisa, Campo Santo: Job fresco | |
| | | | 1324–1347 Ambrogio Lorenzetti active in Siena 1335–1340 Siena, Palazzo Publico | |
| | | | 1333 Annunciation (Uffizi) *c.* 1325 *c.* 1379 Tommaso da Modena | |
| | | | 1346–1352 Treviso, chapter hall of S. Niccolò 1346–1422 Taddeo di Bartolo | |
| | | | 1338–1370 Guariento | |

1 – Head of Christ, from the Crucifixion on the western rood-screen at Naumburg, by the Naumburg Master, *c.* 1260. *Cf. pp. 148, 158*

2 – Paris, Notre-Dame Cathedral. The west front, *c.* 1215. *Cf. pp. 27, 130*

3 – Rheims Cathedral. The portals 1250–1260, the towers *c.* 1300. *Cf. p. 39*

4 – Orvieto Cathedral. Begun after 1285. *Cf. p. 176*

5 – Lichfield Cathedral. The west front, begun *c.* 1280. *Cf. p. 120.*

6 – Cologne Cathedral. Foundation-stone laid 1248, the western portion begun *c.* 1350. Completed after old plans 1842–1880. *Cf. pp. 130, 142*

7 – Magdeburg Cathedral. Begun 1209, consecrated 1363. *Cf. p. 132*

8 – Tarragona Cathedral. Second half of 13th cent. *Cf. pp. 166, 174*

9 – Bolsward (Holland). Friary Church. 13th–14th cent. *Cf. p. 125*

10 – Paris, Notre-Dame. View towards the choir. *C.* 1190. *Cf. p. 27*

11 – Chartres Cathedral. View towards the choir. 1194–1260. *Cf. p. 34*

12 – Florence, Santa Maria Novella. View towards the choir. Begun in 1283 by Fra Sisto and Fra Ristoro. *Cf. p. 177*

13 – Wells Cathedral. View towards the choir. 1192–1230. The great inverted arches at the crossing, a characteristic feature of Wells Cathedral, support the central tower. *Cf. p. 124*

14 – Cologne Cathedral. Consecrated in 1322. The nave was completed in 1842–1880 in the style of the original building. *Cf. p. 142*

15 – Magdeburg Cathedral. The choir was begun in 1209, the choir gallery (bishop's gallery) after 1220. *Cf. p. 134*

16 – Palma de Mallorca. View towards the choir. Early 14th cent., restored *c.* 1900 by Antonio Gaudi. *Cf. p. 166*

17 – Maastricht, Dominican church. The nave, looking westwards. 13th–14th cent. *Cf. p. 125*

18 – Trier. Liebfrauenkirche, seen from the south-east. 1242–1253. *Cf. p. 136*

19 – Pisa. Santa Maria della Spina, from the south-west. 1230–1323.

20 – Linköping Cathedral. *C.* 1260. *Cf. p. 126*

21 – Death of the Virgin. Tympanum relief on the south portal of Strasbourg Cathedral. After 1230. *Cf. p. 141*

22 – Head of Edward II. From the tomb of Edward II in Gloucester Cathedral. *C.* 1330. *Cf. p. 124*

23 – The Papal Palace, Avignon. Bird's eye view from the east. 1334–1353. *Cf. p. 94*

24 – Crac-des-Chevaliers. The ruins of a crusader castle in Syria. Mid-12th to early 13th cent. *Cf. p. 98*

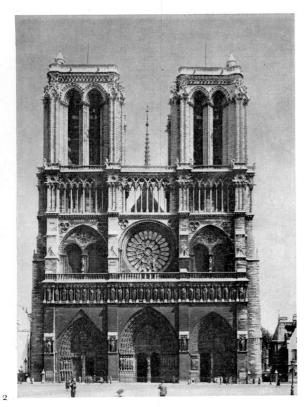

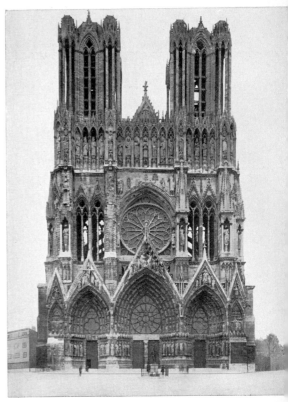

10

12

18

20

23

24

203

Principal Cistercian abbeys
in the 12th and 13th centuries
showing dates of foundation

**CÎTEAUX**

The four earliest sister foundations

Limits of Roman Catholic jurisdiction

Limits of Greek Orthodox jurisdiction

# BIBLIOGRAPHY

## I. GENERAL

*P. d'Ancona, J. Cattaneo and F. Wittgens*, L'arte italiana, 3 vols. Florence, 1932.

*M. Aubert*, L'art gothique, ses origines françaises, in: Actes du XIII^me congrès international d'histoire de l'art. Stockholm, 1933.

*P. v. Baldass, W. Buchowiecki, R. Feuchtmüller, W. Mrazek*, Gotik in Österreich. Vienna, 1961.

*K. Bauch*, Abendländische Kunst. Düsseldorf, 1952.

*J. A. Brutails*, L'archéologie du moyen-âge et ses méthodes. Paris, 1900.

*G. Dehio*, Geschichte der deutschen Kunst, vol. II. Berlin, 1923.

*M. Dvorák*, Idealismus und Naturalismus in der gotischen Skulptur und Malerei. Munich, 1918.

*M. Dvorák*, Geschichte der italienischen Kunst, 2 vols. Munich, 1927–28.

*P. Frankl*, Meinungen über Wesen und Herkunft der Gotik, in: Walter Timmling, Kunstgeschichte und Kunstwissenschaft, Kleine Literaturführer, vol. VI. Leipzig, 1923.

*P. Frankl*, Der Beginn der Gotik und das allgemeine Problem des Stilbeginns, in: Festschrift für Heinrich Wölfflin. Munich, 1924.

*P. Frankl*, The Gothic. Literary Sources and Interpretations through Eight Centuries. Princeton, 1960.

*D. Frey*, Gotik und Renaissance. Augsburg, 1929.

*R. Hamann*, Deutsche und französische Kunst im Mittelalter. Marburg-on-Lahn, 1923.

*Hashagen*, Zur ideengeschichtlichen Stellung des staufischen Zeitalters, in: Deutsche Vierteljahrsschrift für Literaturwissenschaft und Geistesgeschichte, 9 (1931), pp. 350ff.

*Ch. H. Haskins*, The Rise of the Universities. New York, 1923.

*I. Herwegen, OSB*, Kirche und Seele. Die Seelenhaltung des Mysterienkultes und ihr Wandel im Mittelalter. Münster, 1926.

*H. Karlinger*, Die Kunst der Gotik. Berlin, 1926.

*H. Keller*, Die Kunstlandschaften Frankreichs. Wiesbaden, 1963.

*K. Künstle*, Ikonographie der christlichen Kunst, 2 vols. Fribourg, 1928.

*E. Mâle*, L'art religieux du XIII^me siècle en France. Etude sur l'iconographie du moyen-âge. Paris, 1910.

*E. Mâle*, L'art religieux du XII^me siècle en France. Paris, 1922.

*E. Mâle*, L'art religieux de la fin du moyen-âge en France. Paris, 1922.

*E. Mâle*, L'art allemand et l'art français du moyen-âge. Paris, 1922.

*C. Martin*, L'art gothique en France. Paris, 1913.

*A. Mayer*, Liturgie und Geist der Gotik, in: Jahrbuch für Liturgiewissenschaft, VI. Münster, 1926.

*W. Menzel*, Christliche Symbolik, 2 pts. Regensburg, 1854.

*W. Molsdorf*, Christliche Symbolik der mittelalterlichen Kunst. Leipzig, 1926.

*K. Pfister*, Die Welt des Mittelalters. Vienna, 1952.

*W. Pinder*, Die Kunst der deutschen Kaiserzeit. Leipzig, 1937.

*W. Pinder*, Die Kunst der ersten Bürgerzeit. Leipzig, 1939.

*K. Scheffler*, Der Geist der Gotik. Leipzig, 1922.

*J. von Schlosser*, Quellenbuch zur Kunstgeschichte des Mittelalters, in: Quellenschriften zur Kunstgeschichte, new series, VII. Vienna, 1896.

*J. von Schlosser*, Die Kunst des Mittelalters. Berlin-Neubabelsberg, 1926.

*A. Schmarsow*, Kompositionsgesetze in der Kunst des Mittelalters, 2 vols. Bonn–Leipzig, 1922.

*A. Schmarsow*, Italienische Kunst im Zeitalter Dantes. Augsburg, 1928.

*O. Schmitt*, Reallexikon zur deutschen Kunstgeschichte. Stuttgart, 1937.

*H. Schmitz*, Die Gotik im deutschen Geistesleben. Berlin, 1921.

*G. Schnürer*, Kirche und Kultur im Mittelalter, 3 vols. Paderborn, 1924–29.

Schrifttum zur deutschen Kunstgeschichte, ed. Deutscher Verein für Kunstwissenschaft. Berlin, 1934.

*H. Thode*, Franz von Assisi und die Anfänge der Kunst der Renaissance in Italien. 2nd ed. Berlin, 1904.

*P. Toesca*, Storia dell'arte italiana. Turin, 1913–1926.

*A. Venturi*, Storia dell'arte italiana. Milan, 1901–1938.

*W. Vöge*, Die Anfänge des monumentalen Stils im Mittelalter. Strasbourg, 1894.

*G. Weise*, Italien und die geistige Welt der Gotik. Halle, 1939.

*W. Worringer*, Formprobleme der Gotik. Munich, 1912.

*W. Worringer*, Griechentum und Gotik. 3rd ed. Munich, 1928.

*W. Worringer*, Byzantismus und Gotik, in: Festschrift Gzum 60. Geburtstag von Paul Clemen. Bonn, 1926.

# II. ARCHITECTURE

A. GENERAL

*P. Abraham*, Nouvelee explication de l'architecture religieuse gothique, in Gazette des Beaux Arts, 1934.

*E. Adam*, Die Baukunst des Mittelalters, in: Illustrierte Weltkunstgeschichte. Zurich, 1959.

*G. Bandmann*, Mittelalterliche Architektur als Bedeutungsträger. Berlin, 1951.

*P. Booz*, Der Baumeister der Gotik. Munich–Berlin, 1956.

*L. Bruhns*, Christliche Frühzeit und mittelalterliche Dome. Leipzig, 1927.

*K. H. Clasen*, Die gotische Baukunst (Handbuch der Kunstwissenschaft). Potsdam, 1930.

*G. Dehio-Bezold*, Die kirchliche Baukunst des Abendlandes, vol. II. Stuttgart, 1901.

*H. G. Evers*, Tod, Macht und Raum als Bereiche der Architektur. Munich, 1939.

*P. Frankl*, Baukunst des Mittelalters (Handbuch der Kunstwissenschaft). Potsdam, 1926.

*W. Gross*, Zur Mittelalterlichkeit der gotischen Kathedrale, in: Festschrift für Wilhelm Pinder. Leipzig, 1938.

*W. Gross*, Die abendländische Architektur um 1300. Stuttgart, n.d. [1948].

*H. Jantzen*, Über den gotischen Kirchenraum. Fribourg, 1927.

*H. Jantzen*, Zur Beurteilung der gotischen Architektur als Raumkunst, in: Kritische Berichte zur kunstgeschichtlichen Literatur. Leipzig, 1927.

*H. Jantzen*, High Gothic. Translated by James C. Palmes, London, 1962.

*H. Jantzen*, Die Gotik des Abendlandes. Cologne, 1962.

*R. Krautheimer*, Introduction to an 'Iconography' of Medieval Architecture, in: Warburg Journal, v, 1942.

*H. E. Kubach*, Das Triforium, ein Beitrag zur kunstgeschichtlichen Raumkunde Europas im Mittelalter, in: Zeitschrift für Kunstgeschichte, 5, 1936.

*Ch. H. Moore*, Development and Character of Gothic Architecture. New York, 1906.

*E. Panofsky*, Gothic Architecture and Scholasticism. Latrobe, 1951.

*N. Pevsner*, An Outline of European Architecture. 7th ed., Harmondsworth, 1963.

*H. Rose*, Die Baukunst der Zisterzienser. Munich, 1916.

*J. Sauer*, Die Symbolik des Kirchengebäudes und seiner Ausstattung. Freiburg im Breisgau, 1924.

*H. Sedlmayr*, Die Entstehung der Kathedrale. Zurich, 1950.

*O. von Simson*, The Gothic Cathedral. New York, 1956.

*W. Überwasser*, Nach rechtem Maß. Aussagen über den Begriff des Maßes in der Kunst des 12. bis 16. Jhs., in: Jahrbuch der preußischen Kunstsammlungen, 1935.

Wasmuths Lexikon der Baukunst, 5 vols. Berlin, 1929–1937.

*L. L. Behling*, Gestalt und Geschichte des Maßwerks, in: Die Gestalt, no. 16. Halle, 1944.


B. FRANCE

*P. Abraham*, Viollet-le-Duc et le rationalisme médiéval. Paris, 1935.

*P. Abraham*, Nouvelle explication de l'architecture religieuse gothique, in: Gazette des Beaux Arts, 1934/1, p. 255ff.

*H. Adams*, Mont Saint Michel and Chartres. Cambridge (Mass.), 1905.

*M. Aubert*, Senlis. Paris, 1912.

*M. Aubert*, Notre-Dame de Paris, sa place dans l'histoire de l'architecture du XII$^{me}$ au XIV$^{me}$ siècle. 2nd ed. Paris, 1929.

*M. Aubert*, La cathédrale de Metz. Paris, 1931.

*M. Aubert*, L'architecture cistercienne en France. Paris, 1943.

*M. Aubert*, La lumière dans les églises au début de l'époque gothique, in: Archives de l'art français, 1959.

*L. Barbier*, Etude sur la stabilité des absides du Noyon et de Saint-Germain des Prés, in: Bulletin monumental, 89 (1939).

*A. Boinet*, La cathédrale de Bourges. Paris, n.d.

*Bonnenfant*, Notre-Dame d'Evreux. Paris, 1939.

*J. Bony*, Essai sur la spiritualité des deux cathédrales, Notre-Dame de Paris et Sainte-Etienne de Bourges, in: Chercher Dieu. Paris, 1943.

*R. Branner*, Burgundian Gothic Architecture. London, 1960.

*L. Brehier*, La cathédrale de Reims. Paris, 1920.

*Bulteau et Brou*, Monographie de la cathédrale de Chartres. Chartres, 1887–1901.

*P. Clemen–P. Meyer*, Französische Kathedralen. Zurich.

*P. du Colombier*, Les chantiers des cathédrales. Paris, 1953.

*S. Crosby*, L'abbaye royale de Saint-Denis. Paris, 1953.

*L. Demaison*, La cathédrale de Reims. Paris, 1910.

*M. Deshoulières*, La cathédrale de Meaux. Paris, n.d.

*A. Dimier*, Recueil des plans d'églises cisterciennes, 2 vols. Paris, 1949.

G. *Durand*, Monographie de l'église cathédrale Notre-Dame d'Amiens, 2 vols. 1901–1903.

C. *Enlart*, Manuel d'architecture française, 1: Architecture religieuse, 3 vols. Paris, 1919–1924.

G. *Fleury*, La cathédrale du Mans. Paris, n.d. [1901].

C. *Fontaine*, Pontigny, abbaye cistercienne. 1928.

E. *Gall*, Die gotische Baukunst in Frankreich und Deutschland, 2nd. ed. Brunswick, n.d.

L. *Grodecki*, The Transept Portals of Chartres Cathedral: The date of their construction according to archaeological data, in: The Art Bulletin, New York, 1951.

B. *de Guilhermy*, Les Jacobins de Toulouse, in: Annales archéologiques, 6 (1847).

H. R. *Hannloser*, Entwürfe eines Architekten um 1250 aus Reims, in: Actes du xiii$^{me}$ congrès international d'histoire de l'art. Stockholm, 1933.

H. R. *Hannloser*, Villard de Honnecourt. Vienna, 1935.

K. *Heyer*, Das Wunder von Chartres. Basle, 1926.

E. *Houvet*, La cathédrale de Chartres, 7 vols. Paris, n.d.

H. *Jantzen*, Burgundische Gotik, in: Sitzungsbericht d. Bayer. Akad. der Wissenschaften, Philos. Hist. Klasse, anno 1948, no. 5, 1949.

H. *Jantzen*, Kunst der Gotik: Klassische Kathedralen Frankreichs–Chartres, Reims, Amiens. Hamburg, 1957.

H. *Kunze*, Das Fassadenproblem der französischen Früh- und Hochgotik. (Strasbourg Dissertation). Leipzig, 1912.

E. *Lambert*, L'abbatiale de Saint Germer et l'école de Saint-Denis, in: Bulletin monumental, 100 (1941).

E. *Lambert*, L'église et le couvent des Jacobins de Toulouse et l'architecture dominicaine en France, in: Bulletin monumental, 104 (1945).

J. *Laran*, La cathédrale d'Albi. Paris, n.d.

R. *de Lasteyrie*, L'architecture religieuse en France à l'époque gothique. Paris, 1926–27.

V. *Leblanc*, L'église Sainte-Etienne de Beauvais. Paris, 1929.

L. *Lefèvre-Pontalis*, La cathédrale de Coutances, in: Congrès archéologique. 1908.

L. *Lefrançois-Pillion*, La cathédrale d'Amiens, Paris, 1937.

*Abbé Loisel*, La cathédrale de Rouen. Paris, 1913.

E. *Mâle*, L'architecture gothique du midi de la France, in: Revue des deux Mondes, 1926.

E. *Mâle*, Notre-Dame de Chartres. Paris, 1948.

H. *Masson*, L'église Saint-Ouen de Rouen. Rouen, 1930.

H. *Masson*, Le rationalisme dans l'architecture du moyen-âge, in: Bulletin monumental, 94 (1935).

E. *Medding-Alp*, Zur Baugeschichte der Abtei-Kirche von Saint-Denis, in: Zeitschrift für Kunstgeschichte, 1936.

R. *Merlet*, La cathédrale de Chartres. Paris, n.d.

P. *Meyer*, Das Innere der Kathedrale von Reims, in: Das Werk no. 25 (1938), no. 8, pp. 235ff.

F. *Moreau-Nelation*, La cathédrale de Reims. Paris, n.d.

E. *Panofsky*, Abbot Suger on the Abbey Church of St. Denis and its Art Treasures. Princeton, 1946.

A. *Rhein*, L'église Notre-Dame de Mantes. Paris, 1932.

R. *Rey*, L'art gothique du midi de la France. Paris, 1934.

W. *Sauerländer*, Die Kathedrale von Chartres. Stuttgart, n.d. [1954].

W. *Sauerländer*, Von Sens bis Straßburg. Berlin, 1964.

W. *Schöne*, Das Königsportal in Chartres. Stuttgart, 1961.

L. *Schürenberg*, Die kirchliche Baukunst in Frankreich zwischen 1270 und 1380. Berlin, 1934.

L. *Schürenberg*, Der Dom zu Metz. Frankfurt-on-Main, 1940.

A. *Stein*, Pierre de Montereau et la cathédrale de Paris, in: Mémoires de la société nationale des antiquaires de la France, 71 (1911).

J. *Vallery-Radot*, La cathédrale de Bayeux. Paris, n.d.

J. *Verrier*, La cathédrale de Bourges et ses vitraux. Paris, n.d.

E. *Viollet-le-Duc*, Dictionnaire raisonné de L'architecture française du xi$^{me}$ au xvi$^{me}$ siècle, 10 vols. Paris, 1854.

P. *Vitry*, La cathédrale de Reims, architecture et sculpture, 2 vols. Paris, 1919.

P. *Vitry*, G. *Brière*, L'église abbatiale de Saint-Denis. Paris, 1927.

H. *Weber*, Das wechselseitige Verhältnis von Konstruktion und Formung an den Kathedralen Nord-Frankreichs. Hanover, 1957.

C. ENGLAND

E. *Barr*, Große englische Kathedralen. Stuttgart, 1962.

J. *Bilson*, The Architecture of the Cistercians in England, in: Archaeological Journal, 1901.

F. *Bond*, Gothic Architecture in England. London, 1906.

H. *Braun*, An Introduction to English Medieval Architecture. London, 1951.

P. *Brieger*, English Art. Oxford, 1952.

J. *Britton*, Cathedral Antiquities, 14 vols. London, 1814–1835.

G. H. Cook, English Cathedral Series. London, 1948.

K. Escher, Englische Kathedralen. Berlin und Munich, 1929 (with a bibliography).

D. Frey, Englisches Wesen in der bildenden Kunst. Stuttgart–Berlin, 1942.

J. H. Harvey, Gothic England. London, 1947.

J. H. Harvey, The Gothic World. London, 1950.

J. H. Harvey–H. Felton, The English Cathedrals. London, 1950.

J. M. Hastings, The Court Style, in: Architectural Review, January 1949.

M. Hürlimann–P. Meyer, English Cathedrals. London,1950.

C. H. Moore, The Medieval Church Architecture of England. New York, 1912.

N. Pevsner, The Buildings of England. London 1951.

E. S. Prior, History of Gothic Art in England. London, 1900.

O. E. Saunders, A History of English Art in the Middle Ages. Oxford, 1932.

A. H. Thompson, Cathedral-Churches of England. London, 1925.

G. F. Webb, Gothic Architecture in England. London, 1951.

G. F. Webb, Architecture in Britain: The Middle Ages. London, 1956.

G. H. West, Gothic Architecture in England and France. London, 1927.


D. GERMANY, SWITZERLAND, AUSTRIA

E. Adam, Der Turm des Freiburger Münsters, in: Schau-ins-Land, 73 (1955), pp. 18ff.

E. Bachmann, Eine spätstaufische Baugruppe im mittelböhmischen Raum. Brno–Leipzig, 1940.

E. Bachmann, Sudentenländische Kunsträume im 13. Jh. Brno–Leipzig, 1941.

G. Bandmann, Der Kölner Dom und seine Bildwerke. Berlin, 1948.

K. Bauch, Die drei Münster am Oberrhein. 1937.

J. Baum, Zwölf deutsche Dome des Mittelalters. Zurich–Fribourg, 1955.

F. Baumgarten, Das Freiburger Münster. Stuttgart, 1914.

H. Beenken, Die entwicklungsgeschichtliche Stellung der deutschen Baukunst, in: Vorträge der ersten deutschen Kunsthistorikertagung auf Schloß Brühl, 1948, pp. 46ff.

F. Bock, Rheinlands Baudenkmale des Mittelalters. Cologne–Neuß, 1878.

S. Boisserée, Geschichte und Beschreibung des Doms von Köln. 2nd. ed. Munich, 1842.

W. Burmeister, Norddeutsche Backsteindome. Berlin, 1930.

W. Burmeister, Die westfälischen Dome. Munich–Berlin, 1950.

K. Busch, Regensburger Kirchenbaukunst 1160 bis 1280. 1932.

K. H. Clasen–P. Metz, Zehn deutsche Dome. Berlin, 1939.

P. Clemen, Die Katharinenkirche zu Oppenheim a. Rh. Mainz, 1925.

P. Clemen, ed., Der Dom zu Köln. Düsseldorf, 1937.

P. Clemen, Das Münster zu Aachen. Berlin, 1952.

G. Dehio, Geschichte der deutschen Kunst. 1st ed., 1919.

G. Dehio, Das Straßburger Münster. Munich, 1922.

G. Dehio, Der Bamberger Dom. Munich, 1939.

W. R. Deusch, Das Münster zu Basel. Augsburg, 1928.

O. Doering, Deutschlands mittelalterliche Kunstdenkmäler als Geschichtsquelle. Leipzig, 1910.

O. Doering, Der Bamberger Dom. Munich, 1916.

O. Doering, Die Dome von Limburg und Naumburg. Munich, 1920.

R. K. Donin, Die Bettelordenskirchen in Österreich. Baden near Vienna, 1935.

J. Dörrenberg, Das Zisterzienserkloster Maulbronn. Würzburg, 1938.

K. Eckart, 700 Jahre Altenberg (Die Kunstdenkmäler des Rheinlands). Bergisch-Gladbach, 1956.

S. L. Eger, Studien zum gotischen Architekturornament im Mittelrheingebiet. 1940.

H. Eichler, Ein frühgotischer Grundriß der Liebfrauenkirche in Trier, in: Trierer Zeitschrift 22 (1953), pp. 145ff.

M. Eimer, Zum schwäbischen Kirchenbau im Mittelalter, in: Zeitschrift für württembergische Landesgeschichte, 1944/1948.

D. Ellger, Die Baugeschichte der Lübecker Marienkirche 1159–1351, in: D. Ellger und J. Kolbe, St. Marien zu Lübeck und seine Wandmalereien. Neumünster, 1951.

E. Emmering, Die St. Katharinenkirche zu Oppenheim. Oppenheim, 1933.

A. Erler, Das Straßburger Münster im Rechtsleben des Mittelalters. Frankfurt-on-Main, 1954.

H. B. Eydoux, Die Zisterzienserabtei Bebenhausen. Tübingen, 1950.

H. B. Eydoux, Die Klosterbaukunst. Arbeitsbericht der deutsch-französischen Kunsthistorikertagung 1951, in: Bulletin des relations artistiques franco-allemandes. Mainz, 1951.

H. B. Eydoux, L'architecture des églises cisterciennes d'Allemagne. Paris, 1952.

J. Fait, Die Bettelordenskirchen zwischen Elbe und Oder (Dissertation). Greifswald, 1953.

P. Fechter, Deutsche Backsteingotik. Königsberg, 1934.

E. *Fink*, Die gotischen Hallenkirchen in Westfalen. 1934.

P. *Frankl*, Die Stellung der Westtürme des Naumburger Doms, in: Medieval Studies in Memory of Kingsley Porter, II.

K. *Friedrich*, Das Münster zu Ulm. Berlin, 1944.

W. *Funk*, Der Dom zu Bamberg (with extensive bibliography), in: Das Münster, no. 11/12, 1957.

E. *Gall*, Die gotische Baukunst in Frankreich und Deutschland. 1925.

E. *Gall*, Über die Maße der Trierer Liebfrauenkirche, in: Form und Inhalt (Festschrift für O. Schmitt). Stuttgart, 1950.

E. *Gall*, Zur Baugeschichte des Regensburger Doms, in: Zeitschrift für Kunstgeschichte, 17 (1954), pp. 61ff.

E. *Gall*, Dome und Klosterkirchen am Rhein. Munich, 1956.

M. *Geimer*, Die Einwirkungen des Kölner Domchores. Bonn, 1936.

K. *Gerstenberg*, Deutsche Sondergotik. Munich, n.d. [1913].

K. *Gerstenberg*, Das Ulmer Münster. Burg, 1926.

A. *Gessner*, Die Entwicklung des gotischen Kapitells in Südwest- und Westdeutschland im 13. Jh. Würzburg, 1935.

H. *Giesau*, Eine deutsche Bauhütte aus dem Anfang des 13. Jhs. Halle, 1912.

H. *Giesau*, Der Dom zu Naumburg. 1927.

H. *Giesau*, Der Chor des Magdeburger Doms, die Herkunft seines Planes und seine stilistischen Voraussetzungen, in: Jahrbuch Sachsen und Anhalt, vol. 4. Magdeburg, 1928.

H. *Giesau*, Der Dom zu Halberstadt. Burg, 1929.

H. *Giesau*, Der Dom zu Magdeburg. 2nd ed. Burg, 1936.

W. *Greischel*, Der Magdeburger Dom. Berlin–Zurich, n.d. [1939].

W. *Gross*, Die Hochgotik im deutschen Kirchenbau, in: Marburger Jahrbuch für Kunstwissenschaft, VII (1933), pp., 28ff.

L. *Grote*, Das Freiburger Münster. Stuttgart, 1928.

Th. *Hach*, Der Dom zu Lübeck. Lübeck, n.d.

H. *Hahn*, Die Kirche der Zisterzienserabtei Eberbach im Rheingau, in: Nassauische Annalen 1953, vol. 64.

H. *Hahn*, Die frühe Kirchenbaukunst der Zisterzienser. Frankfurt-on-Main, 1957.

R. *Hamann*, Die Elisabethkirche zu Marburg. Burg, 1938.

R. *Hamann and K. Wilhelm-Kästner*, Die Elisabeth-Kirche zu Marburg. 1924.

R. *Hamann and Fr. Rosenfeld*, Der Magdeburger Dom. Berlin, 1910.

R. *Hamann and H. Weigert*, Das Straßburger Münster und seine Bildwerke. Berlin, 1928.

E. *Hansen*, Otterberg und die kirchliche Baukunst der Hohenstauferzeit in der Pfalz. Heidelberg, 1936.

S. *Hausmann*, Denkmäler der Baukunst im Elsaß. Strasbourg, 1905–1906.

E. *Heinen*, Der bergische Dom (Altenberg). 1936.

P. *Heliot*, L'église abbatiale d'Heisterbach et les relations artistiques franco-allemandes au XIII^me siècle. Paris, 1953.

E. *Hempel*, Geschichte der deutschen Baukunst. Munich, 1949.

A. *Horn*, Der Dom zu Regensburg. Bayreuth, 1939.

W. *Hotz*, Die Münster am Oberrhein. Berlin, 1941.

H. *Jantzen*, Das Münster zu Freiburg i. Br. Burg, 1929.

H. *Jantzen*, Das Münster zu Straßburg. Burg, 1933.

H. *Kauffmann*, Die Kölner Domfassade, in: Festschrift 'Der Kölner Dom 1248–1948'. Cologne, 1948.

H. *Kauffmann*, Die Maßwerkhelme des Freiburger Münsters und des Kölner Doms, in: Festschrift für Kurt Bauch. Munich, n.d. [1957].

H. *Kienast*, Deutschland und Frankreich in der Kaiserzeit. Leipzig, 1943.

O. *Kletzl*, Ein unbekannter Pergamentplan der Münsterbauhütte Straßburg, in: Elsaß-Lothringen, VIII (1939), pp. 63ff.

S. *Kömstedt*, Die Anfänge der Gotik in Deutschland. Leipzig, 1926.

H. *Konow*, Die Baukunst der Bettelorden am Oberrhein. (Dissertation). Freiburg im Breisgau, 1938.

E. *Kransen*, Die Klöster des Zisterzienserordens in Bayern. Munich-Pasing, 1953.

R. *Krautheimer*, Die Kirchen der Bettelorden in Deutschland. Cologne, 1925.

W. *Kröning*, Zur Erforschung der Zisterzienser Architektur, in: Zeitschrift für Kunstgeschichte, 1953, pp. 222ff.

H. E. *Kubach*, Rheinische Baukunst der Stauferzeit: Das Triforium und seine Parallelen in Frankreich. Cologne, 1934.

H. E. *Kubach*, Die deutsche Westgrenze und die Baukunst des Mittelalters, in: DAfLV, 2, 1938.

H. *Kunze*, Der gegenseitige Stand der Erforschung der Baugeschichte des Magdeburger Doms. Magdeburg, 1924.

H. *Kunze*, Der Stand unseres Wissens um die Baugeschichte des Straßburger Münsters, in: Elsaß-Lothringen, XVIII (1939), pp. 63ff.

E. *Kuphal*, Der Dom zu Köln. Cologne, 1930.

E. *Lehmann*, Vom Sinn und Wesen der Wandlung in der Raumanordnung der deutschen Kirchen des Mittelalters, in: Zeitschrift für Kunstgeschichte, 1947.

H. *Lichtenberg*, Die Architekturdarstellung in der mittelhochdeutschen Dichtung. Münster, 1931.

H. *Lützeler*, Der Turm des Freiburger Münsters. Fribourg, 1955.

P. *Meißner*, Zur Baugeschichte der Katharinenkirche zu Oppenheim, in: Festschrift für Ernst Neeb. Mainz, 1936.

P. *Meyer*, Schweizerische Münster und Kathedralen des Mittelalters. Zurich, 1945.

W. *Meyer-Barkhausen*, Die Elisabethkirche zu Marburg. Marburg on-Lahn, 1925.

W. *Meyer-Barkhausen*, Zum Grundrißproblem der Elisabethkirche, in: Hessenland 1930, no. 12.

W. *Meyer-Barkhausen*, Das große Jahrhundert kölnischer Kirchenbaukunst 1150–1250. Cologne, 1952.

W. *Graf Metternich*, Die Anfänge der Gotik in Brabant und die Baukunst des 12. bis 15. Jhs. am Niederrhein, in: Annalen des historischen Vereins für den Niederrhein, 15, 1952.

F. *Mühlen*, Die entwicklungsgeschichtliche Stellung der frühen Münsterländer Hallenkirchen, in: Festgabe für Alois Fuchs. Paderborn, 1950, pp. 7ff.

W. *J. Müller*, Mittelalterliche Backsteinornamentik in Mecklenburg 1200–1300. Rostock, 1948.

W. *Neuß*, Rheinische Kirchen im Wiederaufbau. Mönchen-Gladbach, 1951.

E. *Niebelschütz*, Der Magdeburger Dom. Berlin, 1944.

E. *Niebelschütz*, Der Dom zu Lübeck. Berlin, 1944.

E. *Nienholdt*, Die Katharinenkirche zu Oppenheim am Rhein. Berlin, 1947.

W. *Noack*, Die Baurisse zum Freiburger Münsterturm, in: Oberrheinische Kunst 1926–27, vol. 2, pp. 1ff.

W. *Noack*, Die Baumeister des Freiburger Münsters, in: Freiburger Almanach, 1950, pp. 60ff.

W. *Paatz*, Die Marienkirche zu Lübeck. Burg, 1929.

W. *Passarge*, Der Dom und die Severikirche zu Erfurt. Burg, 1936.

H. *Peters*, Der Dom zu Köln. Düsseldorf, 1948.

W. *Pinder*, Der Naumburger Dom und seine Bildwerke. Berlin, 1926.

W. *Pinder*, Der Bamberger Dom und seine Bildwerke. Berlin, 1927.

A. *Pottgiesser*, Die Kirche der Zisterzienserabtei Altenberg. Ratingen, 1950.

*Raichier-Hermann*, Das Ulmer Münster. Stuttgart, 1950.

W. *Rave*, Die Stufenhalle – System westfälischer Hallenkirchen, in: Westfalen, 1934.

W. *Rave*, Westfälische Baukunst. Münster, 1953.

H. *Reinhard*, Das Basler Münster. Basle, 1926.

H. *Reinhard*, Das Münster zu Basel. Burg, 1929.

H. *Reinhard*, La cathédrale de l'évêque Wernher, in: Bulletin de la société des amis de la cathédrale de Strasbourg, 1932, pp. 39ff.

H. *Reinhard*, Das Basler Münster. Basle, 1961.

A. *von Reitzenstein*, Die Baugeschichte des Bamberger Doms, in: Münchener Jahrbuch vol. 11.

H. *Rode*, Kölner Dombibliographie 1942/53, in: Domblatt, I/1954.

H. *Rose*, Die Baukunst der Zisterzienser. Munich, 1916.

H. *Rosemann*, Der Kölner Dom. Cologne, 1931.

H. *Rosemann*, Ausstrahlung der Regensburger Dombauhütte nach dem deutschen Südosten um 1300, in: Festschrift für Wilhelm Pinder, 1938.

J. *A. Schmoll gen. Eisenwerth*, Das Kloster Chorin und die askanische Architektur in der Mark Brandenburg. Berlin, 1961.

J. *A. Schmoll gen. Eisenwerth*, Zisterzienser-Romanik, Kritische Gedanken zur jüngsten Literatur, in: Formositas Romanica – J. Gantner zugeeignet. Frauenfeld, 1958.

J. *A. Schmoll gen. Eisenwerth*, Die mittelalterlichen Bauten der ehem. Zisterzienserabtei auf dem Wörschweiler Klosterberg, in: Beiträge zur saarländischen Archäologie und Kunstgeschichte. Saarbrücken, 1962.

J. *A. Schmoll, gen. Eisenwerth*, Zur Verbreitung der Zisterzienser im Nordosten (mit einem kurzen Bericht über die Grabungsergebnisse in Mariensee/Mark), in: Klosterbaukunst. Mainz, 1951.

P. *F. Schmidt*, Der Dom zu Magdeburg. Magdeburg, 1911.

H. *Schnitzler*, Der Dom zu Aachen. Düsseldorf, 1950.

J. *H. Schröder*, Deutsche Baugeschichte. Augsburg, 1951.

L. *Schürenberg*, Das Freiburger Münster. Berlin, 1941.

R. *Sedlmaier*, St. Marien zu Lübeck in der Baugeschichte der Gotik. Stuttgart, 1951.

O. *Stiehl*, Backsteinbauten in Norddeutschland und Dänemark. Stuttgart, 1923.

*Stockhausen*, Zur ältesten Baugeschichte der Elisabethkirche in Marburg, in: Zeitschrift für Kunstgeschichte, 1940, pp. 175ff.

E. *H. Stückelberg*, Das Münster zu Basel. Basle, 1927.

H. *Thümmler*, Nationale Charaktere europäischer Kunst im Spiegel des italienischen und deutschen Sakralbaus, in: Die Welt als Geschichte, 26, 1951.

H. *Thümmler*, Neue Forschungen zur mittelalterlichen Baukunst in Westfalen, in: Deutsche Kunst und Denkmalspflege, 1952 pp. 97ff.

A. *Verbeek*, Die Abteikirche Heisterbach als zisterziensische und niederrheinische Bauschöpfung. Mainz, 1951.

W. *Venzmer*, Der Dom zu Lübeck. (Dissertation.) Hamburg, 1957.

H. *Vollmer*, Das Münster von Ulm. Karlsruhe, 1943.

*Wachtsmuth*, Der Grundriß der Elisabethkirche zu Marburg, in: Hessenland, 1930.

A. *Wangert*, Maßsystem des Münsters zu Freiburg, in: Schau-ins-Land, 71 (1953), pp. 49ff.

J. *Warncke*, Die St. Marienkirche zu Lübeck. Lübeck, 1936.

H. *Weigert*, Der Dom zu Naumburg. Berlin, 1944.

Th. *Wieschenbrink*, Der Dom des heiligen Ludgerus in Münster, in: Westfalen, 21 (1936).

K. *Wilhelm-Kästner*, Der Dom zu Münster i. W. Berlin, 1921.

K. *Wilhelm-Kästner*, Die Elisabethkirche zu Marburg. Marburg, 1924.

K. *Zahn*, Der Dom zu Regensburg. 1929.

E. L. *Zinsel*, Die Hallenkirchen der hessischen Schule. Darmstadt, 1932.

### E. SPAIN AND PORTUGAL

L. T. *Balbas*, Arquitectura Gótica. (Ars Hispaniae, VII). Madrid, 1952 (with comprehensive bibliography).

M. *Dieulafoy*, Geschichte der Kunst in Spanien und Portugal. 1913.

C. *Enlart*, Les origines françaises de l'architecture gothique en Espagne et Portugal, in: Bulletin archéologique, 1894.

*Feilchenfeld*, Die Meisterwerke der Baukunst in Portugal.

J. *de Figueiredo*, Evolusao da arte em Portugal. 1908.

E. *Lambert*, L'art gothique en Espagne au XII^{me} et XIII^{me} siècle. Paris, 1931.

V. *Lamperéz y Romea*, Historia de la arquitectura cristiana española en la edad media, 3 vols. 3rd ed. Madrid, 1930.

P. *Lavedan*, L'architecture gothique religieuse en Catalogne, Valence et Baléares. Paris, 1935.

M. *Leroy*, Materiales y Documentes de arte español. Barcelona, 1900ff.

L. F. *Marques de Lozoya*, Historia del arte hispanico, 4 vols. Barcelona, 1931–.

L. F. *Marques de Lozoya*, El arte gotico en Espana. Barcelona, 1935.

A. L. *Mayer*, Gotik in Spanien. Leipzig, 1928.

R. *dos Santos*, L'art portugais. Paris, 1938.

H. *Terasse*, L'art hispano-mauresque des origines au XIII^{me} siècle. Paris, 1933.

S. *Viterbo*, Diccionario dos architectos... portuguezes, 3 vols. 1899–1922.

S. *Viterbo*, Artes e artistas em Portugal. Lisbon, 1920.

W. C. *Watson*, Portuguese architecture. London, 1908.

### F. ITALY

W. *Braunfels*, Giottos Campanile, in: Das Münster, 1 (1948), pp. 193ff.

M. *Dvorák*, Geschichte der italienischen Kunst, 2 vols. Munich 1927–28.

C. *Enlart*, Origines françaises de l'architecture gothique en Italie. Paris, 1894.

H. *Keller*, Umbrien. Vienna–Munich, n.d. [1959].

H. *Keller*, Die Kunstlandschaften Italiens. Munich, n.d. [1960].

B. *Kleinschmidt*, Die Basilika San Francesco in Assisi. Berlin, 1915–26.

W. *Krönig*, Hallenkirche in Mittelitalien, in: Kunstgeschichtliches Jahrbuch der Hertziana, II, 1938.

L. F. *de Longhi*, Chiese Cisterciensi. Milan, 1958.

W. *Paatz*, Werden und Wesen der Trecento-Architektur in der Toskana. Burg, 1937.

W. und E. *Paatz*, Die Kirchen von Florenz: ein kunstgeschichtliches Handbuch. Frankfurt-on-Main, 1940.

C. *Ricci*, Mittelalterliche Baukunst in Süditalien. Stuttgart, 1928.

J. P. *Supino*, La basilica San Francesco d'Assisi. Bologna, n.d. [1924].

P. *Toesca*, Storia dell'arte italiana, II. Trecento Turin, n.d. [1951].

A. *Venturi*, Storia dell'arte italiana, vols. 3, 4, Milan, 1901–1940.

P. *Verzone*, S. Andrea di Vercelli e l'arte emiliana, in: Bollettino storico bibliografico subalpino. Turin, 1936, II, pp. 403ff.

R. *Wagner-Rieger*, Die italienische Baukunst zu Beginn der Gotik, 2 vols. Graz-Cologne, 1956–1957.

G. *Weise*, Die geistige Welt der Gotik und ihre Bedeutung für Italien. Halle, 1939.

### G. HOLLAND, BELGIUM, SCANDINAVIA

P. *Clemen*, ed., Belgische Kunstdenkmäler, 2 vols. Munich, 1923.

E. *Hardick*, Prämonstratenser Bauten. (Dissertation Bonn). Tongerloo, 1935.

G. C. *Labouchere*, Oude Kerken in Utrecht. 1938.

S. *Leurs*, Geschiedenis van de vlaamsche Kunst. Antwerp, 1936–.

S. *Leurs*, De Kathedrale Kerk van O. L. Vrouw te Antwerpen. Antwerp, 1938.

J. *Mosmans*, De St. Janskerk te 's-Hertogenbosch. Utrecht, n.d.

M. *Ozinga*, De protestantse Kerkenbouw in Nederland. Amsterdam, 1929.

A. L. *Romdahl* and J. *Roosval*, Svensk Konsthistoria. Stockholm, 1913.

O. *Stiehl*, Backsteinbauten in Norddeutschland und Dänemark. Stuttgart, 1923.

*F. Vermeulen*, Handboek tot de Geschiedenis der nederlandsche Bouwkunst. The Hague, 1928–.

H. SECULAR ARCHITECTURE

*A. E. Brinckmann*, Stadtbaukunst (Handbuch der Kunstwissenschaft). Potsdam, 1924.

*J. Gantner*, Grundformen der europäischen Stadt. Vienna, 1928.

*P. Lavedan*, Histoire de l'urbanisme. 1926.

Manuel d'archéologie française, II: *C. Enlart*, Architecture civile et militaire. 2 vols. Paris, 1929, 1932.

*O. Piper*, Burgenkunde. Munich, 1912.

*H. Rosenau*, The Ideal City in Its Architectural Evolution. 1959.

*C. Sitte*, Der Städtebau nach seinen künstlerischen Grundsätzen. 1922.

## III. SCULPTURE

(for other works on sculpture, see the general works listed under GENERAL and ARCHITECTURE)

A. GENERAL

*W. Messerer*, Das Relief im Mittelalter. Berlin, 1959.

*W. Sauerländer*, Die Skulptur im Mittelalter, in: Illustrierte Weltkunstgeschichte, III. Zurich, 1959.

*W. Vöge*, Die Anfänge des monumentalen Stils im Mittelalter. Strasbourg, 1894.

*W. Vöge*, Bildhauer des Mittelalters. Berlin, 1958.

*O. Walzer*, Das Bildprogramm an mittelalterlichen Kirchenportalen, in: Festschrift für Wilhelm Pinder, Leipzig, 1938, pp. 140ff.

*H. Wilm*, Die gotische Holzfigur. 1940.

*W. Worringer*, Zur Frage der gotischen Monumentalität, in: Zum Geist neuer Literaturforschung (Festschrift für Otto Walzel). Potsdam, 1924, pp. 211ff.

B. FRANCE

*M. Aubert*, Die gotische Plastik Frankreichs 1140 bis 1225. Florence–Munich, 1929.

*M. Aubert*, La sculpture française au moyen-âge. Paris, 1946.

*M. Aubert, M. Beaulieu*, Musée national du Louvre: Description raisonnée des sculptures du moyen-âge, de la renaissance et des temps modernes, I Paris, 1950.

*J. Baum*, Malerei und Plastik des Mittelalters in Deutschland, Frankreich und Britannien (Handbuch der Kunstwissenschaft). Potsdam, 1930.

*A. de Baudot*, La sculpture française au moyen-âge. Paris, 1884.

*W. H. Forsyth*, Medieval Studies of the Virgins in Lorraine, in: Metropolitan Museum Studies, V, pt. II. New York, 1936.

*Abd ul Hak*, La sculpture des porches du transept de la cathédrale de Chartres. 1943.

*D. Jalabert*, La première flore gothique aux chapitaux de Notre-Dame de Paris, in: Gazette des Beaux Arts, 1931, pp. 283ff.

*D. Jalabert*, La flore gothique, ses origines, son évolution du XII^me au XVI^me siècle, in: Bulletin monumental, 91 (1932), pp. 181ff.

*E. Mâle*, Le portail de Senlis et son influence, in: Revue de l'art ancien et moderne, 1911/I, pp. 161f.

*W. Medding*, Die Westportale der Kathedrale von Amiens und ihre Meister. Augsburg, 1930.

*Z. Mintschewa*, Die Entstehung und die Entwicklung der Baldachinformen in Frankreich bis zur Mitte des 13. Jhs. (unpublished dissertation). Vienna, 1935.

*E. Panofsky*, Über die Reihenfolge der vier Meister von Reims, in: Jahrb. für Kunstwissenschaft, 1927, pp. 55ff.

*L. Pillon*, Les sculptures françaises du XII^me siècle. Paris, 1924.

*W. Graf Rothkirch*, Architektur und monumentale Darstellung im Mittelalter. Leipzig, 1938.

*J. Roussel*, La sculpture française, époque gothique. Paris, 1928.

*D. Schmidt*, Portalstudien zur Reimser Kathedrale, in: Münchener Jahrb. der bildenden Kunst, 1960, pp. 38ff.

*J. A. Schmoll gen. Eisenwerth*, Lothringische Madonnenstatuetten des 14. Jhs., in: Variae Formae-Veritas Una (Gerke-Festschrift). Baden-Baden, 1962.

*J. A. Schmoll gen. Eisenwerth*, St. Eustasius in Vergaville – ein unbeachtetes Meisterwerk hochgotischer Skulptur in Lothringen, in: Pantheon, IV, Munich, 1960.

*Ch. Seymour*, XIIIth-century Sculpture at Noyon and the Development of the Gothic Caryatid, in: Gazette des Beaux Arts, 1944 (Memorial vol. for Focillon). pp. 163ff.

*J. Vanuxem*, Autour du triomphe de la vierge du portail de la cathédrale de Senlis, in: Bulletin monumental, 103 (1945), pp. 89ff.

*P. Vitry*, La cathédrale de Reims. 1919.

*P. Vitry*, Die gotische Plastik Frankreichs 1226–1270. Florence–Munich, 1929.

*P. Vitry und G. Brière*, Documents de la sculpture française du moyen-âge. Paris, 1904.

*P. Wilhelm*, Die Marienkrönung am Westportal der Kathedrale von Senlis. (Dissertation). Hamburg, 1941.

### C. ENGLAND

*J. Baum*, Die Malerei und Plastik des Mittelalters in Deutschland, Frankreich und Britannien (Handbuch der Kunstwissenschaft). Potsdam, 1930.

*Count B. Biver*, Tombs of the School of London at the Beginning of the 14th Century, in: Archaeol. Inl., LXVII, 1910.

*K. Clark*. The Gothic Revival. London, 1928.

*F. H. Crossley*, English Church Monuments, 1150–1550. London, 1921.

*A. Gardner*, English Gothic Foliage Sculpture. Cambridge, 1927.

*A. Gardner*, English Medieval Sculpture. Cambridge, 1951.

*A. Gardner*, The Lincoln Angels. Lincoln, 1952.

*A. C. Fryer*, Wooden Monuments Effigies in England and Wales. 1924.

*W. L. Hildburgh*, Iconographical Peculiarities in English Medieval Alabaster Carving, in: Folklore, XLIV, 1933.

*W. L. Hildburgh*, English Alabaster Carvings as Records of the Medieval Religious Drama, in: Archaeology, XCIII, 1949.

*W. H. St. J. Hope*, On the Ealy Working of Alabaster in England, in: Archaeol. Inl., LXI, 1904.

*E. Prior and A. Gardner*, An Account of Medieval Figure-Sculpture in England. Cambridge, 1912.

*L. Stone*, British Sculpture of the Middle Ages. London, 1951.

*L. Stone*, Sculpture in Britain: the Middle Ages. London, 1955.

### D. GERMANY

*J. Baum*, Malerei und Plastik des Mittelalters in Deutschland, Frankreich und Britannien (Handbuch der Kunstwissenschaft). Potsdam, 1930.

*L. Behling*, Die klugen und törichten Jungfrauen von Magdeburg, in: Zeitschrift für Kunstwissenschaft, VIII (1954).

*V. Beyer*, La sculpture strasbourgeoise au XIV^me siècle (Dissertation, Ecole du Louvre). Strasbourg– Paris, 1955.

*B. Boeck*, Der Bamberger Meister, in: Zeitschrift für Kunstgeschichte, 1953.

*H. Beenken*, Der Meister von Naumburg. 1939.

*E. Doberer*, Die deutschen Lettner bis 1300. Vienna, 1946.

*H. von Einem*, Der Mainzer Kopf mit der Binde. 1955.

*H. Giesau*, Die Meißner Bildwerke. Burg, 1936.

*A. Goldschmidt*, Französische Einflüsse in der frühgotischen Skulptur Sachsens, in: Jahrbuch der preußischen Kunstsammlungen, 1899.

*R. Hamann*, Der Naumburger Meister in Noyon, in: Zeitschrift des deutschen Vereins für Kunstwissenschaft, II (1935), pp. 424ff.

*R. Hamann–Mac Lean*, Die Rekonstruktion der Meißener Marienpforte, in: Marburger Jahrbuch für Kunstwissenschaft, 1945, pp. 57ff.

*P. Hinz*, Der Naumburger Meister. 1954.

*H. Jantzen*, Deutsche Bildhauer des 13. Jhs. Leipzig, 1925.

*H. Jantzen*, Die Naumburger Stifterfiguren. Stuttgart, 1959.

*E. Kirchner – Doberer*, Die deutschen Lettner bis 1300 (Dissertation). Vienna, 1916 (with bibliography).

*H. Küas*, Die Naumburger Werkstatt. Berlin, 1937.

*P. Metz*, Der Stifterchor des Naumburger Doms. 1948.

*K. Moritz – Eichborn*, Der Skulpturenzyklus in der Vorhalle des Freiburger Münsters. Strasbourg, 1895.

*G. Münzel*, Der Zyklus der sieben freien Künste in der Vorhalle des Freiburger Münsters, in: Schau-ins-Land, 1950.

*G. Münzel*, Ansätze zur Plastik der Vorhalle des Münsters zu Freiburg, in: Das Münster, 1956, pp. 446ff.

*E. Panofsky*, Deutsche Plastik des 11.–13. Jhs. Munich, 1924.

*W. Pinder*, Deutsche Plastik des 14. Jhs. Munich, 1925.

*Reitzenstein*, Frühgotik der deutschen Plastik, in: Zeitschrift für Ästhetik und allgemeine Kunstwissenschaft, XXV (1931).

*Th. Rensing*, Die Knabenpforte des Bamberger Doms, in: Festgabe für Alois Fuchs. Paderborn, 1950.

*W. Schlesinger*, Meißener Dom und Naumburger Westchor. Munich–Cologne, 1952.

*O. Schmitt*, Oberrheinische Plastik. Fribourg, 1924.

*O. Schmitt*, Die gotischen Skulpturen des Straßburger Münsters. Frankfurt-on-Main, 1924.

*O. Schmitt*, Gotische Skulpturen des Freiburger Münster. 1926.

*J. A. Schmoll gen. Eisenwerth*, Die Köpfe der Slg. Priry in Remiremont: ein Fund zur Straßburger Skulptur der Erwinzeit, in: Pantheon, V, 1963.

*A. Stange*, Idee und Gestalt des Naumburger Westchors. Trier, 1955.

*H. Steuerwald*, Das Rätsel um den Bamberger Reiter. Berlin, 1953.

*H. Weigert*, Die Stilstufen der deutschen Plastik von 1250–1350, in: Marburger Jahrbuch für Kunstwissenschaft, IV (1927), pp. 147ff.

H. *Wentzel*, Die Christus-Johannes-Gruppen des 14.
Jhs. Stuttgart, 1960.

K. A. *Wirth*, Beiträge zum Problem des Samson-
Meisters, in: Zeitschrift für Kunstgeschichte
1957, pp. 25ff.

E. SPAIN

H. *Mahn*, Kathedralplastik in Spanien: Die monumentale Figuralskulptur in Alt-Kastilien, Léon
und Navarra zwischen 1230 und 1380. Reutlingen, 1935.

A. L. *Mayer*, Plastik des Mittelalters in Spanien. 1924.

A. D. *Sanpere* and *J. A. de Lasarte*, Escultura gótica
(Ars Hispaniae, VIII). Madrid, 1956 (with extensive bibliography).

G. *Weise*, Spanische Plastik aus sieben Jahrhunder-
ten. Reutlingen, 1925–27.

F. ITALY

E. *Berteaux*, L'art dans l'Italie méridionale. Paris, 1904.

W. *Biehl*, Toskanische Plastik des frühen und hohen
Mittelalters. Leipzig, 1926.

W. *Braunfels*, Zur Gestaltikonographie der Kanzeln
des Nicola und Giovanni Pisano, in: Das Münster, 2 (1949), pp. 321ff.

G. *Francovich*, Benedetto Antelami. Milan,
1952.

H. *Keller*, Die Bauplastik des Sieneser Doms, in:
Kunstgeschichtl. Jahrbuch der Bibl. Hertziana, 1
(1937), pp. 139ff.

J. *Pope-Henessy*, An Introduction to Italian Sculpture. London, 1955.

J. *Pope-Henessy*, Italian Gothic Sculpture. London,
1955.

P. *Schubring*, Die italienische Plastik des Quatro-
cento. Berlin–Neubabelsberg, 1917.

G. *Swarzenski*, Niccolo Pisano.

G. *Graf Vitzthum* and *W. Volbach*, Malerei und Plastik des Mittelalters in Italien (Handbuch der
Kunstwissenschaft). Potsdam, 1924.

# IV. PAINTING

A. GENERAL

W. *Dahmen*, Gotische Glasfenster. Rhythmus und
Strophenbau. Bonn, 1922.

G. *Dupont und C. Gnudi*, La peinture gothique.
Geneva, 1954.

M. Th. *Engels*, Zur Problematik der mittelalterlichen Glasmalerei, in: Neue deutsche Forschungen. Berlin, 1937.

J. L. *Fischer*, Handbuch der Glasmalerei. Leipzig,
1937.

G. *Haupt*, Die Farbensymbolik in der sakralen Kunst
des abendländischen Mittelalters (Dissertation).
Dresden, 1941.

G. *Heinersdorff*, Die Glasmalerei. Berlin, 1914.

H. *Mersmann*, Die Bedeutung des Rundfensters im
Mittelalter (unpublished dissertation). Vienna.

H. *Schwarz*, Zeichen der Sonne, in: Wort und Wahr-
heit, 1946, no. 9, pp. 364 ff.

H. *Wentzel*, Meisterwerke der Glasmalerei. Berlin,
1951, 1954.

B. FRANCE

H. *Arnold*, Stained Glass of the Middle Ages in England and France. London, 1925.

M. *Aubert*, French Cathedral Windows of the 12th
and 13th century. New York, 1939.

J. *Baum*, Die Malerei und Plastik des Mittelalters in
Deutschland, Frankreich und Britannien (Handbuch der Kunstwissenschaft). Potsdam, 1930.

Y. *Delaporte und E. Houvet*, Les vitraux de la cathédrale de Chartres. Chartres, 1926.

L. *Dimier*, Histoire de la peinture française, moyen-
âge et renaissance, 5 vols. Paris, 1925.

J. *Dupont*, Les primitifs français. Paris, 1937.

J. *Dyer-Spencer*, Les vitraux de la Sainte Chapelle de
Paris, in: Bulletin monumental, 1932, pp. 33ff.

L. *Gillet*, La peinture française, moyen-âge et renaissance. Paris, 1928.

L. *Grodecki*, A Stained Glass Atelier of the 13th Century: A Study of Windows in the Cathedrals of
Bourges, Chartres, and Poitiers.

L. *Grodecki*, The Stained Glass of French Churches,
Translated by Rosemary Edmunds and A.D.B.
Sylvester. London–Paris, 1948.

L. *Grodecki und Lafant*, Les vitraux de Notre-Dame et
de la Sainte-Chapelle de Paris. Paris, 1959.

L. *Grodecki*, Autour de Jean Pucelle, in: Médecine
de France, no. 27.

J. J. *Gruber*, Quelques aspects de l'art et de la technique du vitrail en France. Paris, 1928.

W. *Hausenstein*, Tafelmalerei der alten Franzosen.
Munich, 1923.

P. A. *Lemoisne*, Die gotische Malerei Frankreichs.
Florence–Berlin, 1931.

L. H. *Labande*, Le palais des Papes et les monuments d'Avignon au xiv$^{me}$ siècle. Versailles, 1925.

L. H. *Labande*, Les primitifs français, peintres et
peintres verrières de la Provence occidentale.
Marseilles, 1932.

M. *Laclotte*, L'école d'Avignon. Paris, 1960.

H. *Martin*, Les miniatures françaises du xiii$^{me}$ au
xv$^{me}$ siècle. Paris–Brussels, 1923.

H. *Martin*, Les miniaturistes français. Paris, 1906.

R. *Michel*, Les fresques de la garde-robe du palais des Papes, in: Gazette des Beaux Arts, 1916, pp. 293ff.

J. *Porcher*, Paris 1250, St. Louis et l'art gothique, in: Médecine de France, No. 25.

F. *Quiévreux*, Les vitraux de Bourges, in: Bulletin monumental, 101 (1943), pp. 255ff.

L. *Réau*, La peinture française du XIV$^{me}$ au XVI$^{me}$ siècle. Paris, 1939.

M. *Roques*, Les peintures murales du sud-est de la France. Paris, 1961.

Ch. *Sterling*, La peinture française: les primitifs. Paris, 1938.

Ch. *Sterling*, Les peintres français du moyen-âge. Paris, 1941.

G. *Graf Vitzthum*, Die Pariser Miniaturmaler. Leipzig, 1907.

C. ENGLAND

E. L. *Armitage*, English Stained Glass. London, 1960.

J. *Baum*, Die Malerei und Plastik des Mittelalters in Deutschland, Frankreich und Britannien (Handbuch der Kunstwissenschaft). Potsdam, 1930.

T. *Borenius* und E. W. *Tristram*, English Medieval Painting. Florence–Paris, 1927.

J. D. *Couteur*, English Medieval Painted Glass. London–New York, 1926.

C. R. *Dodwell*, The Canterbury School of Illumination. Cambridge, 1954.

M. A. *Drake*, A History of English Glass Painting. London, 1912.

F. S. *Eden*, Ancient Stained and Painted Glass. London, 1933.

F. *Harrison*, English Manuscripts of the 14th Century (1250–1400). London–New York, 1937.

J. A. *Herbert*, Illuminated Manuscripts. London, 1911.

E. G. *Millar*, English Illuminated Manuscripts from the 10th to the 13th century. Paris–Brussels, 1926 (also in French, Paris, 1926).

E. G. *Millar*, English Illuminated Manuscripts from the 14th to the 15th century. Paris–Brussels, 1928 (also in French, Paris, 1928).

Ph. *Nelson*, Ancient Painted Glass in England. London, 1913.

B. *Rackham*, The Ancient Glass of Canterbury Cathedral. London, 1949.

H. *Read*, English Stained Glass. London, 1926.

H. *Read* und J. *Baker*, English Stained Glass. London, 1950.

M. *Rickert*, Painting in Britain: the Middle-Ages. London, 1954.

G. *Mc N. Rushforth*, Medieval Christian Imagery. Oxford, 1936.

D. E. *Saunders*, English Illumination. Florence, 1930.

E. W. *Tristram*, English Medieval Wall-Painting: The 13th century. Oxford, 1950.

G. F. *Warner*, Illuminated Manuscripts in the British Museum. London, 1899–1903.

Chr. *Woodforde*, English Stained and Painted Glass. Oxford, 1954.

D. GERMANY, AUSTRIA, SWITZERLAND

J. *Baum*, Die Malerei des Mittelalters in Deutschland, Frankreich und Britannien (Handbuch der Kunstwissenschaft). Potsdam, 1930.

E. J. *Beer*, Die Glasmalereien der Schweiz vom 12. bis zum Beginn des 14. Jhs. Basle, 1956.

R. *Bruck*, Die elsässische Glasmalerei. Strasbourg, 1901.

P. *Clemen*, Die romanische Wandmalerei der Rheinlande. Düsseldorf, 1905–.

P. *du Colombier*, L'art allemand. Paris, 1945.

W. R. *Deusch*, Deutsche Malerei des 13. und 14. Jhs. Berlin, 1940.

O. H. *Förster*, Die kölnische Malerei von Meister Wilhelm bis Stephan Lochner. Cologne, 1923.

O. *Fischer*, Geschichte der deutschen Malerei. Munich, 1942.

W. *Frodl*, Die romanische Wandmalerei in Kärnten. Klagenfurt, 1942.

F. *Geiges*, Der mittelalterliche Fensterschmuck des Freiburger Münsters. Freiburg im Breisgau, 1931.

K. *Ginhart*–B. *Grimschitz*, Der Dom zu Gurk. 1930.

C. *Glaser*, Les peintres primitifs allemands. Paris, 1931.

A. *Goldschmidt*, Die deutsche Buchmalerei. Florence, 1928.

B. *Grimschitz*, Die Entstehungszeit der Freskenfolge in der Westempore des Gurker Doms (Gurk, Friesach, Pisweg), in: Carinthia, 1, 1918.

B. *Grimschitz*, Zur Entstehungszeit der Freskenfolge in der Westempore des Gurker Doms, in: Archiv für vaterländische Geschichte und Topographie, 24. und 25. Jahrg. 1936.

G. *Haseloff*, Eine thüringisch-sächsische Malerschule des 13. Jhs. Strasbourg, 1897.

G. *Haseloff*, Die Psalterillustrationen im 13. Jh. 1938.

G. *Haseloff*, Die Glasgemälde der Elisabethkirche zu Marburg.

E. *Heidrich*, Die altdeutsche Malerei. Jena, 1941.

A. *Hulfegger*, Evolution de la peinture en Allemagne et dans l'Europe Centrale. Paris, 1949.

Fr. *Kieslinger*, Glasmalerei in Österreich. Vienna, 1925.

H. *Lehmann*, Zur Geschichte der Glasmalerei in der Schweiz, in: Mitteilungen der antiquarischen Gesellschaft Zürich, 1906–1912.

H. *Th. Musper*, Gotische Malerei nördlich der Alpen. Cologne, 1961.

J. R. *Rahn*, Die Glasgemälde in der Rosette der Kathedrale Lausanne, in: Mitteilungen der antiquarischen Gesellschaft Zürich, 1879.

L. *Réau*, Les primitifs allemands. Paris, 1910.

M. *Sattler*, Alte Glasmalerei in der Schweiz. Zurich, 1953.

R. *Sillib*, F. *Panzer*, A. *Haseloff*, Die manessische Liederhandschrift. Leipzig, 1929.

A. *Stange*, Deutsche Malerei der Gotik, 9 vols. Leipzig-Berlin, 1934–1958.

A. *Stange*, Frühe Kölner Meister. Bonn, 1938.

H. *Swarzenski*, Die lateinischen illuminierten Handschriften des 13. Jhs. an Rhein, Main und Donau. Berlin, 1937.

H. *Wentzel*, Meisterwerke der Glasmalerei, 2nd ed. Berlin, 1954.

H. *Wentzel*, Die Glasmalerei in Schwaben von 1250–1350 (Corpus vitrearum mediaevi, Deutschland, vol. 1). Berlin, 1958.

F. *Winkler*, Altdeutsche Tafelmalerei. Munich, 1942.

W. *Worringer*, Die Anfänge der Tafelmalerei. Leipzig, 1924.


E. SPAIN

J. *Gudiol*, Spanish painting. Toledo–Ohio, 1941.

J. *Gudiol-Ricart*, La pintura gotica en Cataluña. Barcelona, n.d. [1944].

P. *Guinard und J. Baticle*, Histoire de la peinture espagnole du xiime au xixme siècle. Paris, 1950.

J. *Lassaigne*, La peinture espagnole, des fresques romans au Greco. Geneva, 1952.

A. L. *Mayer*, Historia de la pintura espaolña, 2nd ed. Madrid, 1942.

Ch. R. *Post*, A history of Spanish painting. Cambridge (Mass.). 1930.

J. G. *Ricart*, Pintura gotica (Ars Hispaniae, IX). Madrid, n.d. (with extensive bibliography).

M. S. *Sanpere*, Los cuatrocentistes catalanes. Barcelona, 1905–1096.


F. ITALY

P. *d'Ancona*, La miniature italienne du xiime au xviime siècle. Paris–Brussels, 1925.

M. *Aubert*, Die malerische Dekoration der San Francesco-Kirche in Assisi. Ein Beitrag zur Lösung der Cimabue-Frage. Leipzig, 1907.

K. *Bauch*, Die geschichtliche Bedeutung von Giottos Frühstil, in: Mitteilungen des kunsthistorischen Institutes zu Florenz, vii, 1953, pp. 43ff.

E. *Benkard*, Das literarische Porträt des Giovanni Cimabue. Munich, 1917.

B. *Berenson*, Studies in Medieval Painting. New Haven, 1930.

C. *Brandi*, Die Stilentwicklung des Simone Martini, in: Pantheon, 1934, pp. 225ff.

C. *Brandi*, Duccio. Florence, 1951.

C. *Brandi* (ed.), Il restauro della Maestà di Duccio. Rome, 1959.

E. *Carli*, Giotto. Milan–Florence, 1952.

E. *Carli*, Die großen Maler von Siena. Vienna–Munich, 1956.

E. *Cecchi*, I Trecentisti senesi. Rome, 1928.

E. *Cecchi*, Giotto. Milan, 1937.

L. *Coletti*, I primitivi 1: Dall'arte benedittina a Giotto. Novara, 1941. ii: I senesi e i giotteschi. Novara, 1946. iii: I padani. Novara, 1947.

L. *Coletti*, Die frühe italienische Malerei, I: das 12. und 13. Jh. Vienna, 1941.

L. *Coletti*, Gli affreschi della Basilica di Assisi. Bergamo, 1949.

C. H. *Edgell*, A History of Sienese Painting. New York, 1932.

G. *Fiacco*, Giotto e Arnolfo, in: Rivista d'arte 1937, pp. 221ff.

D. *Frey*, Giotto und die maniera greca, Bildgesetzlichkeit und psychologische Deutung, in: Wallraf-Richartz Jahrbuch, xiv (1952), pp. 73ff.

C. *Gnudi*, Giotto. Milan, 1958.

F. *Hermanin*, Le gallerie nazionale italiane, v, 1902 (frescoes of Cavallini in Santa Cecilia, Rome).

Th. *Hetzer*, Giotto. Frankfurt-on-Main, 1941.

C. H. *Isermeyer*, Beitrag zur Bestimmung des Wesens und der Entwicklung Giottos. Berlin, 1938.

H. *Jantzen*, Giotto und die französische Gotik, in: Kunstrundschau, 1938, March no.

H. *Jantzen*, Die zeitliche Abfolge der Paduaner Fresken Giottos, in: Jahrbuch der preußischen Kunstsammlungen, 60 (1939), pp. 187ff.

H. *Jantzen*, Giotto und der gotische Stil, in: Das Werk des Künstlers, 1 (1939/40), pp. 441ff.

B. *Kleinschmidt OFM*, Die Basilika San Francesco in Assisi, 3 vols. Berlin, 1915–1928.

B. *Kleinschmidt OFM*, Die Wandmalereien der Basilika San Francesco in Assisi. Berlin, 1930.

G. *Kugler*, The Italian Schools of Painting, 6th ed. London, 1902.

R. *Longhi*, La mostra del trecento bolognese, in: Paragone, v, 1950, pp. 5ff.

R. *van Marle*, The Development of the Italian Schools of Painting, 18 vols. The Hague, 1924–36.

R. *van Marle*, Simone Martini et les peintres de son école. Strasbourg, 1920.

L. *Martius*, Die Franziskuslegende in der Ober-
kirche von San Francesco in Assisi und ihre
Stellung in der kunstgeschichtlichen Forschung.
Berlin, 1932.

A. *Nicholson*, Cimabue. Princeton, 1932.

R. *Oertel*, Die Frühzeit der italienischen Malerei.
Stuttgart, 1953.

R. *Oertel*, Wende der Giotto-Forschung, in: Zeitschrift für Kunstgeschichte XI, 1943/44, p.1ff.

G. *Paccaghini*, Simone Martini, Milan, 1955.

E. *Panofsky*, Perspektive als symbolische Form, in:
Vorträge der Bibliothek Warburg 1924–25,
pp. 276ff.

A. *de Rinaldis*, Simone Martini. Rome, 1936.

F. *Rintelen*, Giotto und die Giotto-Apokryphen,
2nd ed. Milan, 1923.

E. *Rosenthal*, Giotto in der mittelalterlichen Geistes-
entwicklung. Augsburg, 1924.

M. *Salmi*, Le origini dell'arte di Giotto, in: Rivista
d'arte 1937.

R. *Salvini*, Giotto-bibliografia. Rome, 1938.

R. *Salvini*, Giotto. Milan, 1952.

R. *Salvini*, Tutta la pittura di Giotto. Milan, 1952.

J. *von Schlosser*, Oberitalienische Trecentisten. Leipzig, 1921.

G. *Sinibaldi*, La pittura del Trecento. Florence, 1930.

O. *Siren*, Giotto and some of his Followers. Cambridge, 1917.

O. *Siren*, Toskanische Malerei des 13. Jhs. Leipzig,
1922.

W. *Suida*, Florentinische Maler des 14. Jhs. Strasbourg, 1905.

J. *Strzygowski*, Cimabue und Rom. Vienna, 1888.

H. *Thode*, Franz von Assisi und die Anfänge der
Kunst der Renaissance, 2 nd. ed. Berlin, 1920.

P. *Toesca*, La pittura e la miniatura nella Lombar-
dia. Milan, 1912.

P. *Toesca*, Die florentiner Malerei des 14. Jhs.
Munich, 1929.

P. *Toesca*, Gli affreschi della vita di San Francesco
nel Santuario di Assisi. Florence, 1946.

P. *Toesca*, Gli affreschi dell'antico e del nuovo
testamento nel Santuario di Assisi. Florence, 1947.

P. *Toesca*, Gli affreschi della Capella di San Silvestro
in Santa Croce. Florence, 1947.

P. *Toesca*, Storia dell'arte italiana: Il trecento.
Turin, 1951.

A. *Venturi*, Storia dell'arte italiana. Milan, 1901-1938.

L. *Venturi*, Introduzione all'arte di Giotto, in:
L'arte, V (1919), pp. 49ff.

L. *Venturi*, La peinture italienne: les créateurs de la
Renaissance. Geneva–Paris, 1950.

C. H. *Weigelt*, Die sienesische Malerei des 14. Jhs.
Leipzig, 1930.

J. *Wilpert*, Die römischen Mosaiken und Malereien
der kirchlichen Bauten vom 4. bis 13. Jh.,
4 vols. Freiburg im Breisgau, 1916.

G. *Vitzthum–W. F. Volbach*, Malerei und Plastik des
Mittelalters in Italien (Handbuch der Kunstwissenschaft). Potsdam, 1924.

## ARTS AND CRAFTS

F. *Back*, Ein Jahrtausend künstlerischer Kultur am
Oberrhein. Darmstadt, 1932.

H. *Th. Bossert*, Geschichte des Kunstgewerbes aller
Völker und Zeiten, vols. v, vi. Berlin, 1932, 1935.

J. *Braun*, Das christliche Altargerät. Munich, 1932.

J. *Braun*, Die Reliquiare des christlichen Kults und
ihre Entwicklung. Fribourg, 1940.

W. *Burger*, Abendländische Schmelzarbeiten. Berlin, 1930.

O. *von Falke und H. Frauberger*, Deutsche Schmelz-
arbeit des Mittelalters. 1904.

O. *von Falke*, Der Dreikönigenschrein des Nikolaus
von Verdun im Kölner Domschatz. 1911.

E. G. *Grimme*, Aachener Goldschmiedekunst im
Mittelalter. Cologne, 1957.

K. *Guth-Dreyfus*, Transluzides Email in der ersten
Hälfte des 14. Jhs. an Ober-, Mittel- und
Niederrhein, in: Baseler Studien zur Kunst-
geschichte 9. Basle, 1954.

R. *Koechlin*, Les ivoires gothiques. Paris, 1924.

H. *Kohlhaussen*, Minnekästchen im Mittelalter.
Berlin, 1928.

H. *Kohlhaussen*, Unveröffentliche frühe deutsche
Schmuck- und Minnekästchen, in: Zeitschrift
für Kunstwissenschaft, Berlin, 1949.

H. *Kohlhaussen*, Geschichte des deutschen Kunstgewerbes. Munich, 1955.

H. *Lüer und M. Creutz*, Geschichte der Metallkunst
Stuttgart, 1904, 1909.

E. *Meyer*, Reliquie und Reliquiar im Mittelalter,
in: Festschrift der C. G. Heyse, Berlin, 1950.

M. *Rosenberg*, Geschichte der Goldschmiedekunst
auf technischer Grundlage. Frankfurt-on-Main,
1918-1924.

M. *Sauerlandt*, Werkformen deutscher Kunst.
Königstein, 1926.

K. *Simon*, Figürliches Kunstgerät. Königstein, 1926.

*abacus*

The slab forming the crowning member of a capital.

*alternating supports*

The change in the columnation of the nave arcade in the Romanesque and the Early Gothic, governed by the different structural function of the supports. With the trend towards a unified vaulting system during the High Gothic, alternating supports disappear.

*ambo*

In the early Christian basilica a raised lectern in front of the choir-screen, replaced during the High Gothic by the pulpit.

*apse*

Also choir-head; the — mostly semi-circular or polygonal — termination of the choir, formed by the outer wall of the altar recess.

*arcade*

From Latin *arcus*, an arch. A series of arches supported by piers or columns or placed in front of the wall on attached piers or pilasters as a purely decorative feature (blind arcade). Cf. also transverse arch.

*barrel-vault*

A vault shaped like a semi-circular cylinder, resting on the walls of the vaulted room.

*basilica*

An aisled church, whose nave rises above the aisles and is lit by a clerestory (unlike the hall church or a church built on a central plan).

*belfry*

The fortified dwelling tower of a castle, or the detached hall tower next to a medieval town hall.

*Bible Moraliste, Biblia Pauperum* (Poor Man's Bible)

The term for the series of Biblical scenes — as well as Virtues and Vices, etc. — illustrated in the sculpture and stained glass of the cathedral.

*blind arcade*

The arcading superimposed on a wall as a purely decorative feature, without any openings.

*blind triforium, blind tribune*

Openings in the nave wall, above the ground-floor arcades, without any gallery behind them; their function is purely decorative.

*breviary*

Also *breviarium*, or book of hours: The book containing the prayers to be said by the clergy.

*buttress arch, buttress pier, flying buttress*

The rib-vault distributes the downward thrust of a vault over the piers and clustered piers of the

nave, while the outward thrust of the vaulting is caught by buttress arches which, in turn, transmit it to the buttress piers. Gothic architecture reveals the buttressing and makes it part of the general composition (cf. Fig. 3).

*campanile*

A bell-tower.

*central plan*

A scheme in which, ideally, the different parts of the building are grouped symmetrically around the centre (cf. Fig. 49 and pp. 145 and 163).

*champlevé*

A technique of enamel painting. Hollows cut into a gold or copper base are filled with a coloured glass powder, which fuses with the ground in firing. The outlines are formed by the ridges of metal between the hollows.

*chapter-hall*

The assembly room of the monks.

*chevet*

A series of radiating chapels linked by the choir ambulatory.

*choir, choir-head, ambulatory, choir-chapels, choir-screens.* Cf. also 'apse'.

The term 'choir' is generally used for the portion of the church beyond the crossing, originally reserved for the singers and for the clergy. Its eastern termination, which contains the altar, is called the choir-head. Already in the Romanesque the choir was surrounded by an ambulatory — whose ceiling is usually lower than that of the choir — and radiating chapels, which in the High Gothic become the chevet (cf. Figs. 7, 15, 16, 20). Sometimes the choir is separated from the ambulatory by the choir-screen, a comparatively low wall frequently decorated with sculpture (Plate p. 83); the separation towards the nave is by means of the rood-screen, which stands behind the principal altar.

*ciborium*

A lidded chalice in which the Consecrated Host is preserved.

*clerestory*

The nave windows of a basilica church. Cf. basilica.

*cloisonné*

An enamel technique, named after the strips of metal — cloisons — which are soldered to a copper or golden base. The areas between the cloisons are then filled with a coloured glass flux, and the whole work is fired at a very high temperature.

*cloisters*
The vaulted and arcaded walk around a square adjoining the side of an abbey or cathedral church and surrounded by administrative buildings of the abbey or cathedral chapter.

*clover-leaf choir*
Cf. triapsal choir.

*clustered piers*
Cf. engaged piers.

*crocket*
A flower or bud, with foliage arranged in a cruciform design, surmounting Gothic towers, gables and finials.

*crossing*
The area separating nave, transepts and choir.

*cross-vaulting*
A cross-vault is formed by the interpenetration of two barrel-vaults, which causes the weight of the vaulting caps to rest on the walls. By the introduction of ribs at the points of intersection, the load-bearing function of the vaulting caps is transmitted to these ribs, which divert the thrust and counter-thrust of the vault towards the corners. The entire weight of the vault is thus distributed over four points, which have to be strengthened accordingly, while the rest of the wall ceases to have any load-bearing function.

*Deesis*
Christ in Glory between the Virgin and St. John, as the intercessors for humanity. Though the principal motif of the Last Judgement, this group also appears on its own.

*donjon*
The French term for belfry, the fortified dwelling tower of a castle.

*dormitorium*
The sleeping chamber of the monks.

*Ecce Homo*
Cf. Man of Sorrows.

*enamel*
also enamel painting: a technique using coloured glass, ground into a powder which can be used for painting on metal and glass. Hardened in special ovens, it will combine with the specially roughened ground. Cf. also *champlevé* enamel and *cloisonné*.

*engaged pier, engaged column*
A quarter, half, or three-quarter column placed in front of a wall to support the ribs or transverse arches of a vaulting compartment. If several attached columns are grouped around a pier, disguising the core completely, we speak

of a clustered pier (cf. Fig. 25 and Plate p. 131).

*fayence*
A fired earthenware painted with a tin glaze which amalgamates with the body in firing.

*filigree*
Decorative metal work in gold or silver wire, soldered to a metal base.

*finial*
The peak of a gable or pinnacle, often surmounted by a crocket.

*flamboyant*
The last phase of the Gothic in France and England, named after the flame-like patterns of the tracery.

*gisant*
A tomb with a portrait of the deceased in full sculpture.

*Grandes Compagnies, Les*
Bands of mercenaries of different origin, formerly in the service of the kings of England, Navarre and France. Later, in the reigns of Jean le Bon and Charles V, they became the scourge of the French countryside. Between 1366 and 1368 du Guesclin took most of them with him to Spain, where he placed Henry of Transtamare on the throne of Castile with their help.

*grisaille*
Monochrome painting in grey.

*hall church*
An aisled church in which nave and aisles — in contrast to the basilica — are of equal height; lighting, therefore, is from the side windows only (Figs. 21, 31). If the nave is slightly higher — though still without a clerestory — we speak of a pseudo-basilica.

*head reliquary*
A reliquary in the form of a portrait bust in which the skull or part of the skull of a saint is preserved.

*iconography*
The teaching of the meaning, content and history of pictorial representations and of their symbols and attributes.

*jamb*
The sides of a window or portal, cut diagonally into the wall. In the Gothic the jambs serve to display the portal sculpture of the cathedral (cf. reveal).

*keep*
The innermost stronghold of a medieval castle (cf. also belfry and donjon).

*keystone*
The central wedge-shaped stone of an arch or vault, usually decorated with carved foliage or

the portrait bust of a saint; in a vault its function is to transmit the thrust to the supports at the sides.

*lantern*

The turret, or tower, above the crossing, particularly in Romanesque churches.

*lintel*

The upper horizontal termination of a door-way.

*loading gable*

A tall gable above Gothic doors and windows, often filled with tracery.

*Man of Sorrows*

The representation of Christ with the Crown of Thorns, placed before the beholders as the symbol of the Passion and man's salvation.

*nave arcade*

The arcade dividing the nave from the aisles. Cf. also transverse arch and wall arches.

*oblong vaulting*

A vaulting compartment over a rectangular — instead of a square — plan.

*palas*

The owner's quarters of a German medieval castle.

*parlatorium*

The monks' common room, where conversation is permitted.

*Parler art*

The phase in sculpture and architecture inaugurated *c.* 1350 by Peter Parler, of Gmünd, and continued by his sons.

*Pietà*

The Madonna with the dead Christ in her lap.

*porticus*

The pillared porch of the main entrance.

*predella*

The rectangular base of a winged altar.

*Psalter*

Also *Psalterium*. The Book of Psalms used in the liturgy of the church.

*refectory*

The dining-room of a monastery.

*reliquary*

A receptacle for the remains of a saint or for objects touched by him.

*reveal*

The sides of a window or portal, cut at right angles into the wall (cf. also *jamb*).

*ridge rib*

The central rib running along the apex of a vault, particularly in Norman buildings.

*rood-screen*

A screen dividing the choir from the nave. Above it is a gallery — the rood-loft — with a pulpit, from which the Gospel is read to the congregation. In the Gothic, the rood-screen is frequently decorated with sculpture (cf. also choir-screen).

*stucco*

A mixture of plaster, lime and sand, which is fast-setting and therefore gives the artist little time.

While in a malleable state, it is worked with modelling tools, though final details can still be carved after the material has set.

*transverse arch*

The arch dividing the vaulting compartments at a right angle to the main axis. The arches parallel to the main axis are called wall arches.

*triapsal plan*

A church built on a cruciform plan, whose transepts — like the choir — have a semi-circular termination. If transepts and choir are very short and the apses therefore very close, we speak of a clover-leaf choir.

*tribune*

In Romanesque and Early Gothic churches the gallery above the aisles which opens into arcades towards the nave. Structurally, the tribunes serve the function of buttressing arches, namely the support of the nave vault. In the High Gothic flying buttresses, also developed into a decorative feature, make tribunes unnecessary.

*triforium*

From Early French *trifoire*, pierced work. A narrow passage along the nave wall, opening into a series of arcades. It serves the articulation of the wall rather than any practical function (cf. also blind arcade). Cf. Appx. Pl. 17.

*trumeau pier*

The centre pier of a wide portal — often displaying a statue — which supports the tympanum.

*tumba*

A free-standing sarcophagus in stone or bronze.

*tympanum*

The area between the lintel and the arch above a door-way, often decorated in relief.

*wall arches*

The arches along the wall at the sides of the vaulting compartments, whose weight they support. Cf. also transverse arch.

# INDEX